More's
UTOPIA
and Its Critics

Ligeia Gallagher

Loyola University, Chicago

Scott, Foresman and Company

Chicago   Atlanta   Dallas   Palo Alto   Fair Lawn, N. J.

Acknowledgments

The author is deeply grateful to the following publishers
for permission to reprint the critical essays in this volume:

A. & C. Black, Ltd.: "The Roots of More's Socialism," *Thomas More and His Utopia* by Karl Kautsky, translated by H. J. Stenning, 1927.

Jonathan Cape, Ltd.: "The Meaning of *Utopia*" and "*Utopia* and the Problems of 1516," *Thomas More* by R. W. Chambers, 1935.

The Dublin Publishing Company: Richard O'Sullivan, "Social Life and Theories of St. Thomas More," *Dublin Review*, 199 (July 1936).

Harvard University Press: Reprinted by permission of the publishers from *The Praise of Pleasure* by Edward Surtz, S. J. Copyright, 1957, by The President and Fellows of Harvard College.

Princeton University Press: "Introduction," *Citizen Thomas More and His Utopia* by Russell Ames, 1949. Reprinted by permission. Copyright, 1949, by Princeton University Press.

Random House: From the Preface to *A Man for All Seasons* by Robert Bolt. Copyright © 1960, 1962 by Robert Bolt. Reprinted by permission of Random House, Inc.

Russell & Russell, Inc.: Letter to Ulrich von Hutten, *The Epistles of Erasmus, From His Earliest Letters to His Fifty-First Year*, 3 vols., translated by Francis Morgan Nichols, 1962.

University of North Carolina Press: David M. Bevington, "Dialogue in *Utopia:* Two Sides to the Question," *Studies in Philology*, 58 (July 1961).

The map of Utopia and the Utopian Alphabet, which appear on the front and back covers, originally appeared in Thomas More's *Utopia*, published in 1516. Originals courtesy of the Berg Collection of the New York Public Library.

Introduction

Mankind can be considered an experiment in solidarity. Paradoxically, even our most intimate struggles to know and realize the self are dependent on our relations with other human beings. That is why Aristotle completed his study of the good man (his *Ethics*) with a study of the good society (his *Politics*) and why Plato wrote the first great utopia, *The Republic.* Defined as "any place, state, or situation of ideal perfection, any visionary scheme or system for an ideally perfect social order," a utopia derives its name from the famous book which is considered in this text.

More's title, *Utopia,* was a humanist jest: his scholar friends recognized its Greek origin (*ou,* not; *topos,* place) and the fictional, make-believe nature of the island. Yet the imaginative truth of the book was immediately apparent, whether to the uninitiated who wanted to fit out actual expeditions to the island, or to the more sophisticated who perceived its brilliant social satire and felt its strong appeal for reform.

The humorous deception of the place-names in *Utopia,* or Nowhere, is only part of the indirection employed by More. The fictional framework, the dialog structure, the many ironies lead to ambiguity; and critics have ascribed to More varied and conflicting attitudes toward the ideas he presents in the work. H. G. Wells thought it "one of the most profoundly inconsistent of books"[1] in its mingling of Socialist and Communist forms with unimaginative, individualistic Whiggery. T. E. Bridgett, one of the finer Catholic apologists for More, asked, "But what can be the purpose of arguing by induction from a work which was put out as a *jeu d'esprit* when the writer has left hundreds of pages in which his real belief is expressed without ambiguity?"[2]

None of the critics appearing in this text doubts the value of induction from *Utopia.* Their very diversity of opinion and the conviction with which they argue leads to controversy, a controversy which is intended to stimulate personal discussion and writing on the student's part. It can hardly be emphasized too much that, despite the widening of range he should experience in reading the critics, it remains the student's responsibility to confront More's reality in *Utopia* with his own reality. Certainly the vital way in which ideas are taken up, analyzed, assimilated, modified, or discarded by the critics should be an example of what it means to enter the dialog of scholarship.

Part One of *More's UTOPIA and Its Critics* reproduces a modernized version of Robinson's translation (1551) of the original Latin (1516). Part Two assembles opinions of some eminent scholar-humanists about More and his *Utopia:* Erasmus' biographical letter, More's own letter about his book, two other letters, and a laudatory poem. I have not included William Roper's *Life of Sir Thomas More* because it has nothing to say about *Utopia* and is easily available elsewhere. Part Three is a collection of

---

1. "Introduction," *Utopia.* New York: Heritage Press, Limited Editions Club, 1935.
2. *The Life and Writings of Blessed Thomas More.* London: Burns, Oates & Washbourne, Ltd., 1924, p. 105. Cf. Christopher Hollis, *St. Thomas More,* London: Burns & Oates, 1961, who judges the writing of *Utopia* as an imprudence on More's part.

modern views about More and *Utopia*. Serving as a parallel to Erasmus' letter to Hutten about More is Robert Bolt's interpretive essay, which prefaced the published version of his hit play, *A Man for All Seasons*.

The unanimity of educated opinion in the sixteenth century vanishes in the twentieth-century essays, which were chosen chiefly because they point to a remarkable range of opinion and interpretation. One of the more startling interpretations is the Marxist-Soviet one that claims More, who for many is a Christian saint, as the first English communist and the father of Utopian Socialism. I have included a selection from the classic Marxist criticism of Karl Kautsky and one from a contemporary Soviet magazine, *News,* by Vyacheslav Volgin, the vice-president of the U.S.S.R. Academy of Science. To them More was a critic of the emerging capitalist system and a prophet of modern socialism and communism. Richard O'Sullivan and Edward Surtz represent a view of *Utopia* as essentially religious and philosophical. David M. Bevington and Richard W. Chambers are humanists who emphasize the literary and ironic quality of the work. Finally, Russell Ames views More as an exponent of the best aspects of rising capitalism, and the *Utopia* as an attack on decadent feudalism.

At the end of the book are a list of the principal dates in More's life, study questions, topics for papers, and a bibliography.

Throughout the text the figures in slashes — for example, /156/ — indicate the end of pages in the original text; brackets denote my editorial insertions. I wish to thank the authors and publishers who gave permission to reprint materials here. I am especially grateful to Dr. Agnes Donohue and Miss Barbara Donaker for their help in preparing the manuscript.

Contents

Utopia
by
Thomas
More

Book I

Henry the Eighth, the unconquered King of England, a prince adorned
with all the virtues that become a great monarch, having some differences
of no small consequence with Charles, the most serene prince of Castile,
sent me into Flanders, as his ambassador, for treating and composing
matters between them. I was colleague and companion to that incompara-
ble man Cuthbert Tonstal, whom the king with such universal applause
lately made Master of the Rolls; but of whom I will say nothing; not because I fear that the testimony of a friend will be suspected, but rather
because his learning and virtues are too great for me to do them justice,
and so well known, that they need not my commendations unless I would,
according to the proverb, "Show the sun with a lantern." Those that were
appointed by the prince to treat with us met us at Bruges, according to
agreement; they were all worthy men. The Margrave of Bruges was their
head, and the chief man among them; but he that was esteemed the wisest,
and that spoke for the rest, was George Temse, the Provost of Casselsee;
both art and nature had concurred to make him eloquent: he was very
learned in the law; and as he had a great capacity, so by a long practice
in affairs he was very dextrous at unravelling them. After we had several
times met without coming to an agreement, they went to Brussels for some
days to know the prince's pleasure. And since our business would admit
it, I went to Antwerp. While I was there, among many that visited me,
there was one that was more acceptable to me than any other, Peter Giles,
born at Antwerp, who is a man of great honor, and of a good rank in his
town, though less than he deserves; for I do not know if there be anywhere
to be found a more learned and a better bred young man: for as he is both
a very worthy and a very knowing person, so he is so civil to all men, so
particularly kind to his friends, and so full of candor and affection, that
there is not perhaps above one or two anywhere to be found that is in all
respects so perfect a friend. He is extraordinarily modest, there is no
artifice in him; and yet no man has more of a prudent simplicity: his
conversation was so pleasant and so innocently cheerful, that his company
in a great measure lessened my longings to go back to my country, and to
my wife and children, which an absence of four months had quickened
very much. One day as I was returning home from Mass at St. Mary's,
which is the chief church, and the most frequented of any in Antwerp,
I saw him by accident talking with a stranger, who seemed past the
flower of his age; his face was tanned, he had a long beard, and his cloak
was hanging carelessly about him, so that by his looks and habit I concluded he was a seaman. As soon as Peter saw me, he came and saluted me;
and as I was returning his civility, he took me aside, and pointing to him
with whom he had been discoursing, he said, "Do you see that man? I
was just thinking to bring him to you." I answered, "He should have been
very welcome on your account." "And on his own too," replied he, "if
you knew the man, for there is none alive that can give so copious an
account of unknown nations and countries as he can do; which I know you

very much desire." Then said I, "I did not guess amiss, for at first sight I took him for a seaman." "But you are much mistaken," said he, "for he has not sailed as a seaman, but as a traveller, or rather a philosopher. This Raphael, who from his family carries the name of Hythloday,[1] is not ignorant of the Latin tongue, but is eminently learned in the Greek, having applied himself more particularly to that than to the former, because he had given himself much to philosophy, in which he knew that the Romans have left us nothing that is valuable, except what is to be found in Seneca and Cicero. He is a Portuguese by birth, and was so desirous of seeing the world, that he divided his estate among his brothers, run the same hazard as Americus Vesputius, and bore a share in three of his four voyages, that are now published, only he did not return with him in his last, but obtained leave of him almost by force, that he might be one of those twenty-four who were left at the farthest place at which they touched, in their last voyage to New Castle. The leaving him thus did not a little gratify one that was more fond of travelling than of returning home, to be buried in his own country; for he used often to say, that the way to heaven was the same from all places; and he that had no grave, had the heaven still over him. Yet this disposition of mind had cost him dear, if God had not been very gracious to him; for after he, with five Castilians, had travelled over many countries, at last, by some strange good fortune, he got to Ceylon, and from thence to Calicut, where he very happily found some Portuguese ships; and, beyond all men's expectations, returned to his native country." When Peter had said this to me, I thanked him for his kindness, in intending to give me the acquaintance of a man whose conversation he knew would be so acceptable; and upon that Raphael and I embraced each other. After these civilities were past which are usual with strangers upon their first meeting, we all went to my house, and entering into the garden, sat down on a green bank, and entertained one another in discourse. He told us, that when Vesputius had sailed away, he and his companions that stayed behind in New Castle, by degrees insinuated themselves into the affections of the people of the country, meeting often with them, and treating them gently: and at last they not only lived among them without danger, but conversed familiarly with them; and got so far into the heart of the prince, whose name and country I have forgot, that he both furnished them plentifully with all things necessary, and also with the conveniences of travelling; both boats when they went by water, and wagons when they travelled over land: he sent with them a very faithful guide, who was to introduce and recommend them to such other princes as they had a mind to see: and after many days' journey, they came to towns, and cities, and to commonwealths, that were both happily governed and well peopled. Under the equator, and as far as on both sides of it as the sun moves, there lay vast deserts that were parched with the perpetual heat of the sun; the soil was withered, all things looked dismally, and all places were either quite uninhabited, or abounded with wild beasts and serpents, and some few men, that were neither less wild nor less cruel than the beasts themselves. But as they went farther, a new scene opened, all things grew

---

1. Derived from the Greek *hythlos*, "idle talk or nonsense"; and *daios*, "knowing, cunning."

milder, the air less burning, the soil more verdant, and even the beasts were less wild: and at last there were nations, towns, and cities, that had not only mutual commerce among themselves, and with their neighbors, but traded both by sea and land, to very remote countries. There they found the conveniences of seeing many countries on all hands, for no ship went any voyage into which he and his companions were not very welcome. The first vessels that they saw were flat-bottomed, their sails were made of reeds and wicker woven close together, only some were of leather; but afterwards they found ships made with rounded keels, and canvas sails, and in all respects like our ships; and the seamen understood both astronomy and navigation. He got wonderfully into their favor, by showing them the use of the needle, of which till then they were utterly ignorant. They sailed before with great caution, and only in summer-time, but now they count all seasons alike, trusting wholly to the loadstone, in which they are perhaps more secure than safe; so that there is reason to fear that this discovery, which was thought would prove so much to their advantage, may by their imprudence become an occasion of much mischief to them. But it were too long to dwell on all that he told us he had observed in every place; it would be too great a digression from our present purpose: whatever is necessary to be told, concerning those wise and prudent institutions which he observed among civilized nations, may perhaps be related by us on a more proper occasion. We asked him many questions concerning all these things, to which he answered very willingly; only we made no inquiries after monsters, than which nothing is more common; for everywhere one may hear of ravenous dogs and wolves, and cruel man-eaters; but it is not so easy to find states that are well and wisely governed.

As he told us of many things that were amiss in those new-discovered countries, so he reckoned up not a few things from which patterns might be taken for correcting the errors of these nations among whom we live; of which an account may be given, as I have already promised, at some other time; for at present I intend only to relate those particulars that he told us of the manners and laws of the Utopians: but I will begin with the occasion that led us to speak of that commonwealth. After Raphael had discoursed with great judgment on the many errors that were both among us and these nations; had treated of the wise institutions both here and there, and had spoken as distinctly of the customs and government of every nation through which he had passed, as if he had spent his whole life in it; Peter being struck with admiration, said, "I wonder, Raphael, how it comes that you enter into no king's service, for I am sure there are none to whom you would not be very acceptable: for your learning and knowledge, both of men and things, is such, that you would not only entertain them very pleasantly, but be of great use to them, by the examples you could set before them, and the advices you could give them; and by this means you would both serve your own interest, and be of great use to all your friends" — "As for my friends," answered he, "I need not be much concerned, having already done for them all that was incumbent on me; for when I was not only in good health, but fresh and young, I distributed that among my kindred and friends which other people do not part with till they are old and sick; when they then unwillingly give that which they can enjoy no longer themselves. I think my friends ought to rest contented with this, and not to expect that for their sakes I should enslave myself to any king whatsoever" — "Soft and fair," said Peter, "I do not mean that you should be a slave to any king, but only that you should assist them, and be useful to them." — "The change of the word," said he, "does not alter the matter." — "But term it as you will," replied Peter, "I do not see any other way in which you can be so useful, both in private and to your friends, and to the public, and by which you can make your own condition happier." — "Happier!" answered Raphael, "is that to be compassed in a way so abhorrent to my genius? Now I live as I will, to which I believe few courtiers can pretend. And there are so many that court the favor of great men, that there will be no great loss if they are not troubled either with me or with others of my temper." Upon this, said I, "I perceive, Raphael, that you neither desire wealth nor greatness; and indeed I value and admire such a man much more than I do any of the great men in the world. Yet I think you would do what would well become a generous and philosophical a soul as yours is, if you would apply your time and thoughts to public affairs, even though you may happen to find it a little uneasy to yourself: and this you can never do with so much advantage, as by being taken into the counsel of some great prince, and putting him on noble and worthy actions, which I know you would do if you were in such a post; for the springs both of good and evil flow from the prince, over a whole nation, as from a lasting fountain. So much learning as you have, even without practice in affairs, or so great a practice as you have had, without any other learning, would render you a very fit counsellor to any king whatsoever." — "You are doubly mistaken, my dear More," said he, "both in your opinion of me, and in the judgment you make of things: for as I have not that capacity that you fancy I have; so, if I had it, the public would not be one jot the better, when I had sacrificed my quiet to it. For most princes apply themselves more to affairs of war than to the useful arts of peace; and in these I neither have any knowledge, nor do I much desire it: they are generally more set on acquiring new kingdoms, right or wrong, than on governing well those they possess. And among the ministers of princes, there are none that are not so wise as to need no assistance, or at least that do not think themselves so wise, that they imagine they need none; and if they court any, it is only those for whom the prince has much personal favor, whom by their fawnings and flatteries they endeavor to fix to their own interests: and indeed Nature has so made us, that we all love to be flattered, and to please ourselves with our own notions. The old crow loves his young, and the ape her cubs. Now if in such a Court, made up of persons who envy all others, and only admire themselves, a person should but propose anything that he had either read in history, or observed in his travels, the rest would think that the reputation of their wisdom would sink, and that their interest would be much depressed, if they could run it down: and if all other things failed, then they would fly to this, that such or such things pleased our ancestors, and if were well for us if we could but match them. They would set up their rest on such an answer, as a sufficient confutation of all that could be said; as if it were a great misfortune, that any should be found wiser than his ancestors; but though they willingly let go all the good things that were among those of former ages, yet if better things are proposed they cover themselves obstinately with this excuse of reverence to past times. I have met with these proud, morose, and absurd judgments of things in many places, particularly once in England." — "Were you ever there?" said I. — "Yes, I was," answered he, "and stayed some months there, not long after the rebellion in the west was suppressed with a great slaughter of the poor people that were engaged in it."[2]

"I was then much obliged to that reverend prelate, John Morton,[3] Archbishop of Canterbury, Cardinal, and Chancellor of England: a man," said he, "Peter (for More knows well what he was), that was not less venerable for his wisdom and virtues, than for the high character he bore. He was of a middle stature, not broken with age; his looks begot reverence rather than fear; his conversation was easy, but serious and grave; he sometimes took pleasure to try the force of those that came as suitors to him upon business, by speaking sharply, though decently to them, and by that he discovered their spirit and presence of mind, with which he was much delighted, when it did not grow up to impudence, as bearing a great resemblance to his own temper; and he looked on such persons as the fittest men for affairs. He spoke both gracefully and weightily; he was eminently skilled in the law, had a vast understanding, and a prodigious memory; and those excellent talents with which Nature had furnished him, were improved by study and experience. When I was in England the king depended much on his counsels, and the government seemed to be chiefly supported by him; for from his youth he had been all along practiced in affairs; and having passed through many traverses of fortune, he had with great cost acquired a vast stock of wisdom, which is not soon lost when it is purchased so dear. One day when I was dining with him there happened to be at table one of the English lawyers, who took occasion to run out in a high commendation of the severe execution of justice upon thieves, who, as he said, were then hanged so fast, that there were sometimes twenty on one gibbet; and upon that he said he could not wonder enough how it came to pass, that since so few escaped, there were yet as many thieves left who were still robbing in all places. Upon this, I took the boldness to speak freely before the Cardinal, said, there was no reason to wonder at the matter, since this way of punishing thieves was neither just in itself nor good for the public, for as the severity was too great, so the remedy was not effectual; simple theft not being so great a crime that it ought to cost a man his life, no punishment how severe soever being able to restrain those from robbing who can find out no other way of livelihood. 'In this,' said I, 'not only you in England, but a great part of the world imitate some ill masters that are readier to chastise their scholars than to teach them. There are dreadful punishments enacted against thieves, but it were much better to make such good provisions by which every man might be put in a method how to live, and so be preserved from the fatal necessity of stealing and of dying for it.' — 'There has been

---

2. About two thousand rebels were slain in this rebellion of 1497.
3. As a boy of twelve and thirteen, More lived in the household of Cardinal Morton (1420-1500) and was later sent to Oxford by him.

care enough taken for that,' said he, 'there are many handicrafts, and there is husbandry, by which they may make a shift to live unless they have a greater mind to follow ill courses.' — 'That will not serve your turn,' said I, 'for many lose their limbs in civil or foreign wars, as lately in the Cornish rebellion, and some time ago in your wars with France, who being thus mutilated in the service of their king and country, can no more follow their old trades, and are too old to learn new ones: but since wars are only accidental things, and have intervals, let us consider those things that fall out every day. There is a great number of noblemen among you, that are themselves idle as drones, that subsist on other men's labor, on the labor of their tenants, whom, to raise their revenues, they pare to the quick. This indeed is the only instance of their frugality, for in all other things they are prodigal, even to the beggaring of themselves: but besides this, they carry about with them a great number of idle fellows, who never learned any art by which they may gain their living; and these, as soon as either their lord dies, or they themselves fall sick, are turned out of doors; for your lords are readier to feed idle people, than to take care of the sick; and often the heir is not able to keep together so great a family as his predecessor did. Now when the stomachs of those that are thus turned out of doors, grow keen, they rob no less keenly; and what else can they do? for when, by wandering about, they have worn out both their health and their clothes, and are tattered, and look ghastly, men of quality will not entertain them, and poor men dare not do it; knowing that one who has been bred up in idleness and pleasure, and who was·used to walk about with his sword and buckler, despising all the neighborhood with an insolent scorn, as far below him, is not fit for the spade and mattock: nor will he serve a poor man for so small a hire, and in so low a diet as he can afford to give him.' To this he answered, 'This sort of men ought to be particularly cherished, for in them consists the force of the armies for which we have occasion; since their birth inspires them with a nobler sense of honor, than is to be found among tradesmen or plowmen.' — 'You may as well say,' replied I, 'that you must cherish thieves on the account of wars, for you will never want the one as long as you have the other; and as robbers prove sometimes gallant soldiers, so soldiers often prove brave robbers; so near an alliance there is between those two sorts of life. But this bad custom, so common among you, of keeping many servants, is not peculiar to this nation. In France there is yet a more pestiferous sort of people, for the whole country is full of soldiers, still kept up in time of peace; if such a state of a nation can be called a peace: and these are kept in pay upon the same account that you plead for those idle retainers about noblemen; this being a maxim of those pretended statesmen that it is necessary for the public safety, to have a good body of veteran soldiers ever in readiness. They think raw men are not to be depended on, and they sometimes seek occasions for making war, that they may train up their soldiers in the art of cutting throats; or as Sallust observed, for keeping their hands in use, that they may not grow dull by too long an intermission. But France has learned to its cost, how dangerous it is to feed such beasts. The fate of the Romans, Carthaginians, and Syrians, and many other nations and cities, which were both overturned and quite.

ruined by those standing armies, should make others wiser: and the folly of this maxim of the French, appears plainly even from this, that their trained soldiers often find your raw men prove too hard for them; of which I will not say much, lest you may think I flatter the English. Every day's experience shows, that the mechanics in the towns, or the clowns in the country, are not afraid of fighting with those idle gentlemen, if they are not disabled by some misfortune in their body, or dispirited by extreme want, so that you need not fear that those well-shaped and strong men (for it is only such that noblemen love to keep about them, till they spoil them) who now grow feeble with ease, and are softened with their effeminate manner of life, would be less fit for action if they were well bred and well employed. And it seems very unreasonable, that for the prospect of a war, which you need never have but when you please, you should maintain so many idle men, as will always disturb you in time of peace, which is ever to be more considered than war. But I do not think that this necessity of stealing arises only from hence; there is another cause of it more peculiar to England.'—'What is that?' said the Cardinal. —'The increase of pasture,' said I, 'by which your sheep, which are naturally mild, and easily kept in order, may be said now to devour men, and unpeople, not only villages, but towns; for wherever it is found that the sheep of any soil yield a softer and richer wool than ordinary, there the nobility and gentry, and even those holy men the abbots, not contented with the old rents which their farms yielded, nor thinking it enough that they, living at their ease, do no good to the public, resolve to do it hurt instead of good. They stop the course of agriculture, destroying houses and towns, reserving only the churches, and enclose grounds that they may lodge their sheep in them. As if forests and parks had swallowed up too little of the land, those worthy countrymen turn the best inhabited places into solitudes; for when an insatiable wretch, who is a plague to his country, resolves to inclose many thousand acres of ground, the owners, as well as tenants, are turned out of their possessions, by tricks, or by main force, or being wearied out with all usage, they are forced to sell them. By which means those miserable people, both men and women, married and unmarried, old and young, with their poor but numerous families (since country business requires many hands), are all forced to change their seats, not knowing whither to go; and they must sell almost for nothing their household stuff, which could not bring them much money, even though they might stay for a buyer. When that little money is at an end, for it will be soon spent; what is left for them to do, but either to steal and so to be hanged (God knows how justly), or to go about and beg? And if they do this, they are put in prison as idle vagabonds; while they would willingly work, but can find none that will hire them; for there is no more occasion for country labor, to which they have been bred, when there is no arable ground left. One shepherd can look after a flock, which will stock an extent of ground that would require many hands, if it were to be plowed and reaped. This likewise in many places raises the price of corn. The price of wool is also risen, that the poor people who were wont to make cloth are no more able to buy it; and this likewise makes many of them idle. For since the increase of pasture God has punished the avarice of the owners, by a rot among the sheep, which has destroyed vast numbers of them; to us it might have seemed more just had it fell on the owners themselves. But suppose the sheep should increase ever so much, their price is not like to fall; since though they cannot be called a monopoly, because they are not engrossed by one person, yet they are in so few hands, and these are so rich, that as they are not pressed to sell them sooner than they have a mind to it, so they never do it till they have raised the price as high as possible. And on the same account it is, that the other kinds of cattle are so dear, because many villages being pulled down, and all country labor being much neglected, there are none who make it their business to breed them. The rich do not breed cattle as they do sheep, but buy them lean, and at low prices; and after they have fattened them on their grounds, sell them again at high rates. And I do not think that all the inconveniences this will produce are yet observed; for as they sell the cattle dear, so if they are consumed faster than the breeding countries from which they are bought can afford them, then the stock must decrease, and this must needs end in great scarcity; and by these means this your island, which seemed as to this particular the happiest in the world, will suffer much by the cursed avarice of a few persons; besides this, the rising of grain makes all people lessen their families as much as they can; and what can those who are dismissed by them do, but either beg or rob? And to this last, a man of a great mind is much sooner drawn than to the former. Luxury likewise breaks in apace upon you, to set forward your poverty and misery; there is an excessive vanity in apparel, and great cost in diet; and that not only in noblemen's families, but even among tradesmen, among the farmers themselves, and among all ranks of persons. You have also many infamous houses, and besides those that are known, the taverns and alehouses are no better; add to these, dice, cards, tables, football, tennis, and quoits, in which money runs fast away; and those that are initiated into them, must in the conclusion betake themselves to robbing for a supply. Banish these plagues, and give orders that those who have dispeopled so much soil, may either rebuild the villages they have pulled down, or let out their grounds to such as will do it; restrain those engrossings of the rich, that are as bad almost as monopolies; leave fewer occasions to idleness; let agriculture be set up again, and the manufacture of the wool be regulated, that so there may be work found for those companies of idle people whom want forces to be thieves, or who now being idle vagabonds, or useless servants, will certainly grow thieves at last. If you do not find a remedy to these evils, it is a vain thing to boast of your severity in punishing theft, which though it may have the appearance of justice, yet in itself is neither just nor convenient. For if you suffer your people to be ill educated, and their manners to be corrupted from their infancy, and then punish them for those crimes to which their first education disposed them, what else is to be concluded from this, but that you first make thieves and then punish them?"

"While I was talking thus, the counsellor who was present had prepared an answer, and had resolved to resume all I had said, according to the formality of a debate, in which things are generally repeated more faithfully than they are answered; as if the chief trial to be made were of men's memories. 'You have talked prettily for a stranger,' said he, 'having heard of many things among us which you have not been able to consider well; but I will make the whole matter plain to you, and will first repeat in order all that you have said, then I will show how much your ignorance of our affairs has misled you, and will in the last place answer all your arguments. And that I may begin where I promised there were four things—' 'Hold your peace,' said the Cardinal, 'this will take up too much time; therefore we will at present ease you of the trouble of answering, and reserve it to our next meeting, which shall be to-morrow, if Raphael's affairs and yours can admit it. But, Raphael,' said he to me, 'I would gladly know upon what reason it is that you think theft ought not to be punished by death? Would you give way to it? Or do you propose any other punishment that will be more useful to the public? For since death does not restrain theft, if men thought their lives would be safe, what fear or force could restrain ill men? On the contrary, they would look on the mitigation of the punishment as an invitation to commit more crimes.' I answered, 'It seems to me a very unjust thing to take away a man's life for a little money; for nothing in the world can be of equal value with a man's life: and if it is said, that it is not for the money that one suffers, but for his breaking the law, I must say, extreme justice is an extreme injury; for we ought not to approve of these terrible laws that make the smallest offences capital, nor of that opinion of the Stoics, that makes all crimes equal, as if there were no difference to be made between the killing a man and the taking his purse, between which, if we examine things impartially, there is no likeness nor proportion. God has commanded us not to kill, and shall we kill so easily for a little money? But if one shall say, that by the law we are only forbid to kill any, except when the laws of the land allow of it; upon the same grounds, laws may be made in some cases to allow of adultery and perjury: for God having taken from us the right of disposing, either of our own or of other people's lives, if it is pretended that the mutual consent of man in making laws can authorize manslaughter in cases in which God has given us no example, that it frees people from the obligation of the divine law, and so makes murder a lawful action; what is this, but to give a preference to human laws before the divine? And if this is once admitted, by the same rule men may in all other things put what restrictions they please upon the laws of God. If by the Mosaical law, though it was rough and severe, as being a yoke laid on an obstinate and servile nation, men were only fined, and not put to death for theft, we cannot imagine that in this new law of mercy, in which God treats us with the tenderness of a father, He has given us a greater license to cruelty than He did to the Jews. Upon these reasons it is, that I think putting thieves to death is not lawful; and it is plain and obvious that it is absurd, and of ill consequence to the commonwealth, that a thief and a murderer should be equally punished; for if a robber sees that his danger is the same, if he is convicted of theft as if he were guilty of murder, this will naturally incite him to kill the person whom otherwise he would only have robbed, since if the punishment is the same, there is more security, and less danger of discovery, when he that can best make it is put out of the way; so that terrifying thieves too much, provokes them to cruelty.

" 'But as to the question, what more convenient way of punishment can be found? I think it is much easier to find that out, than to invent anything that is worse; why should we doubt but the way that was so long in use among the old Romans, who understood so well the arts of government, was very proper for their punishment? They condemned such as they found guilty of great crimes, to work their whole lives in quarries, or to dig in mines with chains about them. But the method that I liked best, was that which I observed in my travels in Persia, among the Polylerits,[4] who are a considerable and well-governed people. They pay a yearly tribute to the King of Persia; but in all other respects they are a free nation, and governed by their own laws. They lie far from the sea, and are environed with hills; and being contented with the productions of their own country, which is very fruitful, they have little commerce with any other nation; and as they, according to the genius of their country, have no inclination to enlarge their borders; so their mountains, and the pension they pay to the Persian, secure them from all invasions. Thus they have no wars among them; they live rather conveniently than with splendor, and may be rather called a happy nation, than either eminent or famous; for I do not think that they are known so much as by name to any but their next neighbors. Those that are found guilty of theft among them, are bound to make restitution to the owner, and not as it is in other places, to the prince, for they reckon that the prince has no more right to the stolen goods than the thief; but if that which was stolen is no more in being, then the goods of the thieves are estimated, and restitution being made out of them, the remainder is given to their wives and children: and they themselves are condemned to serve in the public works, but are neither imprisoned, nor chained, unless there happened to be some extraordinary circumstances in their crimes. They go about loose and free, working for the public. If they are idle or backward to work, they are whipped; but if they work hard, they are well used and treated without any mark of reproach, only the lists of them are called always at night, and then they are shut up. They suffer no other uneasiness, but this of constant labor; for as they work for the public, so they are well entertained out of the public stock, which is done differently in different places. In some places, whatever is bestowed on them, is raised by a charitable contribution; and though this way may seem uncertain, yet so merciful are the inclinations of that people, that they are plentifully supplied by it; but in other places, public revenues are set aside for them; or there is a constant tax of a poll-money raised for their maintenance. In some places they are set to no public work, but every private man that has occasion to hire workmen, goes to the market-places and hires them of the public, a little lower than he would do a freeman: if they go lazily about their task, he may quicken them with the whip. By this means there is always some piece of work or other to be done by them; and beside their livelihood, they earn somewhat still to the public. They all wear a peculiar habit, of one certain color, and their hair is cropped a little above their ears, and a piece of one of their ears is cut off. Their friends are allowed to give them either meat,

---

4. Derived from the Greek *polus leros,* "much nonsense."

drink, or clothes, so they are of their proper color; but it is death, both to the giver and taker, if they give them money; nor is it less penal for any freeman to take money from them, upon any account whatsoever: and it is also death for any of these slaves (so they are called) to handle arms. Those of every division of the country are distinguished by a peculiar mark; which it is capital for them to lay aside, to go out of their bounds, or to talk with a slave of another jurisdiction; and the very attempt of an escape is no less penal than an escape itself; it is death for any other slave to be accessory to it; and if a freeman engages in it he is condemned to slavery. Those that discover it are rewarded; if freemen, in money; and if slaves, with liberty, together with a pardon for being accessory to it; that so they might find their account, rather in repenting of their engaging in such a design, than in persisting in it.

"These are their laws and rules in relation to robbery; and it is obvious that they are as advantageous as they are mild and gentle; since vice is not only destroyed, and men preserved, but they are treated in such a manner as to make them see the necessity of being honest, and of employing the rest of their lives in repairing the injuries they have formerly done to society. Nor is there any hazard of their falling back to their old customs: and so little do travellers apprehend mischief from them, that they generally make use of them for guides, from one jurisdiction to another; for there is nothing left them by which they can rob, or be the better for it, since as they are disarmed, so the very having of money is a sufficient conviction: and as they are certainly punished if discovered, so they cannot hope to escape; for their habit being in all the parts of it different from what is commonly worn, they cannot fly away, unless they would go naked, and even then their cropped ears would betray them. The only danger to be feared from them, is their conspiring against the government: but those of one division and neighborhood can do nothing to any purpose, unless a general conspiracy were laid amongst all the slaves of the several jurisdictions, which cannot be done, since they cannot meet or talk together, nor will any venture on a design where the concealment would be so dangerous, and the discovery so profitable. None are quite hopeless of recovering their freedom, since by their obedience and patience, and by giving good grounds to believe that they will change their manner of life for the future, they may expect at last to obtain their liberty: and some are every year restored to it, upon the good character that is given of them. — When I had related all this, I added, that I did not see why such a method might not be followed with more advantage, than could ever be expected from that severe justice which the counsellor magnified so much. To this he answered, that it could never take place in England, without endangering the whole nation. As he said this, he shook his head, made some grimaces, and held his peace, while all the company seemed of his opinion, except the Cardinal, who said that it was not easy to form a judgment of its success, since it was a method that never yet had been tried. 'But if,' said he, 'when the sentence of death was passed upon a thief, the prince would reprieve him for a while, and make the experiment upon him, denying him the privilege of a sanctuary; and then if it had a good effect upon him, it might take place; and if it did not succeed, the worst would be, to execute the sentence on the condemned persons at last. And I do not see,' added he, 'why it would be either unjust, inconvenient, or at all dangerous, to admit of such a delay: in my opinion, the vagabonds ought to be treated in the same manner; against whom, though we have made many laws, yet we have not been able to gain our end.' When the Cardinal had done, they all commended the motion, though they had despised it when it came from me; but more particularly commended what related to the vagabonds, because it was his own observation.

"I do not know whether it be worth while to tell what followed, for it was very ridiculous; but I shall venture at it, for as it is not foreign to this matter, so some good use may be made of it. There was a jester standing by, that counterfeited the fool so naturally, that he seemed to be really one. The jests which he offered were so cold and dull, that we laughed more at him than at them; yet sometimes he said, as it were by chance, things that were not unpleasant; so as to justify the old proverb, 'That he who throws the dice often, will sometimes have a lucky hit.' When one of the company had said, that I had taken care of the thieves, and the Cardinal had taken care of the vagabonds, so that there remained nothing but that some public provision might be made for the poor, whom sickness or old age had disabled from labor. 'Leave that to me,' said the fool, 'and I shall take care of them; for there is no sort of people whose sight I abhor more, having been so often vexed with them, and with their sad complaints; but as dolefully soever as they have told their tale, they could never prevail so far as to draw one penny from me: for either I had no mind to give them anything, or when I had a mind to do it, I had nothing to give them: and they now know me so well, that they will not lose their labor, but let me pass without giving me any trouble, because they hope for nothing, no more in faith than if I were a priest: but I would have a law made, for sending all these beggars to monasteries, the men to the Benedictines to be made lay-brothers, and the women to be nuns.' The Cardinal smiled, and approved of it in jest; but the rest liked it in earnest. There was a divine present, who though he was a grave morose man, yet he was so pleased with this reflection that was made on the priests and the monks, that he began to play with the fool, and said to him, 'This will not deliver you from all beggars, except you take care of us friars.'—'That is done already,' answered the fool, 'for the Cardinal has provided for you, by what he proposed for restraining vagabonds, and setting them to work, for I know no vagabonds like you.' This was well entertained by the whole company, who looking at the Cardinal, perceived that he was not ill pleased at it; only the friar himself was vexed, as may be easily imagined, and fell into such a passion, that he could not forbear railing at the fool, and calling knave, slanderer, backbiter, and son of perdition, and then cited some dreadful threatenings out of the Scriptures against him. Now the jester thought he was in his element, and laid about him freely. 'Good friar,' said he, 'be not angry, for it is written, "In patience possess your soul." '—The friar answered (for I shall give you his own words) 'I am not angry, you hangman; at least I do not sin in it, for the Psalmist says, "Be ye angry, and sin not." '—Upon this the Cardinal admonished him gently, and wished him to govern his passions. 'No, my lord,' said he, 'I speak not but from a good zeal, which is said, "The zeal of thy house hath eaten me up;" and we sing in our church, that those who mocked Elisha as he went up to the house of God, felt the effects of his zeal; which that mocker, that rogue, that scoundrel, will perhaps feel.' — 'You do this perhaps with a good intention,' said the Cardinal; 'but in my opinion, it were wiser in you, and perhaps better for you, not to engage in so ridiculous a contest with a fool.' — 'No, my lord,' answered he, 'that were not wisely done; for Solomon, the wisest of men, said. "Answer a fool according to his folly;" which I now do, and show him the ditch into which he will fall, if he is not aware of it; for if the many mockers of Elisha, who was but one bald man, felt the effect of his zeal, what will become of one mocker of so many friars, among whom there are so many bald men?[5] We have likewise a Bull, by which all that jeer us are excommunicated.' — When the Cardinal saw that there was no end of this matter, he made a sign to the fool to withdraw, turned the discourse another way; and soon after rose from the table, and dismissing us, went to hear causes.

"Thus, Master More, I have run out into a tedious story, of the length of which I had been ashamed, if, as you earnestly begged it of me, I had not observed you to hearken to it, as if you had no mind to lose any part of it. I might have contracted it, but I resolved to give it to you at large, that you might observe how those that despised what I had proposed, no sooner perceived that the Cardinal did not dislike it, but presently approved of it, fawned so on him, and flattered him to such a degree, that they in good earnest applauded those things that he only liked in jest. And from hence you may gather, how little courtiers would value either me or my counsels."

To this I answered, "You have done me a great kindness in this relation; for as everything has been related by you, both wisely and pleasantly, so you have made me imagine that I was in my own country, and grown young again, by recalling that good Cardinal to my thoughts, in whose family I was bred from my childhood: and though you are upon other accounts very dear to me, yet you are the dearer, because you honor his memory so much; but after all this I cannot change my opinion; for I still think that if you could overcome that aversion which you have to the Courts of Princes, you might, by the advice which it is in your power to give, do a great deal of good to mankind; and this is the chief design that every good man ought to propose to himself in living; for your friend Plato thinks that nations will be happy, when either philosophers become kings, or kings become philosophers, it is no wonder if we are so far from that happiness, while philosophers will not think it their duty to assist kings with their councils." — "They are not so base-minded," said he, "but that they would willingly do it: many of them have already done it by their books, if those that are in power would but hearken to their good advice. But Plato judged right, that except kings themselves became philosophers, they who from their childhood are corrupted with false notions, would never fall in entirely with the councils of philosophers, and this he himself found to be true in the person of Dionysius.

5. See II Kings 11:23. The "bald head" is a reference to the tonsure.

"Do not you think, that if I were about any king, proposing good laws to him, and endeavoring to root out all the cursed seeds of evil that I found in him, I should either be turned out of his Court, or at least laughed at for my pains? For instance, what could it signify if I were about the King of France, and were called into his cabinet-council, where several wise men, in his hearing, were proposing many expedients; as by what arts and practices Milan may be kept; and Naples, that had so oft slipped out of their hands, recovered; how the Venetians, and after them the rest of Italy, may be subdued; and then how Flanders, Brabant, and all Burgundy, and some other kingdoms which he has swallowed already in his designs, may be added to his empire. One proposes a league with the Venetians, to be kept as long as he finds his account in it, and that he ought to communicate councils with them, and give them some share of the spoil, till his success makes him need or fear them less, and then it will be easily taken out of their hands. Another proposes the hiring the Germans, and the securing the Switzers by pensions. Another proposes the gaining the Emperor by money, which is omnipotent with him. Another proposes a peace with the King of Arragon, and in order to cement it, the yielding up the King of Navarre's pretensions. Another thinks the Prince of Castile is to be wrought on, by the hope of an alliance; and that some of his courtiers are to be gained to the French faction by pensions. The hardest point of all is what to do with England: a treaty of peace is to be set on foot, and if their alliance is not to be depended on, yet is to be made as firm as possible; and they are to be called friends, but suspected as enemies; therefore the Scots are to be kept in readiness, to be let loose upon England on every occasion: and some banished nobleman is to be supported underhand (for by the league it cannot be done avowedly) who has a pretension to the crown, by which means that suspected prince may be kept in awe. Now when things are in so great a fermentation, and so many gallant men are joining councils, how to carry on the war, if so mean a man as I should stand up, and wish them to change all their councils, to let Italy alone, and stay at home, since the kingdom of France was indeed greater than could be well governed by one man; that therefore he ought not to think of adding others to it: and if after this, I should propose to them the resolutions of the Achorians,[6] a people that lie on the south-east of Utopia, who long ago engaged in war, in order to add to the dominions of their prince another kingdom, to which he had some pretensions by an ancient alliance. This they conquered, but found that the trouble of keeping it was equal to that by which it was gained; that the conquered people were always either in rebellion or exposed to foreign invasions, while they were obliged to be incessantly at war, either for or against them, and consequently could never disband their army; that in the meantime they were oppressed with taxes, their money went out of the kingdom, their blood was spilled for the glory of their king, without procuring the least advantage to the people, who received not the smallest benefit from it even in time of peace; and that their manners being corrupted by a long war, robbery and murders everywhere abounded, and their laws fell into contempt; while their king, distracted with the care of two kingdoms, was the

6. Derived from the Greek *a-choros,* "no place."

less able to apply his mind to the interests of either. When they saw this, and that there would be no end to these evils, they by joint councils made an humble address to their king, desiring him to choose which of the two kingdoms he had the greatest mind to keep, since he could not hold both; for they were too great a people to be governed by a divided king, since no man would willingly have a groom that should be in common between him and another. Upon which the good prince was forced to quit his new kingdom to one of his friends (who was not long after dethroned), and to be contented with his old one. To this I would add, that after all those warlike attempts, the vast confusions, and the consumption both of treasure and of people that must follow them; perhaps upon some misfortune, they might be forced to throw up all at last; therefore it seemed much more eligible that the king should improve his ancient kingdom all he could, and make it flourish as much as possible; that he should love his people, and be beloved of them; that he should live among them, govern them gently, and let other kingdoms alone, since that which had fallen to his share was big enough, if not too big for him. Pray how do you think would such a speech be heard?"—"I confess," said I, "I think not very well."

"But what," said he, "if I should sort with another kind of ministers, whose chief contrivances and consultations were, by what art the prince's treasures might be increased. Where one proposes raising the value of specie when the king's debts are large, and lowering it when his revenues were to come in, that so he might both pay much with a little, and in a little receive a great deal: another proposes a pretence of a war, that money might be raised in order to carry it on, and that a peace be concluded as soon as that was done; and this with such appearances of religion as might work on the people, and make them impute it to the piety of their prince, and to his tenderness for the lives of his subjects. A third offers some old musty laws, that have been forgotten by all the subjects, so they had been also broken by them; and proposes the levying the penalties of these laws, that as it would bring in a vast treasure, so there might be a very good pretence for it, since it would look like the executing a law, and the doing of justice. A fourth proposes the prohibiting of many things under severe penalties, especially such as were against the interest of the people, and then the dispensing with these prohibitions upon great compositions, to those who might find their advantage in breaking them. This would serve two ends, both of them acceptable to many; for as those whose avarice led them to transgress would be severely fined, so the selling licenses dear would look as if a prince were tender of his people, and would not easily, or at low rates, dispense with anything that might be against the public good. Another proposes that the judges must be made sure, that they may declare always in favor of the prerogative, that they must be often sent for to Court, that the king may hear them argue those points in which he is concerned; since how unjust soever any of his pretensions may be, yet still some one or other of them, either out of contradiction to others, or the pride of singularity, or to make their court, would find out some pretence or other to give the king a fair color to carry the point; for if the judges but differ in opinion, the clearest thing in the world is made by that means disputable, and truth being once brought in question, the king may then take advantage to expound the law for his own profit; while the judges that stand out will be brought over, either out of fear or modesty; and they being thus gained, all of them may be sent to the bench to give sentence boldly, as the king would have it; for fair pretences will never be wanting when sentence is to be given in the prince's favor. It will either be said that equity lies of his side, or some words in the law will be found sounding that way, or some forced sense will be put on them; and when all other things fail, the king's undoubted prerogative will be pretended, as that which is above all law; and to which a religious judge ought to have a special regard. Thus all consent to that maxim of Crassus,[7] that a prince cannot have treasure enough, since he must maintain his armies out of it; that a king, even though he would, can do nothing unjustly; that all property is in him, not excepting the very persons of his subjects; and that no man has any other property, but that which the king out of his goodness thinks fit to leave him. And they think it is the prince's interest, that there be as little of this left as may be, as if it were his advantage that his people should have neither riches nor liberty; since these things make them less easy and less willing to submit to a cruel and unjust government; whereas necessity and poverty blunts them, makes them patient, beats them down, and breaks that height of spirit, that might otherwise dispose them to rebel. Now what if after all these propositions were made, I should rise up and assert, that such councils were both unbecoming a king, and mischievous to him: and that not only his honor but his safety consisted more in his people's wealth, than in his own; if I should show that they choose a king for their own sake, and not for his; that by his care and endeavors they may be both easy and safe; and that therefore a prince ought to take more care of his people's happiness than of his own, as a shepherd is to take more care of his flock than of himself. It is also certain, that they are much mistaken that think the poverty of a nation is a means of public safety. Who quarrel more than beggars? Who does more earnestly long for a change, than he that is uneasy in his present circumstances? And who run to create confusion with so desperate a boldness, as those who have nothing to lose, hope to gain by them? If a king should fall under such contempt or envy, that he could not keep his subjects in their duty, but by oppression and ill usage, and by rendering them poor and miserable, it were certainly better for him to quit his kingdom, than to retain it by such methods, as makes him while he keeps the name of authority, lose the majesty due to it. Nor is it so becoming the dignity of a king to reign over beggars, as over rich and happy subjects. And therefore Fabricius, a man of a noble and exalted temper, said, he would rather govern rich men, than be rich himself; since for one man to abound in wealth and pleasure, when all about him are mourning and groaning, is to be a gaoler and not a king. He is an unskilful physician, that cannot cure one disease without casting his patient into another: so he that can find no other way for correcting the errors of his people, but by taking from them the conveniences of life, shows that he knows not

---

7. The saying is attributed to the rich Crassus, M. Licinius Crassus Dives, a contemporary of Cicero.

what it is to govern a free nation. He himself ought rather to shake off his sloth, or to lay down his pride; for the contempt or hatred that his people have for him, takes its rise from the vices in himself. Let him live upon what belongs to him, without wronging others, and accommodate his expense to his revenue. Let him punish crimes, and by his wise conduct let him endeavor to prevent them, rather than be severe when he has suffered them to be too common; let him not rashly revive laws that are abrogated by disuse, especially if they have been long forgotten, and never wanted; and let him never take any penalty for the breach of them, to which a judge would not give way in a private man, but would look on him as a crafty and unjust person for pretending to it. To these things I would add, that law among the Macarians,[8] a people that lie not far from Utopia, by which their king, on the day on which he begins to reign, is tied by an oath confirmed by solemn sacrifices, never to have at once above a thousand pounds of gold in his treasures, or so much silver as is equal to that in value. This law, they tell us, was made by an excellent king, who had more regard to the riches of his country than to his own wealth; and therefore provided against the heaping up of so much treasure, as might impoverish the people. He thought that a moderate sum might be sufficient for any accident; if either the king had occasion for it against rebels, or the kingdom against the invasion of an enemy; but that it was not enough to encourage a prince to invade other men's rights, a circumstance that was the chief cause of his making that law. He also thought that it was a good provision for that free circulation of money, so necessary for the course of commerce and exchange: and when a king must distribute all those extraordinary accessions that increase treasure beyond the due pitch, it makes him less disposed to oppress his subjects. Such a king as this will be the terror of ill men, and will be beloved by all the good.

"If, I say, I should talk of these or such like things, to men that had taken their bias another way, how deaf would they be to all I could say?" – "No doubt, very deaf," answered I; "and no wonder, for one is never to offer propositions or advice that we are certain will not be entertained. Discourses so much out of the road could not avail anything, nor have any effect on men whose minds were prepossessed with different sentiments. This philosophical way of speculation is not unpleasant among friends in a free conversation, but there is no room for it in the Courts of Princes where great affairs are carried on by authority." – "That is what I was saying," replied he, "that there is no room for philosophy in the Courts of Princes." – "Yes, there is," said I, "but not for this speculative philosophy that makes everything to be alike fitting at all times: but there is another philosophy that is more pliable, that knows its proper scene, accommodates itself to it, and teaches a man with propriety and decency to act that part which has fallen to his share. If when one of Plautus's comedies is upon the stage and a company of servants are acting their parts, you should come out in the garb of a philosopher, and repeat out of 'Octavia's discourse of Seneca's to Nero,' would it not be better for you to say nothing than by mixing things of such different natures to make an impertinent

---

8. Derived from the Greek *makarios*, "blessed."

tragi-comedy? For you spoil and corrupt the play that is in hand when you mix with it things of an opposite nature, even though they are much better. Therefore go through with the play that is acting the best you can, and do not confound it because another that is pleasanter comes into your thoughts. It is even so in a commonwealth, and in the councils of princes; if ill opinions cannot be quite rooted out, and you cannot cure some received vice according to your wishes, you must not therefore abandon the commonwealth, for the same reasons you should not forsake the ship in a storm because you cannot command the winds. You are not obliged to assault people with discourses that are out of their road, when you see that their received notions must prevent your making an impression upon them. You ought rather to cast about and to manage things with all the dexterity in your power, so that if you are not able to make them go well they may be as little ill as possible; for except all men were good everything cannot be right, and that is a blessing that I do not at present hope to see."
—"According to your arguments," answered he, "all that I could be able to do would be to preserve myself from being mad while I endeavored to cure the madness of others; for if I speak truth, I must repeat what I have said to you; and as for lying, whether a philosopher can do it or not, I cannot tell, I am sure I cannot do it. But though these discourses may be uneasy and ungrateful to them, I do not see why they should seem foolish or extravagant: indeed if I should either propose such things as Plato has contrived in his commonwealth, or as the Utopians practice in theirs, though they might seem better, as certainly they are, yet they are so different from our establishment, which is founded on property, there being no such thing among them, that I could not expect that it would have any effect on them; but such discourses as mine, which only call past evils to mind and give warning of what may follow, have nothing in them that is so absurd that they may not be used at any time, for they can only be unpleasant to those who are resolved to run headlong the contrary way; and if we must let alone everything as absurd or extravagant which by reason of the wicked lives of many may seem uncouth, we must, even among Christians, give over pressing the greatest part of those things that Christ hath taught us, though He has commanded us not to conceal them, but to proclaim on the house-tops that which He taught in secret. The greatest parts of His precepts are more opposite to the lives of the men of this age than any part of my discourse has been; but the preachers seemed to have learned that craft to which you advise me, for they observing that the world would not willingly suit their lives to the rules that Christ has given, have fitted His doctrine as if it had been a leaden rule, to their lives, that so some way or other they might agree with one another. But I see no other effect of this compliance except it be that men become more secure in their wickedness by it. And this is all the success that I can have in a Court, for I must always differ from the rest, and then I shall signify nothing; or if I agree with them, I shall then only help forward their madness. I do not comprehend what you mean by your casting about, or by the bending and handling things so dextrously, that if they go not well they may go as little ill as may be; for in Courts they will not bear with a man's holding his peace or conniving at what others do.

A man must barefacedly approve of the worst counsels, and consent to the blackest designs: so that he would pass for a spy, or possibly for a traitor, that did but coldly approve of such wicked practices: and therefore when a man is engaged in such a society, he will be so far from being able to mend matters by his casting about, as you call it, that he will find no occasions of doing any good: the ill company will sooner corrupt him, than be the better for him: or if notwithstanding all their ill company, he still remains steady and innocent, yet their follies and knavery will be imputed to him; and by mixing counsels with them, he must bear his share of all the blame that belongs wholly to others.

"It was no ill simile by which Plato set forth the unreasonableness of a philosopher's meddling with government. If a man, says he, was to see a great company run out every day into the rain, and take delight in being wet; if he knew that it would be to no purpose for him to go and persuade them to return to their houses, in order to avoid the storm, and that all that could be expected by his going to speak to them would be that he himself should be as wet as they, it would be best for him to keep within doors; and since he had not influence enough to correct other people's folly, to take care to preserve himself.

"Though to speak plainly my real sentiments, I must freely own, that as long as there is any property, and while money is the standard of all other things, I cannot think that a nation can be governed either justly or happily: not justly, because the best things will fall to the share of the worst men; nor happily, because all things will be divided among a few (and even these are not in all respects happy), the rest being left to be absolutely miserable. Therefore when I reflect on the wise and good constitution of the Utopians, among whom all things are so well governed, and with so few laws; where virtue hath its due reward, and yet there is such an equality, that every man lives in plenty; when I compare with them so many other nations that are still making new laws, and yet can never bring their constitution to a right regulation, where notwithstanding every one has his property; yet all the laws that they can invent have not the power either to obtain or preserve it, or even to enable men certainly to distinguish what is their own from what is another's; of which the many lawsuits that every day break out, and are eternally depending, give too plain a demonstration; when, I say, I balance all these things in my thoughts, I grow more favorable to Plato, and do not wonder that he resolved not to make any laws for such as would not submit to a community of all things: for so wise a man could not but foresee that the setting all upon a level was the only way to make a nation happy, which cannot be obtained so long as there is property: for when every man draws to himself all that he can compass, by one title or another, it must needs follow, that how plentiful soever a nation may be, yet a few dividing the wealth of it among themselves, the rest must fall into indigence. So that there will be two sorts of people among them, who deserve that their fortunes should be interchanged; the former useless, but wicked and ravenous; and the latter, who by their constant industry serve the public more than themselves, sincere and modest men. From whence I am persuaded, that till property is taken away there can be no equitable or just distribution of

things, nor can the world be happily governed: for as long as that is
maintained, the greatest and the far best part of mankind will be still
oppressed with a load of cares and anxieties. I confess without taking it
quite away, those pressures that lie on a great part of mankind may be
made lighter; but they can never be quite removed. For if laws were made
to determine at how great an extent in soil, and at how much money every
man must stop, to limit the prince that he might not grow too great, and to
restrain the people that they might not become too insolent, and that none
might factiously aspire to public employments, which ought neither to be
sold, nor made burthensome by a great expense; since otherwise those that
serve in them would be tempted to reimburse themselves by cheats and
violence, and it would become necessary to find out rich men for undergoing those employments which ought rather to be trusted to the wise.
These laws, I say, might have such effects, as good diet and care might have
on a sick man, whose recovery is desperate: they might allay and mitigate
the disease, but it could never be quite healed, nor the body politic be
brought again to a good habit, as long as property remains; and it will fall
out as in a complication of diseases, that by applying a remedy to one sore,
you will provoke another; and that which removes the one ill symptom
produces others, while the strengthening one part of the body weakens the
rest." — "On the contrary," answered I, "it seems to me that men cannot live
conveniently, where all things are common: how can there be any plenty,
where every man will excuse himself from labor? For as the hope of gain
doth not excite him, so the confidence that he has in other men's industry
may make him slothful: if people come to be pinched with want, and yet
cannot dispose of anything as their own; what can follow upon this but
perpetual sedition and bloodshed, especially when the reverence and
authority due to magistrates falls to the ground? For I cannot imagine
how that can be kept up among those that are in all things equal to one
another." — "I do not wonder," said he, "that it appears so to you, since
you have no notion, or at least no right one, of such a constitution: but
if you had been in Utopia with me, and had seen their laws and rules, as
I did, for the space of five years, in which I lived among them; and during
which time I was so delighted with them, that indeed I should never have
left them, if it had not been to make the discovery of that new world to
the Europeans; you would then confess that you had never seen a people
so well constituted as they." — "You will not easily persuade me," said Peter,
"that any nation in that new world is better governed than those among
us. For as our understandings are not worse than theirs, so our government, if I mistake not, being more ancient, a long practice has helped us
to find out many conveniences of life: and some happy chances have discovered other things to us, which no man's understanding could ever
have invented." — "As for the antiquity, either of their government, or of
ours," said he, "you cannot pass a true judgment of it, unless you had
read their histories; for if they are to be believed, they had towns among
them before these parts were so much as inhabited. And as for those
discoveries, that have been either hit on by chance, or made by ingenious
men, these might have happened there as well as here. I do not deny but
we are more ingenious than they are, but they exceed us much in industry

and application. They knew a little concerning us before our arrival
among them; they call us all by a general name of the nations that lie
beyond the Equinoctial Line; for their Chronicle mentions a shipwreck
that was made on their coast 1,200 years ago; and that some Romans and
Egyptians that were in the ship, getting safe ashore, spent the rest of their'
days amongst them; and such was their ingenuity, that from this single
opportunity they drew the advantage of learning from those unlooked-
for guests, and acquired all the useful arts that were then among the
Romans, and which were known to these shipwrecked men: and by the
hints that they gave them, they themselves found out even some of those
arts which they could not fully explain; so happily did they improve that
accident, of having some of our people cast upon their shore. But if such
an accident has at any time brought any from thence into Europe, we have
been so far from improving it, that we do not so much as remember it;
as in after-times perhaps it will be forgot by our people that I was ever
there. For though they from one such accident made themselves masters
of all the good inventions that were among us; yet I believe it would be
long before we should learn or put in practice any of the good institutions
that are among them. And this is the true cause of their being better governed, and living happier than we, though we come not short of them in
point of understanding or outward advantages." — Upon this I said to him,
"I earnestly beg you would describe that island very particularly to us.
Be not too short, but set out in order all things relating to their soil, their
rivers, their towns, their people, their manners, constitutions, laws, and,
in a word, all that you imagine we desire to know. And you may well
imagine that we desire to know everything concerning them, of which
we are hitherto ignorant." — "I will do it very willingly," said he, "for I
have digested the whole matter carefully; but it will take up some time." —
"Let us go then," said I, "first and dine, and then we shall have leisure
enough." He consented. We went in and dined, and after dinner came
back, and sat down in the same place. I ordered my servants to take care
that none might come and interrupt us. And both Peter and I desired
Raphael to be as good as his word. When he saw that we were very intent
upon it, he paused a little to recollect himself, and began in this manner.

Book II

The island of Utopia is in the middle two hundred miles broad, and
holds almost at the same breadth over a great part of it; but it grows
narrower towards both ends. Its figure is not unlike a crescent: between its
horns, the sea comes in eleven miles broad, and spreads itself into a great
bay, which is environed with land to the compass of about five hundred
miles wide, and is well secured from winds. In this bay there is no great
current, the whole coast is, as it were, one continued harbor, which gives
all that live in the island great convenience for mutual commerce; but the
entry into the bay, occasioned by rocks on the one hand, and shallows on
the other, is very dangerous. In the middle of it there is one single rock

which appears above water, and may therefore be easily avoided, and on the top of it there is a tower in which a garrison is kept; the other rocks lie under water and are very dangerous. The channel is known only to the natives, so that if any stranger should enter into the bay, without one of their pilots, he would run great danger of shipwreck, for even they themselves could not pass it safe, if some marks that are on the coast did not direct their way; and if these should be but a little shifted, any fleet that might come against them, how great soever it were, would be certainly lost. On the other side of the island there are likewise many harbors; and the coast is so fortified, both by nature and art, that a small number of men can hinder the descent of a great army. But they report (and there remains good marks of it to make it credible) that this was no island at first, but a part of the continent. Utopus that conquered it (whose name it still carries, for Abraxa[9] was its first name) brought the rude and uncivilized inhabitants into such a good government, and to that measure of politeness, that they now far excel all the rest of mankind; having soon subdued them, he designed to separate them from the continent, and to bring the sea quite round them. To accomplish this, he ordered a deep channel to be dug fifteen miles long; and that the natives might not think he treated them like slaves, he not only forced the inhabitants, but also his own soldiers, to labor in carrying it on. As he set a vast number of men to work, he beyond all men's expectations brought it to a speedy conclusion. And his neighbors who at first laughed at the folly of the undertaking, no sooner saw it brought to perfection, than they were struck with admiration and terror.

There are fifty-four cities in the island, all large and well built: the manners, customs, and laws of which are the same, and they are all contrived as near in the same manner as the ground on which they stand will allow. The nearest lie at least twenty-four miles distance from one another, and the most remote are not so far distant, but that a man can go on foot in one day from it, to that which lies next it. Every city sends three of their wisest senators once a year to Amaurot,[10] to consult about their common concerns; for that is chief town of the island, being situated near the centre of it, so that it is the most convenient place for their assemblies. The jurisdiction of every city extends at least twenty miles: and where the towns lie wider, they have much more ground: no town desires to enlarge its bounds, for the people consider themselves rather as tenants than landlords. They have built over all the country, farmhouses for husbandmen, which are well contrived, and are furnished with all things necessary for country labor. Inhabitants are sent by turns from the cities to dwell in them; no country family has fewer than forty men and women in it, besides two slaves. There is a master and mistress set over every family; and over thirty families there is a magistrate. Every year twenty of this family come back to the town, after they have stayed two years in the country; and in their room there are other twenty sent from the town, that they may learn country work from those that have been already one

---

9. The significance of the name Abraxa is rather vague. It may be derived from the Greek "not rained upon," and thus extend the meaning of the river Anider (without water).
10. Derived from the Greek *amauros*, "dim, uncertain."

year in the country, as they must teach those that come to them the next from the town. By this means such as dwell in those country farms are never ignorant of agriculture, and so commit no errors, which might otherwise be fatal, and bring them under a scarcity of grain. But though there is every year such a shifting of the husbandmen, to prevent any man being forced against his will to follow that hard course of life too long; yet many among them take such pleasure in it, that they desire to continue it in many years. These husbandmen till the ground, breed cattle, hew wood, and convey it to the towns, either by land or water, as is most convenient. They breed an infinite multitude of chickens in a very curious manner; for the hens do not sit and hatch them, but vast number of eggs are laid in a gentle and equal heat, in order to be hatched, and they are no sooner out of the shell, and able to stir about, but they seem to consider those that feed them as their mothers, and follow them as other chickens do the hen that hatched them. They breed very few horses, but those they have are full of mettle, and are kept only for exercising their youth in the art of sitting and riding them; for they do not put them to any work, either of plowing or carriage, in which they employ oxen; for though their horses are stronger, yet they find oxen can hold out longer; and as they are not subjected to so many diseases, so they are kept upon a less charge, and with less trouble; and even when they are so worn out, that they are no more fit for labor, they are good meat at last. They sow no grain, but that which is to be their bread; for they drink either wine, cider, or perry,[11] and often water, sometimes boiled with honey or liquorice, with which they abound; and though they know exactly how much grain will serve every town, and all that tract of country which belongs to it, yet they sow much more, and breed more cattle than are necessary for their consumption; and they give that overplus of which they make no use to their neighbors. When they want anything in the country which it does not produce, they fetch that from the town, without carrying anything in exchange for it. And the magistrates of the town take care to see it given them; for they meet generally in the town once a month, upon festival day. When the time of harvest comes, the magistrates in the country send to those in the towns, and let them know how many hands they will need for reaping the harvest; and the number they call for being sent to them, they commonly dispatch it all in one day.

Of their towns, particularly Amaurot

He that knows one of their towns, knows them all, they are so like one another, except where the situation makes some difference. I shall therefore describe one of them; and none is so proper as Amaurot; for as none is more eminent, all the rest yielding in precedence to this, because it is the seat of their supreme council; so there was none of them better known to me, I having lived five years altogether in it.[12]

---

11. A drink made from the juice of pears.
12. More may be referring here to the five-year visit which his eminent humanist friend, Erasmus, paid to England. Erasmus is sometimes identified with Hythloday, and More's *Utopia* was dedicated to his friend.

It lies upon the side of a hill, or rather a rising ground; its figure is almost square, for from the one side of it, which shoots up almost to the top of the hill, it runs down in a descent for two miles to the river Anider;[13] but it is a little broader the other way that runs along by the bank of that river. The Anider rises about eighty miles above Amaurot in a small spring at first; but other brooks falling into it, of which two are more considerable than the rest. As it runs by Amaurot, it is grown half a mile broad; but it still grows larger and larger, till after sixty miles course below it, it is lost in the ocean, between the town and the sea, and for some miles above the town, it ebbs and flows every six hours, with a strong current. The tide comes up for about thirty miles so full, that there is nothing but salt water in the river, the fresh water being driven back with its force; and above that, for some miles, the water is brackish; but a little higher, as it runs by the town, it is quite fresh; and when the tide ebbs, it continues fresh all along to the sea. There is a bridge cast over the river, not of timber, but of fair stone, consisting of many stately arches; it lies at that part of the town which is farthest from the sea, so that ships without any hindrance lie all along the side of the town. There is likewise another river that runs by it, which though it is not great, yet it runs pleasantly, for it rises out of the same hill on which the town stands, and so runs down through it, and falls into the Anider. The inhabitants have fortified the fountain-head of this river, which springs a little without the towns; that so if they should happen to be beseiged, the enemy might not be able to stop or divert the course of the water, nor poison it; from thence it is carried in earthen pipes to the lower streets; and for those places of the town to which the water of that small river cannot be conveyed, they have great cisterns for receiving the rain-water, which supplies the want of the other. The town is compassed with a high and thick wall, in which there are many towers and forts; there is also a broad and deep dry ditch, set thick with thorns, cast round three sides of the town, and the river is instead of a ditch on the fourth side. The streets are very convenient for all carriage, and are well sheltered from the winds. Their buildings are good, and are so uniform, that a whole side of a street looks like one house. The streets are twenty feet broad; there lie gardens behind all their houses; these are large but enclosed with buildings, that on all hands face the streets; so that every house has both a door to the street, and a back door to the garden. Their doors all have two leaves, which, as they are easily opened, so they shut of their own accord; and there being no property among them, every man may freely enter into any house whatsoever. At every ten years end they shift their houses by lots. They cultivate their gardens with great care, so that they have both vines, fruits, herbs, and flowers in them; and all is so well ordered, and so finely kept, that I never saw gardens anywhere that were both so fruitful and so beautiful as theirs. And this humor of ordering their gardens so well, is not only kept up by the pleasure they find in it, but also by an emulation between the inhabitants of the several streets, who vie with each other; and there is indeed nothing belonging to the whole town that is both more useful and more pleasant. So that he who founded the town, seems to have taken

---

13. Derived from the Greek *an-hydor*, "without water."

care of nothing more than of their gardens; for they say, the whole scheme of the town was designed at first by Utopus, but he left all that belonged to the ornament and improvement of it, to be added by those that should come after him, that being too much for one man to bring to perfection. Their records, that contain the history of their town and state, are preserved with an exact care, and run backwards 1,760 years. From these it appears that their houses were at first low and mean, like cottages, made of any sort of timber, and were built with mud walls and thatched with straw. But now their houses are three stories high: the fronts of them are faced either with stone, plastering, or brick; and between the facings of their walls they throw in their rubbish. Their roofs are flat, and on them they lay a sort of plaster, which costs very little, and yet is so tempered that it is not apt to take fire, and yet resists the weather more than lead. They have great quantities of glass among them, with which they glaze their windows. They use also in their windows a thin linen cloth, that is so oiled or gummed that it both keeps out the wind and gives free admission to the light.

Thirty families choose every year a magistrate, who was anciently called the Syphogrant, but is now called the Philarch; and over every ten Syphogrants, with the families subject to them, there is another magistrate, who was anciently called the Tranibor,[14] but of late the Archphilarch. All the Syphogrants, who are in number two hundred, choose the Prince out of a list of four, who are named by the people of the four divisions of the city; but they take an oath before they proceed to an election, that they will choose him whom they think most fit for the office. They give their voices secretly, so that it is not known for whom every one gives his suffrage. The Prince is for life, unless he is removed upon suspicion of some design to enslave the people. The Tranibors are new chosen every year, but yet they are for the most part continued. All their other magistrates are only annual. The Tranibors meet every third day, and oftener if necessary, and consult with the Prince, either concerning the affairs of the state in general, or such private differences as may arise sometimes among the people; though that falls out but seldom. There are always two Syphogrants called into the council-chamber, and these are changed every day. It is a fundamental rule of their government, that no conclusion can be made in anything that relates to the public, till it has been first debated three several days in their council. It is death for any to meet and consult concerning the state, unless it be either in their ordinary council, or in the assembly of the whole body of the people.

These things have been so provided among them, that the Prince and the Tranibors may not conspire together to change the government, and enslave the people; and therefore when anything of great importance is set on foot, it is sent to the Syphogrants; who after they have communicated it to the families that belong to their divisions, and have considered it among themselves, make report to the senate; and upon great occasions, the matter is referred to the council of the whole island. One rule observed in their council, is, never to debate a thing on the same day in which it is

---

14. *Philarch* is derived from the Greek word meaning chief of a tribe or clan. The derivation of *Syphogrant* and *Tranibor* is not known.

first proposed; for that is always referred to the next meeting, that so men may not rashly, and in the heat of discourse, engage themselves too soon, which might bias them so much, that instead of consulting the good of the public, they might rather study to support their first opinions, and by a perverse and preposterous sort of shame, hazard their country rather than endanger their own reputation, or venture the being suspected to have wanted foresight in the expedients that they at first proposed. And therefore to prevent this, they take care that they may rather be deliberate than sudden in their motions.

Of their trades, and manner of life

Agriculture is that which is so universally understood among them, that no person, either man or woman, is ignorant of it; they are instructed in it from their childhood, partly by what they learn at school, and partly by practice; they being led out often into the fields, about the town, where they not only see others at work, but are likewise exercised in it themselves. Besides agriculture, which is so common to them all, every man has some peculiar trade to which he applies himself, such as the manufacture of wool, or flax, masonry, smith's work, or carpenter's work; for there is no sort of trade that is in great esteem among them. Throughout the island they wear the same sort of clothes without any other distinction, except what is necessary to distinguish the two sexes, and the married and unmarried. The fashion never alters; and as it is neither disagreeable nor uneasy, so it is suited to the climate, and calculated both for their summers and winters. Every family makes their own clothes; but all among them, women as well as men, learn one or other of the trades formerly mentioned. Women, for the most part, deal in wool and flax, which suit best their weakness, leaving the ruder trades to the men. The same trades generally pass down from father to son, inclinations often following descent; but if any man's genius lies another way, he is by adoption translated into a family that deals in the trade to which he is inclined: and when that is to be done, care is taken not only by his father, but by the magistrate, that he may be put to a discreet and good man. And if after a person has learned one trade, he desires to acquire another, that is also allowed, and is managed in the same manner as the former. When he has learned both, he follows that which he likes best, unless the public has more occasion for the other.

The chief, and almost the only business of the Syphogrants, is to take care that no man may live idle, but that every one may follow his trade diligently; yet they do not wear themselves out with perpetual toil, from morning to night, as if they were beasts of burden, which as it is indeed a heavy slavery, so it is everywhere the common course of life amongst all mechanics except the Utopians; but they dividing the day and night into twenty-four hours, appoint six of these for work; three of which are before dinner; and three after. They then sup, and at eight o'clock, counting from noon, go to bed and sleep eight hours. The rest of their time besides that taken up in work, eating and sleeping, is left to every man's discretion; yet they are not to abuse that interval to luxury and idleness, but must employ it in some proper exercise according to their various inclinations, which is for the most part reading. It is ordinary to have public lectures every morning before daybreak; at which none are obliged to appear but those who are marked out for literature; yet a great many, both men and women of all ranks, go to hear lectures of one sort or other, according to their inclinations. But if others, that are not made for contemplation, choose rather to employ themselves at that time in their trades, as many of them do, they are not hindered, but are rather commended, as men that take care to serve their country. After supper, they spend an hour in some diversion, in summer in their gardens, and in winter in the halls where they eat; where they entertain each other, either with music or discourse. They do not so much as know dice, or any such foolish and mischievous games: they have, however, two sorts of games not unlike our chess; the one is between several numbers, in which one number, as it were, consumes another: the other resembles a battle between the virtues and the vices, in which the enmity in the vices among themselves, and their agreement against virtue, is not unpleasantly represented; together with the special oppositions between the particular virtues and vices; as also the methods by which vice either openly assaults or secretly undermines virtue; and virtue on the other hand resists it. But the time appointed for labor is to be narrowly examined, otherwise you may imagine, that since there are only six hours appointed for work, they may fall under a scarcity of necessary provisions. But it is so far from being true, that this time is not sufficient for supplying them with plenty of all things, either necessary or convenient; that it is rather too much; and this you will easily apprehend, if you consider how great a part of all other nations is quite idle. First, women generally do little, who are the half of mankind; and if some few women are diligent, their husbands are idle: then consider the great company of idle priests, and of those that are called religious men; add to these all rich men, chiefly those that have estates inland, who are called noblemen and gentlemen, together with their families, made up of idle persons, that are kept more for show than use; add to these, all those strong and lusty beggars, that go about pretending some disease, in excuse for their begging; and upon the whole account you will find that the numbers of those by whose labors mankind is supplied, is much less than you perhaps imagined. Then consider how few of those that work are employed in labors that are of real service; for we who measure all things by money, give rise to many trades that are both vain and superfluous, and serve only to support riot and luxury. For if those who work were employed only in such things as the conveniences of life require, there would be such an abundance of them, that the prices of them would sink, that tradesmen could not be maintained by their gains; if all those who labor about useless things, were set to more profitable employments, and if all they that languish out their lives in sloth and idleness, every one of whom consumes as much as any two of the men that are at work, were forced to labor, you may easily imagine that a small proportion of time would serve for doing all that is either necessary, profitable, or pleasant to mankind, especially while pleasure is kept within its due bounds. This appears very plainly in Utopia, for there, in a great city, and in all the territory that lies round it, you can scarce find five hundred, either men or women, by their age and strength, are capable of labor, that are not engaged in it; even the Syphogrants, though excused by the law, yet do not excuse themselves, but work, that by their examples they may excite the industry of the rest of the people. The like exemption is allowed to those, who being recommended to the people by the priests, are by the secret suffrages of the Syphogrants privileged from labor, that they may apply themselves wholly to study; and if any of these fall short of those hopes that they seemed at first to give, they are obliged to return to work. And sometimes a mechanic, that so employs his leisure hours, as to make a considerable advancement in learning, is eased from being a tradesman, and ranked among their learned men. Out of these they choose their ambassadors, their priests, their Tranibors, and the Prince himself; anciently called their Barzanes,[15] but is called of late their Ademus.[16]

And thus from the great numbers among them that are neither suffered to be idle, nor to be employed in any fruitless labor, you may easily make the estimate how much may be done in those few hours in which they are obliged to labor. But besides all that has already been said, it is to be considered that the needful arts among them are managed with less labor than anywhere else. The building or the repairing of houses among us employs many hands, because often a thriftless heir suffers a house that his father built to fall into decay, so that his successor must, at a great cost, repair that which he might have kept up with a small charge: it frequently happens, that the same house which one person built at a vast expense, is neglected by another, who thinks he has a more delicate sense of the beauties of architecture; and he suffering it to fall to ruin, builds another at no less charge. But among the Utopians, all things are so regulated that men very seldom build upon a new piece of ground; and are not only very quick in repairing their houses, but show their foresight in preventing their decay: so that their buildings are preserved very long, with but little labor; and thus the builders to whom that care belongs are often without employment, except the hewing of timber and the squaring of stones, that the materials may be in readiness for raising a building very suddenly, when there is any occasion for it. As to their clothes, observe how little work is spent in them: while they are at labor, they are clothed with leather and skins, cast carelessly about them, which will last seven years; and when they appear in public they put on an upper garment, which hides the other; and these are all of one color, and that is the natural color of the wool. As they need less woollen cloth than is used anywhere else, so that which they make use of is much less costly. They use linen cloth more; but that is prepared with less labor, and they value cloth only by the whiteness of the linen, or by the cleanness of the wool, without much regard to the fineness of the thread: while in other places, four or five upper garments of woollen cloth, of different colors, and as many vests of silk, will scarce serve one man; and while those that are nicer think ten too few, every man there is content with one, which very often serves him two

---

15. *Barzanes* has not been definitely explained. It may mean "son of Zeus."
16. Derived from the Greek *a-demos,* "without a people."

years. Nor is there anything that can tempt a man to desire more; for if he had them, he would neither be the warmer, nor would he make one jot the better appearance for it. And thus, since they are all employed in some useful labor, and since they content themselves with fewer things, it falls out that there is a great abundance of all things among them: so that it frequently happens, that for want of other work, vast numbers are sent out to mend the highways. But when no public undertaking is to be performed, the hours of working are lessened. The magistrates never engage the people in unnecessary labor, since the chief end of the constitution is to regulate labor by the necessities of the public, and to allow all the people as much time as public needs permit for freeing and developing their minds, in which they think the happiness of life consists.

Of their traffic

But it is now time to explain to you the mutual intercourse of this people, their commerce, and the rules by which all things are distributed among them.

As their cities are composed of families, so their families are made up of those that are nearly related to one another. Their women, when they grow up, are married out; but all the males, both children and grandchildren, live still in the same house, in great obedience to their common parent, unless age has weakened his understanding; and in that case, he that is next to him in age comes in his room. But lest any city should become either too great, or by accident be dispeopled, provision is made that none of their cities may become above six thousand families, besides those of the country around it. No family may have less than ten, and more than sixteen persons in it; but there can be no determined number for the children under age. This rule is easily observed, by removing some of the children of a more fruitful couple to any other family that does not abound so much in them. By the same rule, they supply cities that do not increase so fast, from others that breed faster; and if there is any increase over the whole island, then they draw out a number of their citizens out of the several towns, and send them over to the neighboring continent; where, if they find that the inhabitants have more soil than they can well cultivate, they fix a colony, taking the inhabitants into their society, if they are willing to live with them; and where they do that of their own accord, they quickly enter into their method of life, and conform to their rules, and this proves a happiness to both nations: for according to their constitution, such care is taken of the soil, that it becomes fruitful enough for both, though it might be otherwise too narrow and barren for any one of them. But if the natives refuse to conform themselves to their laws, they drive them out of these bounds which they mark out for themselves, and use force if they resist. For they account it a very just cause of war, for a nation to hinder others from possessing a part of that soil, of which they make no use, but which is suffered to lie idle and uncultivated; since every man has by the law of Nature a right to such a waste portion of the earth as is necessary for his subsistence. If an accident has so lessened the number of inhabitants of any of their towns, that it cannot be made up from the other towns of the island, without diminishing them too much, which is said to have fallen out but twice since they were first a people, when great numbers were carried off by the plague; the loss is then supplied by recalling as many as are wanted from their colonies; for they will abandon these, rather than suffer the towns in the island to sink too low.

But to return to their manner of living in society, the oldest man of every family, as has been already said, is its governor. Wives serve their husbands, and children their parents, and always the younger serves the elder. Every city is divided into four equal parts, and in the middle of each there is a market-place: what is brought thither, and manufactured by the several families, is carried from thence to houses appointed for that purpose, in which all things of a sort are laid by themselves; and thither every father goes and takes whatsoever he or his family stand in need of, without either paying for it, or leaving anything in exchange. There is no reason for giving a denial to any person, since there is such plenty of everything among them; and there is no danger of a man's asking for more than he needs; they have no inducements to do this, since they are sure that they shall always be supplied. (It is the fear of want that makes any of the whole race of animals either greedy or ravenous; but besides fear, there is in man a pride that makes him fancy it a particular glory to excel others in pomp and excess.) But by the laws of the Utopians, there is no room for this. Near these markets there are others for all sorts of provisions, where there are not only herbs, fruits, and bread, but also fish, fowl, and cattle. There are also, without their towns, places appointed near some running water, for killing their beasts, and for washing away their filth; which is done by their slaves: for they suffer none of their citizens to kill their cattle, because they think that pity and good-nature, which are among the best of those affections that born with us, are much impaired by the butchering of animals: nor do they suffer anything that is foul or unclean to be brought within their towns, lest the air should be infected by ill smells which might prejudice their health. In every street there are great halls that lie at an equal distance from each other, distinguished by particular names. The Syphogrants dwell in those that are set over thirty families, fifteen lying on one side of it, and as many on the other. In these halls they all meet and have their repasts. The stewards of every one of them come to the market-place at an appointed hour; and according to the number of those that belong to the hall, they carry home provisions. But they take more care of their sick than of any others: these are lodged and provided for in public hospitals: they have belonging to every town four hospitals, that are built without their walls, and are so large that they may pass for little towns: by this means, if they had ever such a number of sick persons, they could lodge them conveniently, and at such a distance, that such of them as are sick of infectious diseases may be kept so far from the rest that there can be no danger of contagion. The hospitals are furnished and stored with all things that are convenient for the ease and recovery of the sick; and those that are put in them are looked after with such tender and watchful care, and are so constantly attended by their skilful physicians, that as none is sent to them against their will, so there is scarce one in a whole town that, if he should fall ill, would not choose rather to go thither than lie sick at home.

After the steward of the hospitals has taken for the sick whatsoever the physician prescribes, then the best things that are left in the market are distributed equally among the halls, in proportion to their numbers, only, in the first place, they serve the Prince, the chief priest, the Tranibors, the ambassadors, and strangers, if there are any, which indeed falls out but seldom, and for whom there are houses well furnished, particularly appointed for their reception when they come among them. At the hours of dinner and supper, the whole Syphogranty being called together by sound of trumpet, they meet and eat together, except only such as are in the hospitals, or lie sick at home. Yet after the halls are served, no man is hindered to carry provisions home from the market-place; for they know that none does that but for some good reason; for though any that will may eat at home, yet none does it willingly, since it is both ridiculous and foolish for any to give themselves the trouble to make ready an ill dinner at home, when there is a much more plentiful one made ready for him so near hand. All the uneasy and sordid services about these halls are performed by their slaves; but the dressing and cooking their meat, and the ordering their tables, belong only to the women, all those of every family taking it by turns. They sit at three or more tables, according to their number; the men sit towards the wall, and the women sit on the other side, that if any of them should be taken suddenly ill, which is no uncommon case amongst women with child, she may, without disturbing the rest, rise and go to the nurse's room, who are there with the sucking children; where there is always clean water at hand, and cradles in which they may lay the young children, if there is occasion for it, and a fire that they may shift and dress them before it. Every child is nursed by its own mother, if death or sickness does not intervene; and in that case the Syphogrants' wives find out a nurse quickly, which is no hard matter; for any one that can do it offers herself cheerfully; for as they are much inclined to that piece of mercy, so the child whom they nurse considers the nurse as its mother. All the children under five years old sit among the nurses, the rest of the younger sort of both sexes, till they are fit for marriage, either serve those that sit at table; or if they are not strong enough for that, stand by them in great silence, and eat what is given them; nor have they any other formality of dining. In the middle of the first table, which stands across the upper end of the hall, sit the Syphogrant and his wife; for that is the chief and most conspicuous place; next to him sit two of the most ancient, for there go always four to a mess. If there is a temple within that Syphogranty, the priest and his wife sit with the Syphogrant above all the rest: next them there is a mixture of old and young, who are so placed, that as the young are set near others, so they are mixed with the more ancient; which they say was appointed on this account, that the gravity of the old people, and the reverence that is due to them might restrain the younger from all indecent words and gestures. Dishes are not served up to the whole table at first, but the best are first set before the old, whose seats are distinguished from the young, and after them all the rest are served alike. The old men distribute to the younger any foods that happen to be set before them, if there is not such an abundance of them that the whole company may be served alike.

Thus old men are honored with a particular respect; yet all the rest fare as well as they. Both dinner and supper are begun with some lecture of morality that is read to them; but it is so short, that it is not tedious nor uneasy to them to hear it: from hence the old men take occasion to entertain those about them, with some useful and pleasant enlargements; but they do not engross the whole discourse so to themselves, during their meals, that the younger may not put in for a share: on the contrary, they engage them to talk, that so they may in that free way of conversation find out the force of every one's spirit, and observe his temper. They despatch their dinners quickly, but sit long at supper; because they go to work after the one, and are to sleep after the other, during which they think the stomach carries on the concoction more vigorously. They never sup without music; and there is always fruit served up after meat; while they are at table, some burn perfumes, and sprinkle about fragrant ointments and sweet waters: in short, they want nothing that may cheer up their spirits: they give themselves a large allowance that way, and indulge themselves in all such pleasures as are attended with no evil consequences. Thus do those that are in the towns live together; but in the country, where they live at great distance, every one eats at home, and no family wants any necessary sort of provision, for it is from them that provisions are sent unto those that live in the towns.

Of the travelling of the Utopians

If any man has a mind to visit his friends that live in some other town, or desires to travel and see the rest of the country, he obtains leave very easily from the Syphogrant and Tranibors, when there is no particular occasion for him at home: such as travel, carry with them a passport from the Prince, which both certifies the license that is granted for travelling, and limits the time of their return. They are furnished with a wagon and a slave, who drives the oxen, and looks after them: but unless there are women in the company, the wagon is sent back at the end of the journey as a needless encumbrance: while they are on the road, they carry no provisions with them; yet they want nothing, but are everywhere treated as if they were at home. If they stay in any place longer than a night, every one follows his proper occupation, and is very well used by those of his own trade: but if any man goes out of the city to which he belongs, without leave, and is found rambling without a passport, he is severely treated, he is punished as a fugitive, and sent home disgracefully; and if he falls again into the like fault, is condemned to slavery. If any man has a mind to travel only over the precinct of his own city, he may freely do it with his father's permission and his wife's consent; but when he comes into any of the country houses, if he expects to be entertained by them, he must labor with them and conform to their rules: and if he does this, he may freely go over the whole precinct; being thus as useful to the city to which he belongs, as if he were still within it. Thus you see that there are no idle

persons among them, nor pretences of excusing any from labor. There are
no taverns, no alehouses nor brothels among them; nor any other occasions of corrupting each other, of getting into corners, or forming themselves into parties: all men live in full view, so that all are obliged, both to
perform their ordinary task, and to employ themselves well in their spare
hours. And it is certain that a people thus ordered must live in great
abundance of all things; and these being equally distributed among them,
no man can want, or be obliged to beg.

In their great council at Amaurot, to which there are three sent from
every town once a year, they examine what towns abound in provisions,
and what are under any scarcity, that so the one may be furnished from
the other; and this is done freely, without any sort of exchange; for
according to their plenty or scarcity, they supply, or are supplied from
one another; so that indeed the whole island is, as it were, one family.
When they have thus taken care of their whole country, and laid up stores
for two years, which they do to prevent the ill consequences of an un-
favorable season, they order an exportation of the overplus, both of grain,
honey, wool, flax, wood, wax, tallow, leather, and cattle; which they send
out commonly in great quantities to other nations. They order a seventh
part of all these goods to be freely given to the poor of the countries to
which they send them, and sell the rest at moderate rates. And by this
exchange, they not only bring back those few things that they need at
home (for indeed they scarce need anything but iron), but likewise a
great deal of gold and silver; and by their driving this trade so long, it is
not to be imagined how vast a treasure they have got among them: so
that now they do not much care whether they sell off their merchandise
for money in hand, or upon trust. A great part of their treasure is now in
bonds; but in all their contracts no private man stands bound, but the
writing runs in the name of the town; and the towns that owe them money,
raise it from those private hands that owe it to them, lay it up in their
public chamber, or enjoy the profit of it till the Utopians call for it; and
they choose rather to let the greatest part of it lie in their hands who make
advantage of it, than to call for it themselves: but if they see that any of
their other neighbors stand more in need of it, then they call it in and lend
it to them: whenever they are engaged in war, which is the only occasion
in which their treasure can be usefully employed, they make use of it
themselves. In great extremities or sudden accidents they employ it in
hiring foreign troops, whom they more willingly expose to danger than
their own people: they give them great pay, knowing well that this will
work even on their enemies, that it will engage them either to betray their
own side, or at least desert it, and that it is the best means of raising mutual
jealousies among them: for this end they have an incredible treasure;
but they do not keep it as a treasure, but in such a manner as I am almost
afraid to tell, lest you think it so extravagant, as to be hardly credible.
This I have the more reason to apprehend, because if I had not seen it
myself, I could not have been easily persuaded to have believed it upon
any man's report.

It is certain that all things appear incredible to us, in proportion as
they differ from own customs. But one who can judge aright, will not

wonder to find, that since their constitution differs so much from ours, their value of gold and silver should be measured by a very different standard; for since they have no use for money among themselves, but keep it as a provision against events which seldom happen, and between which there are generally long intervening intervals; they value it no farther than it deserves, that is, in proportion to its use. So that it is plain, they must prefer iron either to gold or silver: for men can no more live without iron, than without fire or water; but Nature has marked out no use for the other metals, so essential as not easily to be disposed with. The folly of men has enhanced the value of gold and silver, because of their scarcity. Whereas, on the contrary, it is their opinion that Nature, as an indulgent parent, has freely given us all the best things in great abundance, such as water and earth, but has laid up and hid from us the things that are vain and useless.

If these metals were laid up in any tower in the kingdom, it would raise a jealousy of the Prince and Senate, and give birth to that foolish mistrust into which the people are apt to fall, a jealousy of their intending to sacrifice the interest of the public to their own private advantage. If they should work it into vessels, or any sort of plate, they fear that the people might grow too fond of it, and so be unwilling to let the plate be run down, if a war made it necessary to employ it in paying their soldiers. To prevent all these inconveniences, they have fallen upon an expedient, which as it agrees with their other policy, so is it very different from ours, and will scarce gain belief among us, who value gold so much, and lay it up so carefully. They eat and drink out of vessels of earth, or glass, which make an agreeable appearance though formed of brittle materials: while they make their chamber-pots and close-stools of gold and silver; and that not only in their public halls, but in their private houses: of the same metals they likewise make chains and fetters for their slaves; to some of which, as a badge of infamy, they hang an ear-ring of gold, and make others wear a chain or a coronet of the same metal; and thus they take care, by all possible means, to render gold and silver of no esteem. And from hence it is, that while other nations part with their gold and silver, as unwillingly as if one tore out their bowels, those of Utopia would look on their giving in all they possess of those metals, when there were any use for them but as the parting with a trifle, or as we would esteem the loss of a penny. They find pearls on their coast; and diamonds and carbuncles on their rocks; they do not look after them, but if they find them by chance, they polish them, and with them they adorn their children, who are delighted with them, and glory in them during their childhood; but when they grow to years, and see that none but children use such baubles, they of their own accord, without being bid by their parents, lay them aside; and would be as much ashamed to use them afterwards, as children among us, when they come to years, are of their puppets and other toys.

I never saw a clearer instance of the opposite impressions that different customs make on people, than I observed in the ambassadors of the Anemolians,[17] who came to Amaurot when I was there. As they came to

---

17. Derived from the Greek *anemolios*, "windy."

treat of affairs of great consequence, the deputies from several towns met together to wait for their coming. The ambassadors of the nations that lie near Utopia, knowing their customs, and that fine clothes are in no esteem among them, that silk is despised, and gold is a badge of infamy, use to come very modestly clothed; but the Anemolians lying more remote, and having had little commerce with them, understanding that they were coarsely clothed, and all in the same manner, took it for granted that they had none of those fine things among them of which they made no use; and they being a vain-glorious rather than a wise people, resolved to set themselves out with so much pomp, that they should look like gods, and strike the eyes of the poor Utopians with their splendor. Thus three ambassadors made their entry with an hundred attendants, all clad in garments of different color, and the greater part in silk; the ambassadors themselves, who were of the nobility of their country, were in cloth of gold, and adorned with massy chains, ear-rings and rings of gold: their caps were covered with bracelets set full of pearls and other gems: in a word, they were set out with all those things that, among the Utopians, were either the badges of slavery, the marks of infamy, or the playthings of children. It was not unpleasant to see, on the one side, how they looked big, when they compared their rich habits with the plain clothes of the Utopians, who were come out in great numbers to see them make their entry: and, on the other, to observe how much they were mistaken in the impression which they hoped this pomp would have made on them. It appeared so ridiculous a show to all that had never stirred out of their country, and had not seen the customs of other nations, that though they paid some reverence to those that were the most meanly clad, as if they had been the ambassadors, yet when they saw the ambassadors themselves, so full of gold and chains, they looked upon them as slaves, and forbore to treat them with reverence. You might have seen the children, who were grown big enough to despise their playthings, and who had thrown away their jewels, call to their mothers, push them gently, and cry out, "See that great fool that wears pearls and gems, as if he were yet a child." While their mothers very innocently replied, "Hold your peace, this I believe is one of the ambassador's fools." Others censured the fashion of their chains, and observed that they were of no use; for they were too slight to bind their slaves, who could easily break them; and besides hung so loose about them, that they thought it easy to throw them away, and so get from them. But after the ambassadors had stayed a day among them, and saw so vast a quantity of gold in their houses, which was as much despised by them as it was esteemed in other nations, and beheld more gold and silver in the chains and fetters of one slave than all their ornaments amounted to, their plumes fell, and they were ashamed of all that glory for which they had formerly valued themselves, and accordingly laid it aside; a resolution that they immediately took, when on their engaging in some free discourse with the Utopians, they discovered their sense of such things and their other customs. The Utopians wonder how any man should be so much taken with the glaring doubtful lustre of a jewel or a stone, that can look up to a star, or to the sun himself; or how any should value himself because his cloth is made of a finer thread: for how fine soever that thread may be, it was once no better than the fleece of a sheep, and that sheep was a sheep still for all its wearing it. They wonder much to hear that gold which in itself is so useless a thing, should be everywhere so much esteemed, that even men for whom it was made, and by whom it has its value, should yet be thought of less value than this metal. That a man of lead, who has no more sense than a log of wood, and is as bad as he is foolish, should have many wise and good men to serve him, only because he has a great heap of that metal; and that if it should happen that by some accident or trick of law (which sometimes produces as great changes as chance itself) all this wealth should pass from the master to the meanest varlet of his whole family, he himself would very soon become one of his servants, as if he were a thing that belonged to his wealth, and so were bound to follow its fortune. But they much more admire and detest the folly of those who when they see a rich man, though they neither owe him anything, nor are in any sort dependent on his bounty, yet merely because he is rich give him little less than divine honors; even though they know him to be so covetous and base-minded, that notwithstanding all his wealth, he will not part with one farthing of it to them as long as he lives.

These and such like notions has that people imbibed, partly from their education, being bred in a country whose customs and laws are opposite to all such foolish maxims, and partly from their learning and studies; for though there are but few in any town that are so wholly excused from labor as to give themselves entirely up to their studies, these being only such persons as discover from their childhood an extraordinary capacity and disposition for letters; yet their children, and a great part of the nation, both men and women, are taught to spend those hours in which they are not obliged to work in reading: and this they do through the whole progress of life. They have all their learning in their own tongue, which is both a copious and pleasant language, and in which a man can fully express his mind. It runs over a great tract of many countries, but it is not equally pure in all places. They had never so much as heard of the names of any of those philosophers that are so famous in these parts of the world, before we went among them; and yet they had made the same discoveries as the Greeks, both in music, logic, arithmetic, and geometry. But as they are almost in everything equal to the ancient philosophers, so they far exceed our modern logicians; for they have never yet fallen upon the barbarous niceties that our youth are forced to learn in those trifling logical schools that are among us; they are so far from minding chimeras, and fantastical images made in the mind, that none of them could comprehend what we meant when we talked to them of a man in the abstract, as common to all men in particular (so that though we spoke of him as a thing that we could point at with our fingers, yet none of them could perceive him), and yet distinct from every one, as if he were some monstrous Colossus or giant. Yet for all this ignorance of these empty notions, they knew astronomy, and were perfectly acquainted with the motions of the heavenly bodies, and have many instruments, well contrived and divided, by which they very accurately compute the course and positions of the sun, moon, and stars. But for the cheat, of divining by the stars by their oppositions or conjunctions, it has not so much as entered into their thoughts. They have a particular sagacity, founded upon much observation, in judging of the weather, by which they know when they may look for rain, wind, or other alterations in the air; but as to the philosophy of these things, the causes of the saltness of the sea, of its ebbing and flowing, and of the origin and nature both of the heavens and the earth; they dispute of them, partly as our ancient philosophers have done, and partly upon some new hypothesis, in which, as they differ from them, so they do not in all things agree among themselves.

As to moral philosophy, they have the same disputes among them as we have here: they examine what are properly good both for the body and the mind, and whether any outward thing can be called truly good, or if that term belong only to the endowments of the soul. They inquire likewise into the nature of virtue and pleasure; but their chief dispute is concerning the happiness of a man, and wherein it consists? Whether in some one thing, or in a great many? They seem, indeed, more inclinable to that opinion that places, if not the whole, yet the chief part of a man's happiness in pleasure; and, what may seem more strange, they make use of arguments even from religion, notwithstanding its severity and roughness, for the support of that opinion so indulgent to pleasure; for they never dispute concerning happiness without fetching some arguments from the principles of religion, as well as from natural reason, since without the former they reckon that all our inquiries after happiness must be but conjectural and defective.

These are their religious principles, that the soul of man is immortal, and that God of His goodness has designed that it should be happy; and that He has therefore appointed rewards for good and virtuous actions, and punishments for vice, to be distributed after this life. Though these principles of religion are conveyed down among them by tradition, they think that even reason itself determines a man to believe and acknowledge them, and freely confess that if these were taken away no man would be so insensible as not to seek after pleasure by all possible means, lawful or unlawful; using only this caution, that a lesser pleasure might not stand in the way of a greater, and that no pleasure ought to be pursued that should draw a great deal of pain after it; for they think it the maddest thing in the world to pursue virtue, that is a sour and difficult thing; and not only to renounce the pleasures of life, but willingly to undergo much pain and trouble, if a man has no prospect of a reward. And what reward can there be for one that has passed his whole life, not only without pleasure but in pain, if there is nothing to be expected after death? Yet they do not place happiness in all sorts of pleasures, but only in those that in themselves are good and honest. There is a party among them who place happiness in bare virtue; others think that our natures are conducted by virtue to happiness, as that which is the chief good of man. They define virtue thus, that it is a living according to Nature, and think that we are made by God for that end; they believe that a man then follows the dictates of Nature when he pursues or avoids things according to the direction of reason; they say that the first dictate of reason is the kindling in us a love and reverence for the Divine Majesty, to whom we owe both all that we have, and all that we can ever hope for. In the next place, reason directs us to keep our minds as free from passion and as cheerful as we can, and that we should consider ourselves as bound by the ties of good-nature and humanity to use our utmost endeavors to help forward the happiness of all other persons; for there never was any man such a morose and severe pursuer of virtue, such an enemy to pleasure that though he set hard rules for men to undergo much pain, many watchings, and other rigors, yet did not at the same time advise them to do all they could, in order to relieve and ease the miserable, and who did not represent gentleness and good-nature as amiable dispositions. And from thence they infer that if a man ought to advance the welfare and comfort of the rest of mankind, there being no virtue more proper and peculiar to our nature, than to ease the miseries of others, to free from trouble and anxiety, in furnishing them with the comforts of life, in which pleasure consists, Nature much more vigorously leads them to do all this for himself. A life of pleasure is either a real evil, and in that case we ought not to assist others in their pursuit of it, but on the contrary, to keep them from it all we can, as from that which is most hurtful and deadly; or it is a good thing, so that we not only may, but ought to help others to it, why then ought not a man to begin with himself? Since no man can be more bound to look after the good of another than after his own; for Nature cannot direct us to be good and kind to others, and yet at the same time to be unmerciful and cruel to ourselves. Thus, as they define virtue to be living according to Nature, so they imagine that Nature prompts all people on to seek after pleasure, as the end of all they do. They also observe that in order to ensure the pleasures of life, Nature inclines us to enter into society; for there is no man so much raised above the rest of mankind as to be the only favorite of Nature, who, on the contrary, seems to have placed on a level all those that belong to the same species. Upon this they infer that no man ought to seek his own conveniences so eagerly as to prejudice others; and therefore they think that not only all agreements between private persons ought to be observed; but likewise that all those laws ought to be kept, which either a good prince has published in due form, or to which a people, that is neither oppressed with tyranny nor circumvented by fraud, has consented, for distributing those conveniences of life which afford us all our pleasures.

They think it is an evidence of true wisdom for a man to pursue his own advantages, as far as the laws allow it. They account it piety to prefer the public good to one's private concerns; but they think it unjust for a man to seek for pleasure, by snatching another man's pleasures from him. And on the contrary, they think it a sign of a gentle and good soul, for a man to dispense with his own advantage for the good of others; and that by this means a good man finds as much pleasure one way, as he parts with another; for as he may expect the like from others when he may come to need it, so if that should fail him, yet the sense of a good action, and the reflections that he makes on the love and gratitude of those whom he has so obliged, gives the mind more pleasure than the body could have found in that from which it had restrained itself. They are also persuaded that God will make up the loss of those small pleasures, with a vast and endless joy, of which religion easily convinces a good soul.

Thus upon an inquiry into the whole matter, they reckon that all our actions, and even all our virtues, terminate in pleasure, as in our chief end and greatest happiness; and they call every motion or state, either of body or mind, in which Nature teaches us to delight, a pleasure. Thus they cautiously limit pleasure only to those appetites to which Nature leads us; for they say that Nature leads us only to those delights to which reason as well as sense carries us, and by which we neither injure any other person, nor lose the possession of greater pleasures, and of such as draw no troubles after them; but they look upon those delights which men by a foolish, though common, mistake call pleasure, as if they could change as easily the nature of things as the use of words; as things that greatly obstruct their real happiness, instead of advancing it, because they so entirely possess the minds of those that are once captivated by them with a false notion of pleasure, that there is no room left for pleasures of a truer or purer kind.

There are many things that in themselves have nothing that is truly delightful; on the contrary, they have a good deal of bitterness in them: and yet from our perverse appetites after forbidden objects, are not only ranked among the pleasures, but are made even the greatest designs of life. Among those who pursue these sophisticated pleasures, they reckon such as I mentioned before, who think themselves really the better for having fine clothes; in which they think they are doubly mistaken, both in the opinion that they have of their clothes, and in that they have of themselves; for if you consider the use of clothes, why should a fine thread be thought better than a coarse one? And yet these men, as if they had some real advantages beyond others, and did not owe them wholly to their mistakes, look big, seem to fancy themselves to be more valuable, and imagine that a respect is due to them for the sake of a rich garment, to which they would not have pretended if they had been more meanly clothed; and even resent it as an affront, if that respect is not paid them. It is also a great folly to be taken with outward remarks of respect, which signify nothing: for what true or real pleasure can one man find in another's standing bare, or making legs to him? Will the bending another man's knees give ease to yours? And will the head's being bare cure the madness of yours? And yet it is wonderful to see how this false notion of pleasure bewitches many who delight themselves with the fancy of their nobility, and are pleased with this conceit, that they are descended from ancestors, who have been held for some successions rich, and who have had great possessions; for this is all that makes nobility at present; yet they do not think themselves a whit less noble, though their immediate parents have left none of this wealth to them, or though they themselves have squandered it away. The Utopians have no better opinion of those who are much taken with gems and precious stones and who account it a degree of happiness, next to a divine one, if they can purchase one that is very extraordinary; especially if it be of that sort of stones that is then in great request; for the same sort is not at all times universally of the same value; nor will men buy it unless it be dismounted and taken out of the gold; the jeweller is then made to give good security, and required solemnly to swear that the stone is true, that by such an exact caution a false one might not be bought instead of a true: though if you were to examine it, your eye could find no difference between the counterfeit and that which is true; so that they are all one to you as much as if you were blind. Or can it be thought that they who heap up an useless mass of wealth, not for any use that it is to bring them, but merely to please themselves with the contemplation of it, enjoy any true pleasure in it? The delight they find is only a false shadow of joy. Those are no better whose error is somewhat different from the former, and who hide it, out of their fear of losing it; for what other name can fit the hiding it in the earth, or rather the restoring it to it again, it being thus cut off from being useful, either to its owner or to the rest of mankind? And yet the owner having hid it carefully, is glad, because he thinks he is now sure of it. If it should be stolen, the owner, though he might live perhaps ten years after the theft, of which he knew nothing, would find no difference between his having or losing it; for both ways it was equally useless to him.

Among those foolish pursuers of pleasure, they reckon all that delight in hunting, in fowling, or gaming: of whose madness they have only heard, for they have no such things among them. But they have asked us, what sort of pleasure is it that men can find in throwing the dice? For if there were any pleasure in it, they think the doing of it so often should give one a surfeit of it: and what pleasure can one find in hearing the barking and howling of dogs, which seem rather odious than pleasant sounds? Nor can they comprehend the pleasure of seeing dogs run after a hare, more than of seeing one dog run after another; for if the seeing them run is that which gives the pleasure, you have the same entertainment to the eye on both these occasions; since that is the same in both cases; but if the pleasure lies in seeing the hare killed and torn by the dogs, this ought rather to stir pity, that a weak, harmless, and fearful hare should be devoured by strong, fierce, and cruel dogs. Therefore all this business of hunting is, among the Utopians, turned over to their butchers; and those, as has been already said, are all slaves; and they look on hunting as one of the basest parts of a butcher's work: for they account it both more profitable and more decent to kill those beasts that are more necessary and useful to mankind; whereas the killing and tearing of so small and miserable an animal can only attract the huntsman with a false show of pleasure, from which he can reap but small advantage. They look on the desire of the bloodshed, even of beasts, as a mark of a mind that is already corrupted with cruelty, or that at least by the frequent returns of so brutal a pleasure must degenerate into it.

Thus, though the rabble of mankind look upon these, and on innumerable other things of the same nature, as pleasures; the Utopians, on the contrary, observing that there is nothing in them truly pleasant, conclude that they are not to be reckoned among pleasures: for though these things may create some tickling in the senses (which seems to be a true notion of pleasure), yet they imagine that this does not arise from the thing itself, but from a depraved custom, which may so vitiate a man's taste, that bitter things may pass for sweet; as women with child think pitch or tallow taste sweeter than honey; but as a man's sense when corrupted, either by a disease or some ill habit, does not change the nature of other things, so neither can it change the nature of pleasure.

They reckon up several sorts of pleasures, which they call true ones: some belong to the body and others to the mind. The pleasures of the mind lie in knowledge, and in that delight which the contemplation of truth carries with it; to which they add the joyful reflections on a well-spent life, and the assured hopes of a future happiness. They divide the pleasures of the body into two sorts; the one is that which gives our senses some real delight, and is performed, either by recruiting nature, and supplying those parts which feed the internal heat of life by eating and drinking; or when nature is eased of any surcharge that oppresses it; when we are relieved from sudden pain, or that which arises from satisfying the appetite which Nature has wisely given to lead us to the propagation of the species. There is another kind of pleasure that arises neither from our receiving what the body requires, nor its being relieved when overcharged, and yet by a secret, unseen virtue affects the senses, raises the passions, and strikes the mind with generous impressions; this is the pleasure that arises from music. Another kind of bodily pleasure is that which results from an undisturbed and vigorous constitution of body, when life and active spirits seem to actuate every part. This lively health, when entirely free from all mixture of pain, of itself gives an inward pleasure, independent of all external objects of delight; and though this pleasure does not so powerfully affect us, nor act so strongly on the senses as some of the others, yet it may be esteemed as the greatest of all pleasures, and almost all the Utopians reckon it the foundation and basis of all the other joys of life; since this alone makes the state of life easy and desirable; and when this is wanting, a man is really capable of no other pleasure. They look upon freedom from pain, if it does not rise from perfect health, to be a state of stupidity rather than of pleasure. This subject has been very narrowly canvassed among them; and it has been debated whether a firm and entire health could be called a pleasure or not? Some have thought that there was no pleasure but what was excited by some sensible motion in the body. But this opinion has been long ago excluded from them, so that now they almost universally agree that health is the greatest of all bodily pleasures; and that as there is a pain in sickness, which is as opposite in its nature to pleasure as sickness itself is to health; so they hold, that health is accompanied with pleasure: and if any should say that sickness is not really pain, but that it only carries pain along with it, they look upon that as a fetch of subtilty, that does not much alter the matter. It is all one, in their opinion, whether it be said that health is in itself a pleasure, or that it begets a pleasure, as fire gives heat; so it be granted, that all those whose health is entire have a true pleasure in the enjoyment of it: and they reason thus—what is the pleasure of eating, but that a man's health which has been weakened, does, with the assistance of food, drive away hunger, and so recruiting itself recovers its former vigor? And being thus refreshed, it finds a pleasure in that conflict; and if the conflict is pleasure, the victory must yet breed a greater pleasure, except we fancy that it becomes stupid as soon as it has obtained that which it pursued, and so

neither knows nor rejoices in its own welfare. If it is said that health cannot be felt, they absolutely deny it; for what man is in health that does not perceive it when he is awake? Is there any man that is so dull and stupid as not to acknowledge that he feels a delight in health? And what is delight but another name for pleasure?

But of all pleasures, they esteem those to be most valuable that lie in the mind; the chief of which arises out of true virtue, and the witness of a good conscience. They account health the chief pleasure that belongs to the body; for they think that the pleasure of eating and drinking, and all the other delights of sense, are only so far desirable as they give or maintain health. But they are not pleasant in themselves, otherwise than as they resist those impressions that our natural infirmities are still making upon us: for as a wise man desires rather to avoid diseases than to take a physic; and to be freed from pain, rather than to find ease by remedies; so it is more desirable not to need this sort of pleasure, than to be obliged to indulge it. If any man imagines that there is a real happiness in these enjoyments, he must then confess that he would be the happiest of all men if he were to lead his life in perpetual hunger, thirst, and itching, and by consequence in perpetual eating, drinking, and scratching himself which any one may easily see would be not only a base, but a miserabl state of life. These are indeed the lowest of pleasures, and the least pure for we can never relish them, but when they are mixed with the contrar pains. The pain of hunger must give us the pleasure of eating; and her the pain outbalances the pleasure; and as the pain is more vehement, it lasts much longer; for as it begins before the pleasure, so it does n cease but with the pleasure that extinguishes it, and both respire togeth They think, therefore, none of those pleasures are to be valued a further than as they are necessary; yet they rejoice in them, and with d gratitude acknowledge the tenderness of the great Author of Natu who has planted in us appetites, by which those things that are necess for our preservation are likewise made pleasant to us. For how miser a thing would life be, if those daily diseases of hunger and thirst wer be carried off by such bitter drugs as we must use for those diseases return seldomer upon us? And thus these pleasant as well as proper of Nature maintain the strength and the sprightliness of our bodies.

They also entertain themselves with the other delights let in at eyes, their ears, and their nostrils, as the pleasant relishes and seasor of life, which Nature seems to have marked out peculiarly for man; no other sort of animals contemplates the figure and beauty of the verse; nor is delighted with smells, any further than as they distin meats by them; nor do they apprehend the concords or discords of so yet in all pleasures whatsoever they take care that a lesser joy do hinder a greater, and that pleasure may never breed pain, which think always follows dishonest pleasures. But they think it madnes man to wear out the beauty of his face, or the force of his natural str to corrupt the sprightliness of his body by sloth and laziness, or to v by fasting; that it is madness to weaken the strength of his consti and reject the other delights of life; unless by renouncing his ow faction, he can either serve the public or promote the happiness of

for which he expects a greater recompense from God. So that they look on such a course of life as the mark of a mind that is both cruel to itself, and ungrateful to the Author of Nature, as if we would not be beholden to Him for His favors, and therefore rejects all His blessings; as one who should afflict himself for the empty shadow of virtue; or for no better end than to render himself capable of bearing those misfortunes which possibly will never happen.

This is their notion of virtue and of pleasure; they think that no man's reason can carry him to a truer idea of them, unless some discovery from Heaven should inspire him with sublimer notions. I have not now the leisure to examine whether they think right or wrong in this matter: nor do I judge it necessary, for I have only undertaken to give you an account of their constitution, but not to defend all their principles. I am sure, that whatsoever may be said of their notions, there is not in the whole world either a better people or a happier government: their bodies are vigorous and lively; and though they are but of a middle stature, and have neither the fruitfullest soil nor the purest air in the world, yet they fortify themselves so well by their temperate course of life, against the unhealthiness of their air, and by their industry they so cultivate their soil, that there is nowhere to be seen a greater increase both of grain and cattle, nor are there anywhere healthier men, and freer from diseases: for one may there see reduced to practice, not only all the art that the husbandman employs in manuring and improving an ill soil, but whole woods plucked up by the roots, and in other places new ones planted, where there were none before. Their principal motive for this is the convenience of carriage, that their timber may be either near their towns, or growing on the banks of the sea, or of some rivers, so as to be floated to them; for it is a harder work to carry wood at any distance over land, than grain. The people are industrious, apt to learn, as well as cheerful and pleasant; and none can endure more labor, when it is necessary; but except in that case they love their ease. They are unwearied pursuers of knowledge; for when we had given them some hints of the learning and discipline of the Greeks, concerning whom we only instructed them (for we know that there was nothing among the Romans, except their historians and their poets, that they would value much), it was strange to see how eagerly they were set on learning that language. We began to read a little of it to them, rather in compliance with their importunity, than out of any hopes of their reaping from it any great advantage. But after a very short trial we found they made such progress, that we saw our labor was like to be more successful than we could have expected. They learned to write their characters, and to pronounce their language so exactly, had so quick an apprehension, they remembered it so faithfully, and became so ready and correct in the use of it, that it would have looked like a miracle if the greater part of those whom we taught had not been men both of extraordinary capacity and of a fit age for instruction. They were for the greatest part chosen from among their learned men, by their chief council, though some studied it of their own accord. In three years' time they became masters of the whole language, so that they read the best of the Greek authors very exactly. I am indeed apt to think that they learned that language the

more easily, from its having some relation to their own. I believe that they were a colony of the Greeks; for though their language comes nearer the Persian, yet they retain many names, both for their towns and magistrates, that are of Greek derivation. I happened to carry a great many books with me, instead of merchandise, when I sailed my fourth voyage; for I was so far from thinking of soon coming back, that I rather thought never to have returned at all, and I gave them all my books, among which were many of Plato's and some of Aristotle's works. I had also Theophrastus on Plants, which, to my great regret, was imperfect; for having laid it carelessly by, while we were at sea, a monkey had seized upon it, and in many places torn out the leaves. They have no books of grammar but Lascares, for I did not carry Theodorus with me; nor have they any dictionaries but Hesichius and Dioscorides. They esteem Plutarch highly, and were much taken with Lucian's wit, and with his pleasant way of writing. As for the poets, they have Aristophanes, Homer, Euripides, and Sophocles of Aldus' edition; and for historians Thucydides, Herodotus and Herodian. One of my companions, Thricius Apinatus, happened to carry with him some of Hippocrates' works, and Galen's Microtechne, which they held in great estimation; for though there is no nation in the world that needs medicine so little as they do, yet there is not any that honors it so much: they reckon the knowledge of it one of the pleasantest and most profitable parts of philosophy, by which, as they search into the secrets of Nature, so they not only find this study highly agreeable, but think that such inquiries are very acceptable to the Author of Nature; and imagine that as He, like the inventors of curious engines amongst mankind, has exposed this great machine of the universe to the view of the only creatures capable of contemplating it, so an exact and curious observer, who admires His workmanship, is much more acceptable to Him than one of the herd, who like a beast incapable of reason, looks on this glorious scene with the eyes of a dull and unconcerned spectator.

The minds of the Utopians when primed with a love for learning, are very ingenious in discovering all such arts as are necessary to carry it to perfection. Two things they owe to us, the manufacture of paper, and the art of printing: yet they are not so entirely indebted to us for these discoveries, but that a great part of the invention was their own. We showed them some books printed by Aldus, we explained to them the way of making paper, and the mystery of printing; but as we had never practised these arts, we described them in a crude and superficial manner. They seized the hints we gave them, and though at first they could not arrive at perfection, yet by making many essays they at last found out and corrected all their errors, and conquered every difficulty. Before this they only wrote on parchment, on reeds, or on the barks of trees; but now they have established the manufactures of paper, and set up printing-presses, so that if they had but a good number of Greek authors they would be quickly supplied with many copies of them: at present, though they have no more than those I have mentioned, yet by several impressions they have multiplied them into many thousands. If any man was to go among them that had some extraordinary talent, or that by much travelling had observed the customs of many nations (which made us to be so well received), he would receive a hearty welcome; for they are very desirous to know the state of the whole world. Very few go among them on the account of traffic, for what can a man carry to them but iron, or gold, or silver, which merchants desire rather to export than import to a strange country: and as for their exportation, they think it better to manage that themselves than to leave it to foreigners, for by this means, as they understand the state of the neighboring countries better, so they keep up the art of navigation, which cannot be maintained but by much practice.

Of their slaves, and of their marriages

They do not make slaves of prisoners of war, except those that are taken in battle; nor of the sons of their slaves, nor of those of other nations: the slaves among them are only such as are condemned to that state of life for the commission of some crime, or, which is more common, such as their merchants find condemned to die in those parts to which they trade, whom they sometimes redeem at low rates; and in other places have them for nothing. They are kept at perpetual labor, and are always chained, but with this difference, that their own natives are treated much worse than others; they are considered as more profligate than the rest, and since they could not be restrained by the advantages of so excellent an education, are judged worthy of harder usage. Another sort of slaves are the poor of the neighboring countries, who offer of their own accord to come and serve them; they treat these better, and use them in all other respects as well as their own countrymen, except their imposing more labor upon them, which is no hard task to those that have been accustomed to it; and if any of these have a mind to go back to their own country, which indeed falls out but seldom, as they do not force them to stay, so they do not send them away empty-handed.

I have already told you with what care they look after their sick, so that nothing is left undone than can contribute either to their ease or health: and for those who are taken with fixed and incurable diseases, they use all possible ways to cherish them, and to make their lives as comfortable as possible. They visit them often, and take great pains to make their time pass off easily: but when any is taken with a torturing and lingering pain, so that there is no hope, either of recovery or ease, the priests and magistrates come and exhort them, that since they are now unable to go on with the business of life, are become a burden to themselves and to all about them, and they have really outlived themselves, they should no longer nourish such a rooted distemper, but choose rather to die, since they cannot live but in much misery: being assured, that if they thus deliver themselves from torture, or are willing that others should do it, they shall be happy after death. Since by their acting thus, they lose none of the pleasures, but only the troubles of life; they think they behave not only reasonably, but in a manner consistent with religion and piety; because they follow the advice given them by their priests, who are the expounders of the will of God. Such as are wrought on by these persuasions, either starve themselves of their own accord, or take opium, and by that means die without pain. But no man is forced on this way of ending his

life; and if they cannot be persuaded to it, this does not induce them to fail
in their attendance and care of them; but as they believe that a voluntary
death, when it is chosen upon such an authority, is very honorable, so
if any man takes away his own life, without the approbation of the priests
and the Senate, they give him none of the honors of a decent funeral, but
throw his body into a ditch.

Their women are not married before eighteen, nor their men before
two-and-twenty, and if any of them run into forbidden embraces before
marriage they are severely punished, and the privilege of marriage is
denied them, unless they can obtain a special warrant from the Prince.
Such disorders cast a great reproach upon the master and mistress of
the family in which they happen, for it is supposed that they have failed
in their duty. The reason for punishing this so severely is, because they
think that if they were not strictly restrained from all vagrant appetites,
very few would engage in a state in which they venture the quiet of their
whole lives, by being confined to one person, and are obliged to endure
all the inconveniences with which it is accompanied. In choosing their
wives they use a method that would appear to us very absurd and ridiculous, but it is constantly observed among them, and is accounted perfectly
consistent with wisdom. Before marriage some grave matron presents
the bride naked, whether she is a virgin or a widow, to the bridegroom;
and after that some grave man presents the bridegroom naked to the
bride. We indeed both laughed at this, and condemned it as very
indecent. But they, on the other hand, wondered at the folly of the men
of all other nations, who, if they were to buy a horse of a small value, are
so cautious that they will see every part of him, and take off his saddle
and all his other tackle, that there may be no secret ulcer hid under any of
them; and that yet in the choice of a wife, on which depends the happiness
or unhappiness of the rest of his life, a man should venture upon trust,
and only see about a hand's-breadth of the face, all the rest of the body
being covered, under which there may lie hid what may be contagious, as
well as loathsome. All men are not so wise as to choose a woman only for
her good qualities; and even wise men consider the body as that which
adds not a little to the mind: and it is certain there may be some such de-
formity covered with the clothes as may totally alienate a man from his
wife when it is too late to part with her. If such a thing is discovered after
marriage, a man has no remedy but patience. They therefore think it is
reasonable that there should be good provision made against such mischievous frauds.

There was so much the more reason for them to make a regulation in
this matter, because they are the only people of those parts that neither
allow of polygamy, nor of divorces, except in the case of adultery, or in-
sufferable perverseness; for in these cases the Senate dissolves the marriage, and grants the injured person leave to marry again; but the guilty
are made infamous, and are never allowed the privilege of a second marriage. None are suffered to put away their wives against their wills, from
any great calamity that may have fallen on their persons; for they look on
it as the height of cruelty and treachery to abandon either of the married
persons when they need most the tender care of their comfort and chiefly

in the case of old age, which as it carries many diseases along with it, so it is a disease of itself. But it frequently falls out that when a married couple do not well agree, they by mutual consent separate, and find out other persons with whom they hope they may live more happily. Yet this is not done without obtaining leave of the Senate, which never admits of a divorce, but upon a strict inquiry made, both by the senators and their wives, into the grounds upon which it is desired; and even when they are satisfied concerning the reasons of it, they go on but slowly, for they imagine that too great easiness in granting leave for new marriages would very much shake the kindness of married people. They punish severely those that defile the marriage-bed. If both parties are married they are divorced, and the injured persons may marry one another, or whom they please; but the adulterer and the adulteress are condemned to slavery. Yet if either of the injured persons cannot shake off the love of the married person, they may live with them still in that state, but they must follow them to that labor to which the slaves are condemned; and sometimes the repentance of the condemned, together with the unshaken kindness of the innocent and injured person, has prevailed so far with the Prince that he has taken off the sentence; but those that relapse after they are once pardoned are punished with death.

Their law does not determine the punishment for other crimes; but that is left to the Senate, to temper it according to the circumstances of the fact. Husbands have power to correct their wives, and parents to chastise their children, unless the fault is so great that a public punishment is thought necessary for striking terror into others. For the most part, slavery is the punishment even of the greatest crimes; for as that is no less terrible to the criminals themselves than death, so they think the preserving them in a state of servitude is more for the interest of the commonwealth than killing them; since as their labor is a greater benefit to the public than their death could be, so the sight of their misery is a more lasting terror to other men than that which would be given by their death. If their slaves rebel, and will not bear their yoke, and submit to the labor that is enjoined them, they are treated as wild beasts that cannot be kept in order, neither by a prison, nor by their chains; and are at last put to death. But those who bear their punishment patiently, and are so much wrought on by that pressure that lies so hard on them that it appears they are really more troubled for the crimes they have committed than for the miseries they suffer, are not out of hope but that at last either the Prince will, by his perogative, or the people by their intercession, restore them again to their liberty, or at least very much mitigate their slavery. He that tempts a married woman to adultery, is no less severely punished than he that commits it; for they believe that a deliberate design to commit a crime, is equal to the fact itself: since its not taking effect does not make the person that miscarried in his attempt at all the less guilty.

They take great pleasure in fools, and as it is thought a base and unbecoming thing to use them ill, so they do not think it amiss for people to divert themselves with their folly: and, in their opinion, this is a great advantage to the fools themselves: for if men were so sullen and severe as not at all to please themselves with their ridiculous behaviour and foolish sayings, which is all that they can do to recommend themselves to others, it could not be expected that they would be so well provided for, nor so tenderly used as they must otherwise be. If any man should reproach another for his being misshaped or imperfect in any part of his body, it would not at all be thought a reflection on the person so treated, but it would be accounted scandalous in him that had upbraided another with what he could not help. It is thought a sign of a sluggish and sordid mind not to preserve carefully one's natural beauty; but it is likewise infamous among them to use paint. They all see that no beauty recommends a wife so much to her husband as the probity of her life, and her obedience: for as some few are catched and held only by beauty, so all are attracted by the other excellences which charm all the world.

As they fright men from committing crimes by punishments, so they invite them to the love of virtue by public honors: therefore they erect statues to the memories of such worthy men as have deserved well of their country, and set these in their market-places, both to perpetuate the remembrance of their actions, and to be an incitement to their posterity to follow their example.

If any man aspires to any office, he is sure never to compass it: they all live easily together, for none of the magistrates is either haughty or cruel. They would rather be called fathers, and by being really so, they well deserve the name; and the people pay them all the marks of honor the more freely, because none are exacted from them. The Prince himself has no distinction, either of garments, or of a crown; but is only distinguished by a sheaf of grain carried before him; as the high priest is also known by his being preceded by a person carrying a wax light.

They have but few laws, and such is their constitution that they need not many. They very much condemn other nations, whose laws, together with the commentaries on them, swell up to so many volumes; for they think it is an unreasonable thing to oblige men to obey a body of laws that are both of such a bulk, and so dark as not to be read and understood by every one of the subjects.

They have no lawyers among them, for they consider them as a sort of people whose profession it is to disguise matters, and to wrest the laws; and therefore they think it is much better that every man should plead his own cause, and trust it to the judge, as in other places the client trusts it to a counsellor. By this means they both cut off many delays, and find out truth more certainly: for after the parties have laid open the merits of the cause, without those artifices which lawyers are apt to suggest, the judge examines the whole matter, and supports the simplicity of such well-meaning persons, whom otherwise crafty men would be sure to run down: and thus they avoid those evils which appear very remarkably among all those nations that labor under a vast load of laws. Every one of them is skilled in their law, for as it is a very short study, so the plainest meaning of which words are capable is always the sense of their laws. And they argue thus: all laws are promulgated for this end, that every man may know his duty; and therefore the plainest and most obvious sense of the words is that which ought to be put upon them; since a more refined exposition cannot be easily comprehended, and would only serve to make the laws become useless to the greater part of mankind, and especially to those who need most the direction of them: for it is all one, not to make a law at all, or to couch it in such terms that without a quick apprehension, and much study, a man cannot find out the true meaning of it; since the generality of mankind are both so dull, and so much employed in their several trades, that they have neither the leisure nor the capacity requisite for such an inquiry.

Some of their neighbors, who are masters of their own liberties, having long ago, by the assistance of the Utopians, shaken off the yoke of tyranny, and being much taken with those virtues which they observe among them, have come to desire that they would send magistrates to govern them; some changing them every year, and others every five years. At the end of their government they bring them back to Utopia, with great expressions of honor and esteem, and carry away others to govern in their stead. In this they seem to have fallen upon a very good expedient for their own happiness and safety; for since the good or ill condition of a nation depends so much upon their magistrates, they could not have made a better choice than by pitching on men whom no advantages can bias; for wealth is of no use to them, since they must so soon go back to their own country; and they being strangers among them, are not engaged in any of their heats or animosities; and it is certain that when public judicatories are swayed, either by avarice or partial affections, there must follow a dissolution of justice, the chief sinew of society.

The Utopians call those nations that come and ask magistrates from them, neighbors; but those to whom they have been of more particular service, friends. And as all other nations are perpetually either making leagues or breaking them, they never enter into an alliance with any state. They think leagues are useless things, and believe that if the common ties of humanity do not knit men together, the faith of promises will have no great effect; and they are the more confirmed in this by what they see among the nations round about them, who are no strict observers of leagues and treaties. We know how religiously they are observed in Europe, more particularly where the Christian doctrine is received, among whom they are sacred and inviolable. Which is partly owing to the justice and goodness of the princes themselves, and partly to the reverence they pay to the popes; who as they are most religious observers of their own promises, so they exhort all other princes to perform theirs; and when fainter methods do not prevail, they compel them to it by the severity of the pastoral censure, and think that it would be the most indecent thing possible if men who are particularly distinguished by the title of the faithful, should not religiously keep the faith of their treaties. But in that new-found world, which is not more distant from us in situation than the people are in their manners and course of life, there is no trusting to leagues, even though they were made with all the pomp of the most sacred ceremonies; on the contrary, they are on this account the sooner broken, some slight pretence being found in the words of the treaties, which are purposely couched in such ambiguous terms that they can never be so strictly bound but they will always find some loophole to escape at; and thus they break both their leagues and their faith. And this is done with such impudence, and those very men who value themselves on having suggested these expedients to their princes, would with a haughty scorn declaim against such craft, or to speak plainer, such fraud and deceit, if they found private men make use of it in their bargains, and would readily say that they deserve to be hanged.

By this means it is, that all sort of justice passes in the world for a low-spirited and vulgar virtue, far below the dignity of royal greatness. Or at least, there are set up two sorts of justice; the one is mean, and creeps on the ground, and therefore becomes none but the lower part of mankind, and so must be kept in severely by many restraints that it may not break out beyond the bounds that are set to it. The other is the particular virtue of princes, which as it is more majestic than that which becomes the rabble, so takes a freer compass; and thus lawful and unlawful are only measured by pleasure and interest. These practices of the princes that lie about Utopia, who make so little account of their faith, seem to be the reasons that determine them to engage in no confederacies; perhaps they would change their mind if they lived among us; but yet though treaties were more religiously observed, they would still dislike the custom of making them; since the world has taken up a false maxim upon it, as if there were no tie of Nature uniting one nation to another, only separated perhaps by a mountain or a river, and that all were born in a state of hostility, and so might lawfully do all that mischief to their neighbors against which there is no provision made by treaties; and that when treaties are made, they do not cut off the enmity, or restrain the license of preying upon each other, if by the unskillfulness of wording them there are not effectual provisos made against them. They, on the other hand, judge that no man is to be esteemed our enemy that has never injured us; and that the partnership of the human nature is instead of a league. And that kindness and good-nature unite men more effectually and with greater strength than any agreements whatsoever; since thereby the engagements of men's hearts become stronger than the bond and obligation of words.

Of their military discipline

They detest war as a very brutal thing; and which, to the reproach of human nature, is more practiced by men than by any sort of beasts. They, in opposition to the sentiments of almost all other nations, think that there is nothing more inglorious than that glory that is gained by war. And therefore though they accustom themselves daily to military exercises and the discipline of war, in which not only their men but their women likewise are trained up, that in cases of necessity they may not be quite useless; yet they do not rashly engage in war, unless it be either to defend themselves, or their friends, from any unjust aggressors; or out of good-nature or in compassion assist an oppressed nation in shaking off the yoke of tyranny. They indeed help their friends, not only in defensive, but also in offensive wars; but they never do that unless they had been consulted before the breach was made, and being satisfied with the grounds on which they went, they had found that all demands of reparation were rejected, so that a war was unavoidable. This they think to be not only just, when one neighbor makes an inroad on another, by public order, and carry away the spoils; but when the merchants of one country are oppressed in another, either under pretense of some unjust laws, or by the perverse wresting of good ones. This they count a juster cause of war than the other, because those injuries are done under some color of laws. This was the only ground of that war in which they engaged with the Nephelogetes against the Aleopolitanes,[18] a little before our time; for the merchants of the former having, as they thought, met with great injustice among the latter, which, whether it was in itself right or wrong, drew on a terrible war, in which many of their neighbors were engaged; and their keenness in carrying it on being supported by their strength in maintaining it, it not only shook some very flourishing states, and very much excited others, but after a series of much mischief ended in the entire conquest and slavery of the Aleopolitanes, who though before the war they were in all respects much superior to the Nephelogetes, were yet subdued; but though the Utopians had assisted them in the war, yet they pretended to no share of the spoil.

But though they so vigorously assist their friends in obtaining reparation for the injuries they have received in affairs of this nature, yet if any such fraud was committed against themselves, provided no violence was done to their persons, they would only on their being refused satisfaction forbear trading with such people. This is not because they consider their neighbors more than their own citizens; but since their neighbors trade every one upon his own stock, fraud is a more sensible injury to them than it is to the Utopians, among whom the public in such a case only suffers. As they expect nothing in return for the merchandises they export but that in which they so much abound, and is of little use to them, the loss does not much affect them; they think therefore it would be too severe to revenge a loss attended with so little inconvenience either to their lives, or their subsistence, with the death of many persons; but if any of their people is either killed or wounded wrongfully, whether it be done by public authority or only by private men, as soon as they hear of it they send ambassadors, and demand that the guilty persons may be delivered up to them; and if that is denied, they declare war; but if it be complied with, the offenders are condemned either to death or slavery.

They would be both troubled and ashamed of a bloody victory over their enemies, and think it would be as foolish a purchase as to buy the most valuable goods at too high a rate. And in no victory do they glory so much as in that which is gained by dexterity and good conduct, without bloodshed. In such cases they appoint public triumphs, and erect trophies to the honor of those who have succeeded; for then do they reckon that a man acts suitably to his nature when he conquers his enemy in such a way as that no other creature but a man could be capable of, and that is by the strength of his understanding. Bears, lions, boars, wolves, and dogs, and all other animals employ their bodily force one against another, in which as many of them are superior to men, both in strength and fierceness, so they are all subdued by his reason and understanding.

---

18. "The Cloudhangers" and "The Citizens of Nowhere," respectively.

The only design of the Utopians in war is to obtain that by force, which if it had been granted them in time would have prevented the war; or if that cannot be done, to take so severe a revenge on those that have injured them that they may be terrified from doing the like for the time to come. By these ends they measure all their designs, and manage them so that it is visible that the appetite of fame or vain-glory does not work so much on them as a just care of their own security.

As soon as they declare war, they take care to have a great many schedules, that are sealed with their common seal, affixed in the most conspicuous places of their enemies' country. This is carried secretly, and done in many places all at once. In these they promise great rewards to such as shall kill the prince, and lesser in proportion to such as shall kill any other persons, who are those on whom, next to the prince himself, they cast the chief balance of the war. And they double the sum to him that, instead of killing the person so marked out, shall take him alive and put him in their hands. They offer not only indemnity, but rewards, to such of the persons themselves that are so marked, if they will act against their countrymen: by this means those that are named in their schedules become not only distrustful of their fellow-citizens, but are jealous of one another, and are much distracted by fear and danger; for it has often fallen out that many of them, and even the Prince himself, have been betrayed by those in whom they have trusted most: for the rewards that the Utopians offer are so unmeasurably great, that there is no sort of crime to which men cannot be drawn by them. They consider the risk that those run who undertake such services, and offer a recompense proportioned to the danger; not only a vast deal of gold, but great revenues in lands, that lie among other nations that are their friends, where they may go and enjoy them very securely; and they observe the promises they make of this kind very religiously. They very much approve of this way of corrupting their enemies, though it appears to others to be base and cruel; but they look on it as a wise course, to make an end of what would be otherwise a long war, without so much as hazarding one battle to decide it. They think it likewise an act of mercy and love to mankind to prevent the great slaughter of those that must otherwise be killed in the progress of the war, both on their own side and on that of their enemies, by the death of a few that are most guilty; and that in so doing they are kind even to their enemies, and pity them no less than their own people, as knowing that the greater part of them do not engage in the war of their own accord, but are driven into it by the passions of their prince.

If this method does not succeed with them, then they sow seeds of contention among their enemies, and animate the prince's brother, or some of the nobility, to aspire to the crown. If they cannot disunite them by domestic broils, then they engage their neighbors against them, and make them set on foot some old pretensions, which are never wanting to princes when they have occasion for them. These they plentifully supply with money, though but very sparingly with any auxiliary troops: for they are so tender of their own people, that they would not willingly exchange one of them, even with the prince of their enemies' country.

But as they keep their gold and silver only for such an occasion, so when that offers itself they easily part with it, since it would be no inconvenience to them though they should reserve nothing of it to themselves. For besides the wealth that they have among them at home, they have a vast treasure abroad, many nations round about them being deep in their debt: so that they hire soldiers from all places for carrying on their wars, but chiefly from the Zapolets,[19] who live five hundred miles east of Utopia. They are a rude, wild, and fierce nation, who delight in the woods and rocks, among which they are born and bred up. They are hardened both against heat, cold and labor, and know nothing of the delicacies of life. They do not apply themselves to agriculture, nor do they care either for their houses or their clothes. Cattle is all that they look after; and for the greatest part they live either by hunting, or upon rapine; and are made, as it were, only for war. They watch all opportunities of engaging in it, and very readily embrace such as are offered them. Great numbers of them will frequently go out, and offer themselves for a very low pay, to serve any that will employ them: they know none of the arts of life, but those that lead to the taking it away; they serve those that hire them, both with much courage and great fidelity; but will not engage to serve for any determined time, and agree upon such terms, that the next day they may go over to the enemies of those whom they serve, if they offer them a greater encouragement: and will perhaps return to them the day after that, upon a higher advance of their pay. There are few wars in which they make not a considerable part of the armies on both sides: so it often falls out that they who are related, and are hired in the same country, and so have lived long and familiarly together, forgetting both their relations and former friendship, kill one another upon no other consideration than that of being hired to it for a little money, by princes of different interests; and such a regard have they for money, that they are easily wrought on by the difference of one penny a day to change sides. So entirely does this avarice influence them; and yet this money, which they value so highly, is of little use to them; for what they purchase thus with their blood, they quickly waste on luxury, which among them is but of a poor and miserable form.

This nation serves the Utopians against all people whatsoever, for they pay higher than any other. The Utopians hold this for a maxim, that as they seek out the best sort of men for their own use at home, so they make use of this worst sort of men for the consumption of war, and therefore they hire them with the offers of vast rewards, to expose themselves to all sorts of hazards, out of which the greater part never returns to claim their promises. Yet they make them good most religiously to such as escape. This animates them to adventure again, whenever there is occasion for it; for the Utopians are not at all troubled how many of these happen to be killed, and reckon it a service done to mankind if they could be a means to deliver the world from such a lewd and vicious sort of people, that seem to have run together as to the drain of human nature. Next to these they are served in their wars with those upon whose account they undertake them, and with the auxiliary troops of their other friends, to whom they

---

19. "The Ready-Sellers." The reference is to the Swiss mercenaries of More's own day.

join a few of their own people, and send some men of eminent and approved virtue to command in chief. There are two sent with him, who during his command are but private men, but the first is to succeed him if he should happen to be either killed or taken; and in case of the like misfortune to him, the third comes in his place; and thus they provide against ill events, that such accidents as may befall their generals may not endanger their armies. When they draw out troops of their own people, they take such out of every city as freely offer themselves, for none are forced to go against their wills, since they think that if any man is pressed that wants courage, he will not only act faintly, but by his cowardice dishearten others. But if an invasion is made on their country they make use of such men, if they have good bodies, though they are not brave; and either put them aboard their ships or place them on the walls of their towns, that being so posted they may find no opportunity of flying away; and thus either shame, the heat of action, or the impossibility of flying, bears down their cowardice; they often make a virtue of necessity and behave themselves well, because nothing else is left them. But as they force no man to go into any foreign war against his will, so they do not hinder those women who are willing to go along with their husbands; on the contrary, they encourage and praise them, and they often stand next their husbands in the front of the army. They also place together those who are related, parents and children, kindred, and those that are mutually allied, near one another; that those whom Nature has inspired with the greatest zeal for assisting one another, may be the nearest and readiest to do it; and it is matter of great reproach if husband or wife survive one another, or if a child survive his parents, and therefore when they come to be engaged in action they continue to fight to the last man, if their enemies stand before them. And as they use all prudent methods to avoid the endangering their own men, and if it is possible let all the action and danger fall upon the troops they hire, so if it becomes necessary for themselves to engage, they then charge with as much courage as they avoided it before with prudence: nor is it a fierce charge at first, but it increases by degrees; and as they continue in action, they grow more obstinate and press harder upon the enemy, insomuch that they will much sooner die than give ground; for the certainty that their children will be well looked after when they are dead, frees them from all that anxiety concerning them which often masters men of great courage; and thus they are animated by a noble and invincible resolution. Their skill in military affairs increases their courage; and the wise sentiments which, according to the laws of their country are instilled into them in their education, give additional vigor to their minds: for as they do not under-value life so as prodigally to throw it away, they are not so indecently fond of it as to preserve it by base and unbecoming methods. In the greatest heat of action, the bravest of their youth, who have devoted themselves to that service, single out the general of their enemies, set on him either openly or by ambuscade, pursue him everywhere, and when spent and wearied out, are relieved by others, who never give over the pursuit; either attacking him with close weapons when they can get near him, or with those which wound at a distance, when others get in between them;

so that unless he secures himself by flight, they seldom fail at last to kill or to take him prisoner. When they have obtained a victory, they kill as few as possible, and are much more bent on taking many prisoners than on killing those that fly before them; nor do they ever let their men so loose in the pursuit of their enemies, as not to retain an entire body still in order; so that if they have been forced to engage the last of their battalions before they could gain the day, they will rather let their enemies all escape than pursue them, when their own army is in disorder; remembering well what has often fallen out to themselves, that when the main body of their army has been quite defeated and broken, when their enemies imagining the victory obtained, have let themselves loose into an irregular pursuit, a few of them that lay for a reserve, waiting a fit opportunity, have fallen on them in their chase, and when straggling in disorder and apprehensive of no danger, but counting the day their own, have turned the whole action, and wresting out of their hands a victory that seemed certain and undoubted, while the vanquished have suddenly become victorious.

It is hard to tell whether they are more dextrous in laying or avoiding ambushes. They sometimes seem to fly when it is far from their thoughts; and when they intend to give ground, they do it so that it is very hard to find out their design. If they see they are ill posted, or are like to be overpowered by numbers, they then either march off in the night with great silence, or by some stratagem delude their enemies: if they retire in the daytime, they do it in such order, that it is no less dangerous to fall upon them in a retreat than in a march. They fortify their camps with a deep and large trench, and throw up the earth that is dug out of it for a wall; nor do they employ only their slaves in this, but the whole army works at it, except those that are then upon the guard; so that when so many hands are at work, a great line and a strong fortification is finished in so short a time that it is scarce credible. Their armour is very strong for defence, and yet is not so heavy as to make them uneasy in their marches; they can even swim with it. All that are trained up to war, practice swimming. Both horse and foot make great use of arrows, and are very expert. They have no swords, but fight with a pole-axe that is both sharp and heavy, by which they thrust or strike down an enemy. They are very good at finding out warlike machines, and disguise them so well, that the enemy does not perceive them till he feels the use of them; so that he cannot prepare such a defence as would render them useless; the chief consideration had in the making them, is that they may be easily carried and managed.

If they agree to a truce, they observe it so religiously that no provocations will make them break it. They never lay their enemies' country waste, nor burn their corn, and even in their marches they take all possible care that neither horse nor foot may tread it down, for they do not know but that they may have use for it themselves. They hurt no man whom they find disarmed, unless he is a spy. When a town is surrendered to them, they take it into their protection: and when they carry a place by storm, they never plunder it, but put those only to the sword that opposed the rendering of it up, and make the rest of the garrison slaves, but for the other inhabitants, they do them no hurt; and if any of them had advised a surrender, they give them good rewards out of the estates of those that they condemn, and distribute the rest among their auxiliary troops, but they themselves take no share of the spoil.

When a war is ended, they do not oblige their friend to reimburse their expenses; but they obtain them of the conquered, either in money, which they keep for the next occasion, or in lands, out of which a constant revenue is to be paid them; by many increases, the revenues which they draw out from several countries on such occasions, is now risen to above 700,000 ducats a year. They send some of their own people to receive these revenues, who have orders to live magnificently, and like princes, by which means they consume much of it upon the place; and either bring over the rest to Utopia, or lend it to that nation in which it lies. This they most commonly do, unless some great occasion, which falls out but very seldom, should oblige them to call for it all. It is out of these lands that they assign rewards to such as they encourage to adventure on desperate attempts. If any prince that engages in war with them is making preparations for invading their country, they prevent him, and make his country the seat of the war; for they do not willingly suffer any war to break in upon their island; and if that should happen, they would only defend themselves by their own people, but would not call for auxiliary troops to their assistance.

Of the religions of the Utopians

There are several sorts of religions, not only in different parts of the island, but even in every town; some worshipping the sun, others the moon, or one of the planets: some worship such men as have been eminent in former times for virtue, or glory, not only as ordinary deities, but as the supreme God: yet the greater and wiser sort of them worship none of these, but adore one eternal, invisible, infinite, and incomprehensible Deity; as a Being that is far above all our apprehensions, that is spread over the whole universe, not by His bulk, but by His power and virtue; Him they call the Father of All, and acknowledge that the beginnings, the increase, the progress, the vicissitudes, and the end of all things come only from Him; nor do they offer divine honors to any but to Him alone. And indeed, though they differ concerning other things, yet all agree in this, that they think there is one supreme Being that made and governs the world, whom they call in the language of their country Mithras.[20] They differ in this, that one thinks the God whom he worships is this supreme Being, and another thinks that his idol is that God; but they all agree in one principle, that whoever is this supreme Being, He is also that great Essence to whose glory and majesty all honors are ascribed by the consent of all nations.

By degrees, they fall off from the various superstitions that are among them, and grow up to that one religion that is the best and most in request; and there is no doubt to be made but that all the others had vanished long ago, if some of those who were minded to lay aside their superstitions had

---

20. This name is close to Mithra, the Persian name for the sun god. It may link the old Utopian language with Persian.

not met with some unhappy accident, which being considered as inflicted by Heaven, made them afraid that the God whose worship had like to have been abandoned, had interposed, and revenged themselves on those who despised their authority.

After they had heard from us an account of the doctrine, the course of life, and the miracles of Christ, and of the wonderful constancy of so many martyrs, whose blood, so willingly offered up by them, was the chief cause of spreading their religion over a vast number of nations; it is not to be imagined how inclined they were to receive it. I shall not determine whether this proceeded from any secret inspiration of God, or whether it was because it seemed so favorable to that community of goods, which is an opinion so particular as well as so dear to them; since they perceived that Christ and His followers lived by that rule, and that it was still kept up in some communities among the sincerest sort of Christians. From whichsoever of these motives it might be, true it is that many of them came over to our religion, and were initiated into it by baptism. But as two of our number were dead, so none of the four that survived were priests; therefore to our great regret, though they were instructed in other matters, they could not partake of those other sacraments, that can only be administered by priests; but they are instructed concerning them, and long most vehemently for them. They have had great disputes among themselves, whether one chosen by them to be a priest would not be thereby qualified to do all the things that belong to that character, even though he had no authority derived from the Pope; and they seemed to be resolved to choose some for that employment, but they had not done it when I left them.

Those among them that have not received our religion, do not fright any from it, and use none ill that goes over to it; so that all the while I was there, only one man was punished on this occasion. He being newly baptized, did, notwithstanding all that we can say to the contrary, dispute publicly concerning the Christian religion with more zeal than discretion; and with so much heat, that he not only preferred our worship to theirs, but condemned all their rites as profane; and cried out against all that adhered to them, as impious and sacrilegious persons, that were to be damned to everlasting burnings. Upon his having frequently preached in this manner, he was seized, and after trial he was condemned to banishment, not for having disparaged their religion, but for his inflaming the people to sedition: for this is one of their most ancient laws, that no man ought to be the worse off for his religion. At the first constitution of their government, Utopos having understood that before his coming among them the old inhabitants had been engaged in great quarrels concerning religion, by which they were so divided among themselves, that he found it an easy thing to conquer them, since instead of uniting their forces against him, every different party in religion fought by themselves; after he had subdued them, he made a law that every man might be of what religion he pleased, and might endeavor to draw others to it by the force of argument, and by amicable and modest ways, but without bitterness against those of other opinions; but that he ought to use no other force but that of persuasion, and was neither to mix with it reproaches nor violence; and such as did otherwise were to be condemned to banishment or slavery.

This law was made by Utopus, not only for preserving the public peace, which he saw suffered much by daily contentions and irreconcilable heats, but because he thought the interest of religion itself required it. He judged it not fit to determine anything rashly, and seemed to doubt whether those different forms of religion might not all come from God, who might inspire men in a different manner, and be pleased with this variety; he therefore thought it indecent and foolish for any man to threaten and terrify another to make him believe what did not appear to him to be true. And supposing that only one religion was really true, and the rest false, he imagined that the native force of truth would at last break forth and shine bright, if supported only by the strength of argument, and attended to with a gentle and unprejudiced mind; while, on the other hand, if such debates were carried on with violence and tumults, as the most wicked are always the most obstinate, so the best and most holy religion might be choked with superstition, as grain is with briars and thorns; he therefore left men wholly to their liberty, that they might be free to believe as they should see cause; only he made a solemn and severe law against such as should so far degenerate from the dignity of human nature as to think that our souls died with our bodies, or that the world was governed by chance, without a wise overruling Providence: for they all formerly believed that there was a state of rewards and punishments to the good and bad after this life; and they now look on those that think otherwise as scarce fit to be counted men, since they degrade so noble a being as the soul, and reckon it no better than a beast's: thus they are far from looking on such men as fit for human society, or to be citizens of a well-ordered commonwealth; since a man of such principles must needs, as oft as he dares do it, despise all their laws and customs: for there is no doubt to be made that a man who is afraid of nothing but the law, and apprehends nothing after death, will not scruple to break through all the laws of his country, either by fraud or force, when by this means he may satisfy his appetites. They never raise any that hold these maxims, either to honors or offices, nor employ them in any public trust, but despise them, as men of base and sordid minds: yet they do not punish them, because they lay this down as a maxim that a man cannot make himself believe anything he pleases; nor do they drive any to dissemble their thoughts by threatenings, so that men are not tempted to lie or disguise their opinions; which being a sort of fraud, is abhorred by the Utopians. They take care indeed to prevent their disputing in defence of these opinions, especially before the common people; but they suffer, and even encourage them to dispute concerning them in private with their priests and other grave men, being confident that they will be cured of those mad opinions by having reason laid before them. There are many among them that run far to the other extreme, though it is neither thought an ill nor unreasonable opinion, and therefore is not at all discouraged. They think that the souls of beasts are immortal, though far inferior to the dignity of the human soul, and not capable of so great a happiness. They are almost all of them very firmly persuaded that good men will be infinitely happy in another state; so that though they are compassionate to all that are sick, yet they lament no man's death, except they see him loth to depart with life; for they look on this as a very ill presage, as if the soul, conscious to itself of guilt, and quite hopeless, was afraid to leave the body, from some secret hints of approaching misery. They think that such a man's appearance before God cannot be acceptable to Him, who being called on, does not go out cheerfully, but is backward and unwilling, and is, as it were, dragged to it. They are struck with horror when they see any die in this manner, and carry them out in silence and with sorrow, and praying God that He would be merciful to the errors of the departed soul, they lay the body in the ground; but when any die cheerfully, and full of hope, they do not mourn for them, but sing hymns when they carry out their bodies, and commending their souls very earnestly to God: their whole behavior is then rather grave than sad, they burn the body and set up a pillar where the pile was made, with an inscription to the honor of the deceased. When they come from the funeral, they discourse of his good life and worthy actions, but speak of nothing oftener and with more pleasure than of his serenity at the hour of death. They think such respect paid to the memory of good men is both the greatest incitement to engage others to follow their example, and the most acceptable worship that can be offered them; for they believe that though by the imperfection of human sight they are invisible to us, yet they are present among us, and hear those discourses that pass concerning themselves. They believe it inconsistent with the happiness of departed souls not to be at liberty to be where they will, and do not imagine them capable of the ingratitude of not desiring to see those friends with whom they lived on earth in the strictest bonds of love and kindness: besides they are persuaded that good men after death have these affections and all other good dispositions increased rather than diminished, and therefore conclude that they are still among the living, and observe all they say or do. From hence they engage in all their affairs with the greater confidence of success, as trusting to their protection; while this opinion of the presence of their ancestors is a restraint that prevents their engaging in ill designs.

They despise and laugh at auguries, and the other vain and superstitious ways of divination, so much observed among other nations; but have great reverence for such miracles as cannot flow from any of the powers of Nature, and look on them as effects and indications of the presence of the supreme Being, of which they say many instances have occurred among them; and that sometimes their public prayers, which upon great and dangerous occasions they have solemnly put up to God, with assured confidence of being heard, have been answered in a miraculous manner.

They think the contemplating God in His works, and the adoring Him for them, is a very acceptable piece of worship to Him.

There are many among them, that upon a motive of religion neglect learning, and apply themselves to no sort of study; nor do they allow themselves any leisure time, but are perpetually employed, believing that by the good things that a man does he secures to himself that happiness that comes after death. Some of these visit the sick; others mend highways, cleanse ditches, repair bridges, or dig turf, gravel, or stones. Others fell and cleave timber, and bring wood, grain, and other necessaries on carts into their towns. Nor do these only serve the public, but they serve even private men, more than the slaves themselves do; for if there is anywhere a rough, hard, and sordid piece of work to be done, from which many are frightened by the labor and loathsomeness of it, if not the despair of accomplishing it, they cheerfully, and of their own accord, take that to their share; and by that means, as they ease others very much, so they afflict themselves, and spend their whole life in hard labor; and yet they do not value themselves upon this, nor lessen other people's credit to raise their own; but by their stooping to such servile employments, they are so far from being despised, that they are so much the more esteemed by the whole nation.

Of these there are two sorts; some live unmarried and chaste, and abstain from eating any sort of flesh; and thus weaning themselves from all the pleasures of the present life, which they account hurtful, they pursue, even by the hardest and painfullest methods possible, that blessedness which they hope for hereafter; and the nearer they approach to it, they are the more cheerful and earnest in their endeavors after it. Another sort of them is less willing to put themselves to much toil, and therefore prefer a married state to a single one; and as they do not deny themselves the pleasure of it, so they think the begetting of children is a debt which they owe to human nature and to their country; nor do they avoid any pleasure that does not hinder labor, and therefore eat flesh so much the more willingly, as they find that by this means they are the more able to work; the Utopians look upon these as the wiser sect, but they esteem the others as the most holy. They would indeed laugh at any man, who from the principles of reason would prefer an unmarried state to a married, or a life of labor to an easy life; but they reverence and admire such as do it from the motives of religion. There is nothing in which they are more cautious than in giving their opinion positively concerning any sort of religion. The men that lead those severe lives are called in the language of their country Brutheskas,[21] which answers to those we call religious.

Their priests are men of eminent piety, and therefore they are but few, for there are only thirteen in every town, one for every temple; but when they go to war, seven of these go out with their forces, and seven others are chosen to supply their room in their absence; but these enter again upon their employment when they return; and those who served in their absence attend upon the high-priest, till vacancies fall by death; for there is one set over all the rest. They are chosen by the people as the other magistrates are, by suffrages given in secret, for preventing of factions; and when they are chosen they are consecrated by the college of priests. The care of all sacred things, the worship of God, and an inspection into the manners of the people, are committed to them. It is a reproach to a man to be sent for by any of them and taken to task for living a dishonorable life. The priests' duty is only to exhort and admonish the people; for the power of correcting and punishing ill men belongs wholly to the Prince and to the other magistrates. The severest thing that the priest does, is the excluding those that are desperately wicked from joining

---

21. The word, as More himself explains, is derived from the Greek, "very devout."

in their worship. There is not any sort of punishment more dreaded by them than this, for as it loads them with infamy, so it fills them with secret horrors, such is their reverence to their religion; nor will their bodies be long exempted from their share of trouble; for if they do not very quickly satisfy the priests of the truth of their repentance, they are seized on by the Senate, and punished for their impiety. The education of youth belongs to the priests, yet they do not take so much care of instructing them in letters as in forming their minds and manners aright; they use all possible methods to infuse very early into the tender and flexible minds of children such opinions as are both good in themselves and will be useful to their country. For when deep impressions of these things are made at that age, they follow men through the whole course of their lives, and conduce much to preserve the peace of the government, which suffers by nothing more than by vices that rise out of bad moral attitudes. The wives of their priests are the most extraordinary women of the whole country; some-times the women themselves are made priests, though that falls out but seldom, nor are any but ancient widows chosen into that order.

None of the magistrates have greater honor paid them than is paid the priests; and if they should happen to commit any crime, they would not be questioned for it. Their punishment is left to God, and to their own consciences; for they do not think it lawful to lay hands on any man, how wicked soever he is, that has been in a peculiar manner dedicated to God; nor do they find any great inconvenience in this, both because they have so few priests, and because these are chosen with much caution, so that it must be a very unusual thing to find one who merely out of regard to his virtue, and for his being esteemed a singularly good man, was raised up to so great a dignity, degenerate into corruption and vice. And if such a thing should fall out, for man is a changeable creature, yet there being few priests, and these having no authority but what rises out of the respect that is paid them, nothing of great consequence to the public can proceed from the indemnity that the priests enjoy.

They have indeed very few of them, lest greater numbers sharing in the same honor might make the dignity of that order which they esteem so highly to sink in its reputation. They also think it difficult to find out many of such an exalted pitch of goodness, as to be equal to that dignity which demands the exercise of more than ordinary virtues. Nor are the priests in greater veneration among them than they are among their neighboring nations, as you may imagine by that which I think gives occasion for it.

When the Utopians engage in battle, the priests who accompany them to the war, apparelled in their sacred vestments, kneel down during the action, in a place not far from the field; and lifting up their hands to heaven, pray, first for peace, and then for victory to their own side, and particularly that it may be gained without the effusion of much blood on either side; and when the victory turns to their side, they run in among their own men to restrain their fury; and if any of their enemies see them, or call to them, they are preserved by that means; and such as can come so near them as to touch their garments, have not only their lives, but their fortunes secured to them; it is upon this account that all the nations round

about consider them so much, and treat them with such reverence, that
they have been often no less able to preserve their own people from the
fury of their enemies, than to save their enemies from their rage; for it
has sometimes fallen out, that when their armies have been in disorder,
and forced to fly, so that their enemies were running upon the slaughter
and spoil, the priests by interposing have separated them from one another, and stopped the effusion of more blood; so that by their mediation
a peace has been concluded on very reasonable terms; nor is there any
nation about them so fierce, cruel, or barbarous as not to look upon their
persons as sacred and inviolable.

The first and the last day of the month, and of the year, is a festival.
They measure their months by the course of the moon, and their years by
the course of the sun. The first days are called in their language the
Cynemernes, and the last the Trapemernes;[22] which answers in our
language to the festival that begins, or ends the season.

They have magnificent temples, that are not only nobly built, but extremely spacious; which is the more necessary, as they have so few of them;
they are a little dark within, which proceeds not from any error in the
architecture, but is done with design; for their priests think that too much
light dissipates the thoughts, and that a more moderate degree of it both
recollects the mind and raises devotion. Though there are many different
forms of religion among them, yet all these, how various soever, agree in
the main point, which is the worshipping the Divine Essence; and therefore there is nothing to be seen or heard in their temples in which the
several persuasions among them may not agree; for every sect performs
those rites that are peculiar to it, in their private houses, nor is there anything in the public worship that contradicts the particular ways of those
different sects. There are no images for God in their temples, so that every
one may represent Him to his thoughts, according to the way of his religion; nor do they call this one God by any other name but that of Mithras,
which is the common name by which they all express the Divine Essence,
whatsoever otherwise they think it to be; nor are there any prayers among
them but such as every one of them may use without prejudice to his own
opinion.

They meet in their temples on the evening of the festival that concludes
a season: and not having yet broken their fast, they thank God for their
good success during that year or month, which is then at an end; and the
next day being that which begins the new season, they meet early in their
temples, to pray for the happy progress of all their affairs during that
period upon which they then enter. In the festival which concludes the
period, before they go to the temple, both wives and children fall on their
knees before their husbands or parents, and confess everything in which
they have either erred or failed in their duty, and beg pardon for it. Thus
all little discontents in families are removed, that they may offer up their
devotions with a pure and serene mind; for they hold it a great impiety to

---

22. *Cynemernes* may possibly be derived from the Greek, "the dog's day of the month," strictly
the night between the old and the new month, when food was placed out at the crossroads,
and the barking of the dogs was taken as the sign of the approach of Hecate. So in like manner,
Trapemernes would mean the turning or closing day of the month.

enter upon them with disturbed thoughts, or with a consciousness of their
bearing hatred or anger in their hearts to any person whatsoever; and
think that they should become liable to severe punishments if they presumed to offer sacrifices without cleansing their hearts, and reconciling
all their differences. In the temples, the two sexes are separated, the men
go to the right hand, and the women to the left; and the males and fe-
males all place themselves before the head master or mistress of that
family to which they belong; so that those who have the government of
them at home may see their deportment in public; and they intermingle
them so, that the younger and the older may be set by one another; for
if the younger sort were all set together, they would perhaps trifle away
that time too much in which they ought to beget in themselves that religious dread of the supreme Being, which is the greatest and almost
the only incitement to virtue.

They offer up no living creature in sacrifice, nor do they think it suitable to the divine Being, from whose bounty it is that these creatures have
derived their lives, to take pleasure in their deaths, or the offering up their
blood. They burn incense and other sweet odors, and have a great number
of wax lights during their worship; not out of any imagination that such
oblations can add anything to the divine Nature, which even prayers
cannot do; but as it is a harmless and pure way of worshipping God, so
they think those sweet savors and lights, together with some other ceremonies, by a secret and unaccountable virtue, elevate men's souls, and
inflame them with greater energy and cheerfulness during the divine
worship.

All the people appear in the temples in white garments, but the priest's
vestments are parti-colored, and both the work and colors are wonderful.
They are made of no rich materials, for they are neither embroidered nor
set with precious stones, but are composed of the plumes of several birds,
laid together with so much care and so neatly, that the true value of them
is far beyond the costliest materials. They say that in the ordering and
placing those plumes some dark mysteries are represented, which pass
down among their priests in a secret tradition concerning them; and that
they are as hieroglyphics, putting them in mind of the blessings that they
have received from God, and of their duties both to Him and to their
neighbors. As soon as the priest appears in those ornaments, they all
fall prostrate on the ground, with so much reverence and so deep a silence
that such as look on cannot but be struck with it, as if it were the effect
of the appearance of a Deity. After they have been for some time in this
posture, they all stand up, upon a sign given by the priest, and sing hymns
to the honor of God, some musical instruments playing all the while.
These are quite of another form than those used among us: but as many
of them are much sweeter than ours, so others are made use of by us. Yet
in one thing they very much exceed us; all their music, both vocal and
instrumental, is adapted to imitate and express the passions, and is so
happily suited to every occasion, that whether the subject of the hymn
be cheerful or formed to soothe or trouble the mind, or to express grief
or remorse, the music takes the impression of whatever is represented,
affects and kindles the passions, and works the sentiments deep into the

hearts of the hearers. When this is done, both priests and people offer up very solemn prayers to God in a set form of words; and these are so composed, that whatsoever is pronounced by the whole assembly may be likewise applied by every man in particular to his own condition; in these they acknowledge God to be the author and governor of the world, and the fountain of all the good they receive, and therefore offer up to Him their thanksgiving; and in particular bless Him for His goodness in ordering it so, that they are born under the happiest government in the world, and are of a religion which they hope is the truest of all others: but if they are mistaken, and if there is either a better government or a religion more acceptable to God, they implore His goodness to let them know it, vowing that they resolve to follow Him whithersoever He leads them. But if their government is the best, and their religion the truest, then they pray that He may fortify them in it, and bring all the world both to the same rules of life, and to the same opinions concerning himself; unless, according to the unsearchableness of His mind, He is pleased with a variety of religions. Then they pray that God may give them an easy passage at last to himself; not presuming to set limits to Him, how early or late it should be; but if it may be wished for, without derogating from His supreme authority, they desire to be quickly delivered, and to be taken to himself, though by the most terrible kind of death, rather than to be detained long from seeing Him by the most prosperous course of life. When this prayer is ended, they all fall down again upon the ground, and after a little while they rise up, go home to dinner, and spend the rest of the day in diversion or military exercises.

Thus I have described to you, as particularly as I could, the constitution of that commonwealth, which I do not only think the best in the world, but indeed the only commonwealth that truly deserves that name. In all other places it is visible, that while people talk of a commonwealth, every man only seeks his own wealth; but there, where no man has any property, all men zealously pursue the good of the public: and, indeed, it is no wonder to see men act so differently; for in other commonwealths, every man knows that unless he provides for himself, how flourishing soever the commonwealth may be, he must die of hunger; so that he sees the necessity of preferring his own concerns to the public; but in Utopia, where every man has a right to everything, they all know that if care is taken to keep the public stores full, no private man can want anything; for among them there is no unequal distribution, so that no man is poor, none in necessity; and though no man has anything, yet they are all rich; for what can make a man so rich as to lead a serene and cheerful life, free from anxieties; neither apprehending want himself, nor vexed with the endless complaints of his wife? He is not afraid of the misery of his children, nor is he contriving how to raise a portion for his daughters, but is secure in this, that both he and his wife, his children and grandchildren, to as many generations as he can fancy, will all live both plentifully and happily; since among them there is no less care taken of those who were once engaged in labor, but grow afterwards unable to follow it, than there is elsewhere of these that continue still employed. I would gladly hear any man compare the justice that is among them with that of all other nations; among whom, may I perish, if I see anything that looks either like justice or equity: for what justice is there in this, that a nobleman, a goldsmith, a banker, or any other man, that either does nothing at all, or at best is employed in things that are of no use to the public, should live in great luxury and splendor, upon what is so ill acquired; and a mean man, a carter, a smith, or a plowman, that works harder even than the beasts themselves, and is employed in labors so necessary, that no commonwealth could hold out a year without them, can only earn so poor a livelihood, and must lead so miserable a life, that the condition of the beasts is much better than theirs? For as the beasts do not work constantly, so they feed almost as well, and with more pleasure; and have no anxiety about what is to come, whilst these men are depressed by a barren and fruitless employment, and tormented with the apprehensions of want in their old age; since that which they get by their daily labor does but maintain them at present, and is consumed as fast as it comes in, there is no overplus left to lay up for old age.

Is not that government both unjust and ungrateful, that is so prodigal of its favors to those that are called gentlemen, or goldsmiths, or such others who are idle, or live either by flattery, or by contriving the arts of vain pleasure; and on the other hand, takes no care of those of a meaner sort, such as plowmen, colliers, and smiths, without whom it could not subsist? But after the public has reaped all the advantage of their service, and they come to be oppressed with age, sickness, and want, all their labors and the good they have done is forgotten; and all the recompense given them is that they are left to die in great misery. The richer sort are often endeavoring to bring the hire of laborers lower, not only by their fraudulent private practices, but by the laws which they procure to be made to that effect; so that though it is a thing most unjust in itself, to give such small rewards to those who deserve so well of the public, yet they have given those hardships the name and color of justice, by procuring laws to be made for regulating them.

Therefore I must say that, as I hope for mercy, I can have no other notion of all the other governments that I see or know, than that they are a conspiracy of the rich, who on pretence of managing the public only pursue their private interests, and devise all the ways and arts they can find out; first, that they may, without danger, preserve all that they have so ill acquired, and then that they may engage the poor to toil and labor for them at as low rates as possible, and oppress them as much as they please. And if they can but prevail to get these contrivances established by the show of public authority, which is considered as the representative of the whole people, then they are accounted laws. Yet these wicked men after they have, by a most insatiable covetousness, divided that among themselves with which all the rest might have been well supplied, are far from that happiness that is enjoyed among the Utopians: for the use as well as the desire of money being extinguished, much anxiety and great occasions of mischief are cut off with it. And who does not see that the frauds, thefts, robberies, quarrels, tumults, contentions, seditions, murders, treacheries, and poisonings, which are indeed rather punished than restrained by the severities of law, would all fall off, if money were not any more valued by the world? Men's fears, solicitudes, cares, labors, and watchings, would all perish in the same moment with the value of money: even poverty itself, for the relief of which money seems most necessary, would fall. But, in order to the apprehending this aright, take one instance.

Consider any year that has been so unfruitful that many thousands have died of hunger; and yet if at the end of that year a survey was made of the granaries of all the rich men that have hoarded up the grain, it would be found that there was enough among them to have prevented all that consumption of men that perished in misery; and that if it had been distributed among them, none would have felt the terrible effects of that scarcity; so easy a thing would it be to supply all the necessities of life, if that blessed thing called money, which is pretended to be invented for procuring them, was not really the only thing that obstructed their being procured!

I do not doubt but rich men are sensible of this, and that they well know how much a greater happiness it is to want nothing necessary than to abound in many superfluities, and to be rescued out of so much misery than to abound with so much wealth; and I cannot think but the sense of every man's interest, added to the authority of Christ's commands, who as He was infinitely wise, knew what was best, and was not less good in discovering it to us, would have drawn all the world over to the laws of the Utopians, if pride, that plague of human nature, that source of so much misery, did not hinder it; for this vice does not measure happiness so much by its own conveniences as by the miseries of others; and would not be satisfied with being thought a goddess, if none were left that were miserable, over whom she might insult. Pride thinks its own happiness shines the brighter by comparing it with the misfortunes of other persons; that by displaying its own wealth, they may feel their poverty the more sensibly. This is that infernal serpent that creeps into the breasts of mortals, and possesses them too much to be easily drawn out; and therefore I am glad that the Utopians have fallen upon this form of government, in which I wish that all the world could be so wise as to imitate them; for they have indeed laid down such a scheme and foundation of policy, that as men live happily under it, so it is like to be of great continuance; for they having rooted out of the minds of their people all the seeds both of ambition and faction, there is no danger of any commotion at home; which alone has been the ruin of many states, that seemed otherwise to be well secured; but as long as they live in peace at home, and are governed by such good laws, the envy of all their neighboring princes, who have often though in vain attempted their ruin, will never be able to put their state into any commotion or disorder.

When Raphael had thus made an end of speaking, though many things occurred to me, both concerning the manners and laws of that people, that seemed very absurd, as well as their way of making war, as in their notions of religion and divine matters; together with several other particulars, but chiefly what seemed the foundation of all the rest, their living in common, without the use of money, by which all nobility, magnificence, splendor, and majesty, which, according to the common opinion, are the true ornaments of a nation, would be quite taken away; yet since I perceived that Raphael was weary, and was not sure whether he could easily bear contradiction, remembering that he had taken notice of some who seemed to think they were bound in honor to support the credit of their own wisdom, by finding out something to censure in all other men's inventions, besides their own; I only commended their constitution, and the account he had given of it in general; and so taking him by the hand, carried him to supper, and told him I would find out some other time for examining this subject more particularly, and for discoursing more copiously upon it; and indeed I shall be glad to embrace an opportunity of doing it. In the meanwhile, though it must be confessed that he is both a very learned man, and a person who has obtained a great knowledge of the world, I cannot perfectly agree to everything he has related; however, there are many things in the Commonwealth of Utopia that I rather wish, than hope, to see followed in our governments.

Sixteenth-
Century
Opinion

Erasmus[1]

Letter to Ulrich von Hutten

Most illustrious Hutten, your love, I had almost said your passion for the genius of Thomas More, — kindled as it is by his writings, which, as you truly say, are as learned and witty as anything can possibly be, — is, I assure you, shared by many others; and moreover the feeling in this case is mutual; since More is so delighted with what you have written, that I am myself almost jealous of you. It is an example of what Plato says of that sweetest wisdom, which excites much more ardent love among men than the most admirable beauty of form. It is not discerned by the eye of sense, but the mind has eyes of its own, so that even here the Greek saying holds true, that out of Looking grows Liking;* and so it comes to pass that people are sometimes united in the warmest affection, who have never seen or spoken to each other. And, as it is a common experience, that for some unexplained reason different people are attracted by different kinds of beauty, so between one mind and another, there seems to be a sort of latent kindred, which causes us to be specially delighted with some minds, and not with others.

As to your asking me to paint you a full-length portrait of More, I only wish my power of satisfying your request were equal to your earnestness in pressing it. For to me too, it will be no unpleasant task to linger awhile in the contemplation of a friend, who is the most delightful character in the world. But, in the first place, it is not /387/ given to every man to be aware of all More's accomplishments; and in the next place, I know not whether he will himself like to have his portrait painted by any artist that chooses to do so. For indeed I do not think it more easy to make a likeness of More than of Alexander the Great, or of Achilles; neither were those heroes more worthy of immortality. The hand of an Apelles is required for such a subject, and I am afraid I am more like a Fulvius or a

---

Letter of Erasmus to Ulrich von Hutten, in *The Epistles of Erasmus, From His Earliest Letters to His Fifty-First Year*, translated by Francis Morgan Nichols. New York: Russell & Russell, Inc., 1962, Vol. III, pp. 387-402.

1. Desiderius Erasmus (c. 1466-1536) was the most brilliant and important leader of continental humanism in the sixteenth century. He was educated in the school of the celebrated humanist Hegius of Deventer; later at the Priory of Augustinian Canons at Steyn, near Gouda, Holland; and later at the University of Paris (where he disapproved of the scholastic method of instruction then prevalent). While in Paris, he became a tutor of the English Lord Mountjoy, with whose help he traveled to England and met More, Colet, Latimer, and other eminent English humanists (1498-1499). Colet especially inspired Erasmus in his life work of restoring theology to its ancient brightness and dignity through a study of the original Greek text of the New Testament and of Aristotle. More, who had also been a student of Colet, remained a life-long friend and sympathizer. On his return to England in 1509, and while in More's home, Erasmus wrote his famous satire *Morae Encomium* (*The Praise of Folly*) and dedicated it, as the pun in the title indicates, to More. The book was a stinging attack on abuses in church and state; it embodied many of the ideas of More's humanist-reformer friends. More's *Utopia*, some seven years later, is concerned with the same problems; and Raphael Hythloday is often identified with Erasmus — *Editor's note.*

*ἐκ τοῦ ὁρᾶν γίνεται ἀνθρώποις ἐρᾶν.   /387/

Rutuba than an Apelles.* Nevertheless I will try to draw you a sketch, rather than a portrait, of the entire man, so far as daily and domestic intercourse has enabled me to observe his likeness and retain it in my memory. But if some diplomatic employment should ever bring you together, you will find out, how poor an artist you have chosen for this commission; and I am afraid you will think me guilty of envy or of wilful blindness in taking note of so few of the many good points of his character.

To begin with that part of him which is least known to you, — in shape and stature More is not a tall man, but not remarkably short, all his limbs being so symmetrical, that no deficiency is observed in this respect. His complexion is fair, his face being rather blonde than pale, but with no approach to redness, except a very delicate flush, which lights up the whole. His hair is auburn inclining to black, or if you like it better, black inclining to auburn; his beard thin, his eyes a bluish grey with some sort of tinting upon them.† This kind of eye is thought to be a sign of the happiest character, and is regarded with favour in England, whereas /388/ with us black eyes are rather preferred. It is said, that no kind of eye is so free from defects of sight. His countenance answers to his character, having an expression of kind and friendly cheerfulness with a little air of raillery. To speak candidly, it is a face more expressive of pleasantry than of gravity or dignity, though very far removed from folly or buffoonery. His right shoulder seems a little higher than his left, especially when he is walking, a peculiarity that is not innate, but the result of habit, like many tricks of the kind. In the rest of his body there is nothing displeasing, — only his hands are a little coarse, or appear so, as compared with the rest of his figure. He has always from his boyhood been very negligent of his toilet, so as not to give much attention even to the things, which according to Ovid are all that men need care about.* What a charm there was in his looks when young, may even now be inferred from what remains; although I knew him myself when he was not more than three and-twenty years old; for he has not yet passed much beyond his fortieth year.† His health is sound rather than robust, but sufficient for any labours suitable to an honourable citizen; and we may fairly hope, that his life may be long, as he has a father living of a great age, but an age full of freshness and vigour.

I have never seen any person less fastidious in his choice of food. As a young man, he was by preference a water-drinker, a practice he derived from his father. But, not to give annoyance to others, he used at table to conceal this habit from his guests by drinking, out of a pewter vessel, either small beer almost as weak as water, or plain water. As to wine, it being the custom, where he was, for the company to invite each other to drink in turn out of the same cup, he used sometimes to sip a little of it,

---

*Vereor ne ipse Fulvii Rutubæque similior sim quam Apellis. In the passage of Horace here alluded to (Sat. II. vii. 96), Fulvius and Rutuba are generally understood to be the names of gladiators, depicted in a popular hand-bill. But Erasmus appears to interpret them as the names of humble artists dealing with such common-place subjects.   /388/

†capilli subnigro flavore sive mavis sufflavo nigrore: barba rarior: oculi subcæsii maculis quibusdam interspersi.   /388/

*Ovid. *de Arte Amandi*, lib. i. 514. Sit bene conveniens et sine labe toga: *etc.*   /389/

†As to the date of More's birth, see note at the end of this epistle, p. 402 [p. 79].   /389/

to avoid appearing to /389/ shrink from it altogether, and to habitu-
ate himself to the common practice. For his eating he has been accustomed to prefer beef and salt meats, and household bread thoroughly
fermented, to those articles of diet which are commonly regarded as
delicacies. But he does not shrink from things that impart an innocent
pleasure, even of a bodily kind, and has always a good appetite for
milk-puddings and for fruit, and eats a dish of eggs with the greatest
relish.

His voice is neither loud nor excessively low, but of a penetrating tone.
It has nothing in it melodious or soft, but is simply suitable for speech,
as he does not seem to have any natural talent for singing, though he takes
pleasure in music of every kind. His articulation is wonderfully distinct,
being equally free from hurry and from hesitation.

He likes to be dressed simply, and does not wear silk, or purple, or gold
chains, except when it is not allowable to dispense with them. He cares
marvellously little for those formalities, which with ordinary people are
the test of politeness; and as he does not exact these ceremonies from
others, so he is not scrupulous in observing them himself, either on
occasions of meeting or at entertainments, though he understands how to
use them, if he thinks proper to do so; but he holds it to be effeminate and
unworthy of a man to waste much of his time on such trifles.

He was formerly rather disinclined to a Court life and to any intimacy
with princes, having always a special hatred of tyranny and a great fancy
for equality; whereas you will scarcely find any Court so well-ordered, as
not to have much bustle and ambition and pretence and luxury, or to be
free from tyranny in some form or other. He could not even be tempted
to Henry the Eighth's Court without great trouble, although nothing could
be desired more courteous or less exacting than this Prince.* He is
naturally fond of liberty /390/ and leisure; but as he enjoys a holiday
when he has it, so whenever business requires it, no one is more vigilant
or more patient.

He seems to be born and made for friendship, of which he is the sincerest and most persistent devotee. Neither is he afraid of that multiplicity
of friends, of which Hesiod disapproves. Accessible to every tender of
intimacy, he is by no means fastidious in choosing his acquaintance,
while he is most accommodating in keeping it on foot, and constant in
retaining it. If he has fallen in with anyone whose faults he cannot cure,
he finds some opportunity of parting with him, untying the knot of
intimacy without tearing it; but when he has found any sincere friends,
whose characters are suited to his own, he is so delighted with their society
and conversation, that he seems to find in these the chief pleasure of life,
having an absolute distaste for tennis and dice and cards, and the other
games with which the mass of gentlemen beguile the tediousness of Time.
If should be added that, while he is somewhat neglectful of his own
interest, no one takes more pains in attending to the concerns of his
friends. What more need I say? If anyone requires a perfect example of
true friendship, it is in More that he will best find it.

---

*cum hoc Principe nec optari quicquam possit civilius ac modestius. It is of interest to observe
this early estimate of King Henry's character.   /390/

In company his extraordinary kindness and sweetness of temper are such as to cheer the dullest spirit, and alleviate the annoyance of the most trying circumstances. From boyhood he was always so pleased with a joke, that it might seem that jesting was the main object of his life; but with all that, he did not go so far as buffoonery, nor had ever any inclination to bitterness. When quite a youth, he wrote farces and acted them. If a thing was facetiously said, even though it was aimed at himself, he was charmed with it, so much did he enjoy any witticism that had a flavour of subtlety or genius. This led to his amusing himself as a young man with epigrams, and taking great delight in /391/ Lucian. Indeed, it was he that suggested my writing the *Moria,* or Praise of Folly, which was much the same thing as setting a camel to dance.

There is nothing that occurs in human life, from which he does not seek to extract some pleasure, although the matter may be serious in itself. If he has to do with the learned and intelligent, he is delighted with their cleverness, if with unlearned or stupid people, he finds amusement in their folly. He is not offended even by professed clowns,* as he adapts himself with marvellous dexterity to the tastes of all; while with ladies generally, and even with his wife, his conversation is made up of humour and playfulness. You would say it was a second Democritus, or rather that Pythagorean philosopher, who strolls in leisurely mood through the market-place, contemplating the turmoil of those who buy and sell. There is no one less guided by the opinion of the multitude, but on the other hand no one sticks more closely to common sense.

One of his amusements is in observing the forms, characters and instincts of different animals. Accordingly there is scarcely any kind of bird, that he does not keep about his residence, and the same of other animals not quite so common, as monkeys, foxes, ferrets, weasels and the like. Beside these, if he meets with any strange object, imported from abroad or otherwise remarkable, he is most eager to buy it, and has his house so well supplied with these objects, that there is something in every room which catches your eye, as you enter it; and his own pleasure is renewed every time that he sees others interested.

When of a sentimental age, he was not a stranger to the /292/ emotions of love, but without loss of character, having no inclination to press his advantage, and being more attracted by a mutual liking than by any licentious object.

He had drunk deep of Good Letters from his earliest years; and when a young man, he applied himself to the study of Greek and of philosophy; but his father was so far from encouraging him in this pursuit, that he withdrew his allowance and almost disowned him, because he thought he was deserting his hereditary study, being himself an expert professor of English Law. For remote as that profession is from true learning, those who become masters of it have the highest rank and reputation among their countrymen; and it is difficult to find any readier way to acquire

---

*Nec offenditur morionibus. The picture of More and his family, painted by Holbein in or about 1527, includes his fool or jester. In the original sketch for this painting, preserved at Basel, there are inscriptions over each figure, probably dictated by More. Above the fool is written *Henricus Patersonus Thomæ Mori Morio Anno* 40. Bridgett, Life of More, p. 148. /392/

fortune and honour. Indeed a considerable part of the nobility of that island has had its origin in this profession, in which it is said that no one can be perfect, unless he has toiled at it for many years. It was natural, that in his younger days our friend's genius, born for better things, should shrink from this study; nevertheless, after he had had a taste of the learning of the Schools, he became so conversant with it, that there was no one more eagerly consulted by suitors; and the income that he made by it was not surpassed by any of those who did nothing else; such was the power and quickness of his intellect.

He also expended considerable labour in perusing the volumes of the orthodox Fathers; and when scarcely more than a youth, he lectured publicly on the *De Civitate Dei* of Augustine before a numerous audience, old men and priests not being ashamed to take a lesson in divinity from a young layman, and not at all sorry to have done so. Meantime he applied his whole mind to religion, having some thought of taking orders, for which he prepared himself by watchings and fastings and prayers and such like exercises; wherein he showed much more wisdom than the generality of people, who rashly engage in so arduous /393/ a profession without testing themselves beforehand. And indeed there was no obstacle to his adopting this kind of life, except the fact that he could not shake off his wish to marry. Accordingly he resolved to be a chaste husband rather than a licentious priest.

When he married, he chose a very young girl, a lady by birth, with her character still unformed, having been always kept in the country with her parents and sisters,—so that he was all the better able to fashion her according to his own habits. Under his direction she was instructed in learning and in every kind of Music, and had almost completely become just such a person as would have been a delightful companion for his whole life, if an early death had not carried her away. She had however borne him several children, of whom three girls, Margaret, Alice and Cecily, and one boy, John, are still living.

More did not however long remain single, but contrary to his friends' advice,* a few months after his wife's death, he married a widow, more for the sake of the management of his household, than to please his own fancy, as she is no great beauty, nor yet young, *nec bella admodum nec puella,* as he sometimes laughingly says, but a sharp and watchful housewife; with whom nevertheless he lives, on as sweet and pleasant terms as if she were as young and lovely as any one could desire; and scarcely any husband obtains from his wife by masterfulness and severity as much compliance as he does by blandishments and jests. Indeed, what more compliance could he have, when he has induced a woman who is already elderly, who is not naturally of a yielding character, and whose mind is occupied with business, to learn to play on the harp, the viol, the spinet and the flute,† and to give up every day a prescribed time to /394/ practice? With similar kindness he rules his whole household, in which there are no tragic incidents, and no quarrels. If anything of the kind should

---

* *licet alio vocantibus amicorum consiliis.* We have here in all probability an allusion to a correspondence between More and the writer, which would have been of no little interest, if it had been preserved.   /394/

† *Cithara, testudine, monochordo, tibiis canere.*   /394/

be likely, he either calms it down, or applies a remedy at once. And in parting with any member of his household he has never acted in a hostile spirit, or treated him as an enemy. Indeed his house seems to have a sort of fatal felicity, no one having lived in it without being advanced to higher fortune, no inmate having ever had a stain upon his character.

It would be difficult to find any one living on such terms with a mother as he does with his stepmother. For his father had brought in one step-mother after another; and he has been as affectionate with each of them as with a mother. He has lately introduced a third, and More swears that he never saw anything better. His affection for his parents, children and sisters* is such, that he neither wearies them with his love, nor ever fails in any kindly attention.

His character is entirely free from any touch of avarice. He has set aside out of his property what he thinks sufficient for his children, and spends the rest in a liberal fashion. When he was still dependent on his profession, he gave every client true and friendly counsel with an eye to their advantage rather than his own, generally advising them, that the cheapest thing they could do was to come to terms with their opponents. If he could not persuade them to do this, he pointed out how they might go to law at least expense; for there are some people whose character leads them to delight in litigation.

In the City of London, where he was born, he acted for some years as judge in civil causes.† This office, which /395/ is by no means burdensome, —inasmuch as the Court sits only on Thursdays before dinner,—is considered highly honorable; and no judge ever disposed of more suits, or conducted himself with more perfect integrity. In most cases he remitted the fees which are due from the litigants, the practice being for the plaintiff to deposit three groats* before the hearing, and the defendant a like sum, and no more being allowed to be exacted. By such conduct he made himself extremely popular in the City.

He had made up his mind to be contented with this position, which was sufficiently dignified without being exposed to serious dangers. He has been thrust more than once into an embassy,† in the conduct of which he has shown great ability; and King Henry in consequence would never

---

* I am inclined to infer from this passage that More's brother, John, of whom we have found some notice in 1511 (see [*The Epistles of Erasmus,*] vol. ii. pp. 43, 50), was no longer living. /395/

† The office, held by More, seems to have been that of Under-Sheriff of London.   /395/

* *Tres drachmas,* translated 'groats' by Nicholas Harpsfield, who wrote a life of More in the time of Queen Mary. Bridgett, Life of More, p. 66.   /396/

† Semel atque iterum extrusus est in legationem, in qua cum se cordatissime gessisset, etc. We do not distinctly know of More having been employed, before this date, upon more than one embassy abroad, which occupied him about six months from May, 1515; see [*The Epistles of Erasmus,* vol. iii] p. 419, and vol. ii. p. 269. His next service of this kind began in August, 1517, shortly after the date of this letter. But Sir James Mackintosh states, on the authority of the City Records, that he had leave from the Common Council of London, 8 May, 1514, to appoint a deputy in his City office during his absence as the King's Ambassador in Flanders; so that an earlier embassy appears to have been at least *proposed.* (See Bridgett, Life of More, p. 68, Mackintosh's Life, p. 35.) The date of this letter to Hutten,—if right as here corrected,—shows, that More was attached to Henry's household somewhat earlier than has been hitherto supposed. In More's letter of February, 1516, there is no sign of his being then at the Court, from which he forwards the news at second hand; but the description, given by Erasmus in the above letter (p. 397), of More's intimacy with the King, appears to be that of an eye-witness. We may therefore conjecture, that this intimacy began before the end of Erasmus's last visit to England, in April, 1517.   /396/

rest until he dragged him into his Court. 'Dragged him,' I say, and with
reason; for no one was ever more ambitious of being admitted into a
Court, than he was anxious to escape it. But as this excellent monarch was
resolved to pack his /396/ household with learned, serious, intelligent
and honest men, he especially insisted upon having More among them, —
with whom he is on such terms of intimacy that he cannot bear to let
him go. If serious affairs are in hand, no one gives wiser counsel; if
it pleases the King to relax his mind with agreeable conversation, no
man is better company. Difficult questions are often arising, which
require a grave and prudent judge; and these questions are resolved by
More in such a way, that both sides are satisfied. And yet no one has
ever induced him to accept a present. What a blessing it would be for
the world, if magistrates like More were everywhere put in office by
sovereigns!

Meantime there is no assumption of superiority. In the midst of so great
a pressure of business he remembers his humble friends; and from time
to time he returns to his beloved studies. Whatever authority he derives
from his rank, and whatever influence he enjoys by the favour of a powerful sovereign, are employed in the service of the public, or in that of his
friends. It has always been part of his character to be most obliging to
every body, and marvellously ready with his sympathy; and this disposition
is more conspicuous than ever, now that his power of doing good is
greater. Some he relieves with money, some he protects by his authority,
some he promotes by his recommendation, while those whom he cannot
otherwise assist are benefited by his advice. No one is sent away in distress,
and you might call him the general patron of all poor people. He counts
it a great gain to himself, if he has relieved some oppressed person, made
the path clear for one that was in difficulties, or brought back into favour
one that was in disgrace. No man more readily confers a benefit, no man
expects less in return. And successful as he is in so many ways, — while
success is generally accompanied by self-conceit, — I have never seen any
mortal being more free from this failing. /397/

I now propose to turn to the subject of those studies which have been the
chief means of bringing More and me together. In his first youth his
principal literary exercises were in verse. He afterwards wrestled for a
long time to make his prose more smooth; practising his pen in every kind
of writing in order to form that style,* the character of which there is no
occasion for me to recall, especially to you, who have his books always in
your hands. He took the greatest pleasure in declamations, choosing some
disputable subject, as involving a keener exercise of mind. Hence, while
still a youth, he attempted a dialogue, in which he carried the defence of
Plato's community even to the matter of wives! He wrote an answer to
Lucian's *Tyrannicide*,† in which argument it was his wish to have me for a
rival, in order to test his own proficiency in this kind of writing.

He published his *Utopia* for the purpose of showing, what are the
things that occasion mischief in commonwealths; having the English

---

* It may be presumed that the writer is speaking of More's Latin style.   /398/
† Declamatio Erasmi quæ Luciani Declamationi respondeat. Erasmi *Opera*, vol. i. p. 271.
/398/

constitution especially in view, which he so thoroughly knows and under-stands. He had written the second book at his leisure, and afterwards, when he found it was required; added the first off-hand. Hence there is some inequality in the style.

It would be difficult to find any one more successful in speaking *ex tempore,* the happiest thoughts being attended by the happiest language; while a mind that catches and anticipates all that passes, and a ready memory, having everything as it were in stock, promptly supply whatever the time, or the occasion, demands. In disputations nothing can be im-agined more acute, so that the most eminent theologians often find their match, when he meets them on their own ground. Hence John Colet, a man of keen and exact judgment, is wont to say in familiar conversation, that /398/ England has only one genius, whereas that island abounds in distinguished intellects.

However averse he may be from all superstition, he is a steady adherent of true piety; having regular hours for his prayers, which are not uttered by rote, but from the heart. He talks with his friends about a future life in such a way as to make you feel that he believes what he says, and does not speak without the best hope. Such is More, even at Court; and there are still people who think that Christians are only to be found in monas-teries! Such are the persons, whom a wise King admits into his household, and into his chamber; and not only admits, but invites, nay, compels them to come in. These he has by him as the constant witnesses and judges of his life, — as his advisers and travelling companions. By these he rejoices to be accompanied, rather than by dissolute young men or by fops, or even by decorated grandees, or by crafty ministers, of whom one would lure him to silly amusements, another would incite him to tyranny, and a third would suggest some fresh schemes for plundering his people. If you had lived at this Court, you would, I am sure, give a new description of Court life, and cease to be *Misaulos;* though you too live with such a prince, that you cannot wish for a better, and have some companions like Stromer and Copp, whose sympathies are on the right side. But what is that small number compared with such a swarm of distinguished men as Mountjoy, Linacre, Pace, Colet, Stokesley, Latimer, More, Tunstall, Clerk,[1] and others like them, any one of whose names signifies at once a world of virtues and accomplishments? However, I have no mean hope, that Albert, who is at this time the one ornament of our Germany, will attach to his household a multitude of persons like himself, and set a notable example to other princes; so that they may exert themselves in their own circles to do the like.

You have now before you an ill-drawn portrait, by a poor artist, of an excellent original! You will be still less pleased /399/ with the portrait, if you come to have a closer acquaintance with More himself. But mean-time I have made sure of this, that you will not be able to charge me with neglecting your command, nor continue to find fault with the

1. These men were contemporaries of Erasmus and More and, like them, scholars and human-ists. They were familiar with Greek and Latin and read many of the classical philosophers in the original. They turned their abilities to public service as teachers and advisers. Colet was the Dean of St. Paul's Cathedral for a period (1504-1519), and Pace and Tunstall were in the diplomatic service for Henry VIII. Lord Mountjoy was a student of Erasmus —*Editor's note.*

shortness of my letters; though even this one has not seemed too long to me in writing it, and will not, I am confident, appear prolix to you, as you read it; our More's sweetness will secure that. However, — not to leave unanswered your last letter, which I read in print before I saw it in writing, — I have been informed of the kindness of the most illustrious Prince Albert by his own letter to me. But how, I should like to know, has it come to pass, that that cup has reached every one by means of your letter before it has come to me? You certainly could not have sent it more safely by any one than by Richard Pace, the ambassador of the English king, whether I was in Brabant or in England.*

You, I see, are doing vigorous battle both with the pen and with the sword, — successfully too, as well as bravely! For I hear you are in great favour with the Cardinal of Gaëta. I am glad that we have good news of *Capnio.†* If Literature allows the name of Franz von Sickingen to die, she may fairly be taxed with ingratitude.‡ /400/

For our own news, there will be another occasion. Only this at present; business is conducted at this Court by the meanest sycophancy, — a trade to which I must confess myself unequal. If there is any one of your acquaintance who wants to learn it, I will point him out a wonderful master of this accomplishment, — one, of whom you may say that he was evidently born for it. Cicero was not a more successful orator than he was a sycophant; and he finds many docile pupils among us! The right time is not come, but before long I will introduce the man to you, so that he may obtain the glory which he well deserves, and of which he is sadly ambitious. He will then be celebrated in the letters of all the learned, as a portent rather than a man. Farewell.

Antwerp, 23 July, [1517].*

It will be seen in the note below, that the year-date assigned to this letter in the *Farrago Epistolarum* is 1519, which is the date of the publication of the volume of Epistles itself. And this year-date has been unsuspectingly assumed to be true by the biographers of Erasmus and of More. I have taken the year-date printed above from the statement in the letter (p. 389), which shows that little more than seventeen years had passed since the first acquaintance of Erasmus with More, which began in the summer of 1499. See vol. i. p. 200. And this correction is confirmed by the

---

* It appears that the Archduke Albert had proposed to present to Erasmus a silver cup, which might have been forwarded to him through the agency of Richard Pace. Pace, who went abroad in October, 1515, was at Zurich in 1516 and at Constance in August, September and October, 1517. Brewer, *Abstracts,* vol. ii. p. 382. He appears to have stayed at Bruges on his way back to England in November, 1517. See [*The Epistles of Erasmus,* vol. iii,] p. 162   /400/

† Capnioni bene esse gaudeo. Capnio is Reuchlin, the Greek word καπνὸς, being equivalent to the German *Rauch,* English *smoke.* The last news about his suit at Rome appears to have been favourable; but we read in Hutten's letter of 21 July, 1517, Epistle 585, which probably crosses this, that the suit was still before the Court. See [*The Epistles of Erasmus,*] vol. ii. pp. 595, 599, 600.   /400/

‡ Franz von Sickingen (Franciscus Sichnius), a distinguished Free Lance, was a supporter of the Protestant movement and a friend of Hutten, who was his guest from 1520 to 1522. The death of Sickingen occurred in May, 1523, during the siege of his castle of Landstuhl by the Imperial army.   /400/

* Antuuerpiæ, Decimo Cal. Augusti. An. M.D.XIX. *Farrago.*   /401/

mention (p. 400) of Pace's foreign residence, which terminated for the time in the autumn of 1517. See pp. 146, 162, 418. It may be observed, that in July, 1518, Erasmus was at Basel; but in July, 1516 and 1517, and also in July, 1519, he was in the Netherlands.

On the other hand the reference (p. 396) to More's *repeated* diplomatic employment might seem to favour the later date; but a probable revision of the letter before publication may account for the expression *semel atque iterum.* Owing to the loss of all the records of the proceedings of the English Privy Council of this period, it is not known at what date More was sworn on the Council, but his attraction to the Court took place before his embassy of 1517, and soon after his return from his first mission to Flanders. A letter of /401/ Ammonius, dated 17 Feb. [1516], (Epistle 377, vol. ii. pp. 242, 243), and More's own letter of about the same date, Epistle 396, show that the latter was then much with Wolsey; and Erasmus's letter to Ammonius, 11 March, [1517], Epistle 532, tells the same tale.

It may be worth while to observe, that the evidence of Erasmus about the age of More (p. 389), which places his birth in 1477, suggests the correction of an assumption which has been made since the discovery in 1868 of a contemporary memorandum relating to the family of Sir John More (Notes and Queries, 17 Oct. 1868). In this document it is stated, that Thomas More was born on *Friday* the 7th of February in the 17th year of Edward IV.; and the 7th of February, 17 Edw. IV. (1478) having occurred on a Saturday, it has been assumed that the day of the week was mistaken, and that More was born on *Saturday,* 7 Feb. 1478. But it is obvious, that the mistake may have been, not in the day of the week, but in the year of the reign, and the birth have taken place on *Friday,* 7 Feb. 16 Edw. IV. 1477. And this last supposition, which agrees with the statement of Erasmus as to More's age, is further confirmed by observing the date of birth of the next-born child of the same mother. John More and Agnes Graunger were married, 24 Ap. 1474, and their children were 1. Jane, born 11 March, 1475, 2. Thomas, born 7 Feb. 1477 (not, as assumed, 1478, within a year before the accepted date of birth of the next child), 3. Agatha, born 31 Jan. 1479, 4. John, born 6 June, 1480, 5. Edward, born 3 Sept. 1481, and 6. Elizabeth, born 22 Sept. 1482. (Compare Bridgett's Life of More, p. 144.) /402/

Thomas More

Letter to Erasmus

. . . Each day I stand by, waiting with eager ears, for news about that business of yours in Sicily. Please God, it may have a happy ending. Master [Cuthbert] Tunstal recently wrote me a most friendly letter. Bless my soul, but his frank and complimentary criticism of my commonwealth has given me more cheer than would an Attic talent. You have no idea how thrilled I am; I feel so expanded, and I hold my head high. For in my daydreams I have been marked out by my Utopians to be their king forever; I can see myself now marching along, crowned with a diadem of wheat, very striking in my Franciscan frock, carrying a handful of wheat as my sacred scepter, thronged by a distinguished retinue of Amaurotians, and, with this huge entourage, giving audience to foreign ambassadors and sovereigns; wretched creatures they are, in comparison with us, as they stupidly pride themselves on appearing in childish garb and feminine finery, laced with that despicable gold, and ludicrous in their purple and jewels and other empty baubles. Yet, I would not want either you or our friend, Tunstal, to judge me by other men, whose character shifts with fortune. Even if heaven has decreed to waft me from my lowly estate to this soaring pinnacle which, I think, defies comparison with that of kings, still you will never find me forgetful of that old friendship I had with you when I was but a private citizen. And if you do not mind making the short trip to visit me in Utopia, I shall definitely see to it that all mortals governed by my kindly rule will show you the honor due to those who, they know, are very dear to the heart of their king.

I was going to continue with this fascinating vision, but the rising Dawn has shattered my dream — poor me! — and shaken me off my throne, and summons me back to the drudgery of the courts. But at least this thought gives me consolation: real kingdoms do not last much longer.

Farewell, dearest Erasmus.

Letter of Thomas More to Erasmus (London, c. 4 December, 1516), Number 11, from *Selected Letters of St. Thomas More,* edited by Elizabeth Frances Rogers. New Haven: Yale University Press, 1961 [29, Allen, 2, 499].

Guillaume Budé[2]

To his English friend Thomas Lupset[1]

Greeting.

I owe you many thanks, my learned young friend Lupset, for having sent me Thomas More's *Utopia,* and so drawn my attention to what is very pleasant, and likely to be very profitable, reading.

It is not long ago since you prevailed upon me (your en- /lxxx/ treaties seconding my own strong inclination) to read the six books of Galen *On the preservation of the Health,* to which that master of the Greek and Latin tongues, Dr. Thomas Linacre[1], has lately rendered the service — or rather, paid the compliment[2] — of translating them from the extant

Letter of Guillaume Budé to Thomas Lupset, in *The "Utopia" of Sir Thomas More,* edited and translated by J. H. Lupton. Oxford: Oxford University Press, 1895, pp. lxxx-xcii.

[1] Thomas Lupset (? 1498-1530), a scholar whom Colet had educated under William Lily, was at this time in Paris, where he graduated in arts. He was superintending the publication of works by more than one of his friends. — See more in the Introduction, ∫ 5, and for the scanty details of his life, Cooper's *Athenae Cantabrigienses,* i. p. 40.   /lxxx/

[2] The name of Guillaume Budé is too well known in the world of letters to need much said about him here. He was born in 1467, and was thus a close contemporary of Erasmus and Colet. He died in 1540. Many characteristics of the man are illustrated in this letter: his vehemence, his aversion from the law (to the profession of which he was originally destined), his fondness for displaying his command of Greek, and the like. He was invited to the court of the French king as urgently as was More to that of the English, and showed the same disinclination to the service; complying only when he believed that the cause of learning would be benefited by his presence at court. At one period of his life, to counteract the effect of too sedentary habits, he devoted himself to active work in building and planting on his two country estates, at Marly and Saint-   /lxxx/   Maur. When so occupied, he loved, says his biographer (in *Batesii Vitae,* p. 234), in words that will illustrate an expression in his letter, 'cursu corpus fatigare.'

As, besides these country villas, he purchased a house in the Rue Saint-Martin, then accounted the best part of Paris, which he pulled down and rebuilt from top to bottom, and lived in such style there that Vives, the Spanish scholar, when he paid him a visit, 'fut ébloui du train que menait l'illustre helléniste,' it is obvious that his invectives against private property must be taken with some qualification.

How far, or whether at all, Budé was inclined to the principles of the Reformation, has been much disputed. He appears to be very guarded in respect of anything said about doctrine. But in the *Epistolae Posteriores* he animadverts, as bitterly as Erasmus might have done, upon the obstructiveness of the haters of the new learning. His great treatise *De Asse,* 1514, was judged by the Spanish Inquisition to require expurgation (Tribbechovius, *De Doctoribus Scholasticis,* 1719, p. 89); and we can hardly wonder at this, after reading the fierce attack (fol. xci vers) upon the late pope, Julius II. It is certain that, after his death, his widow and some of his many children migrated to Geneva, and made profession of the reformed faith. And some not unnaturally thought, as Melanchthon tells us, that this pointed to counsel given in that direction by Budé, before his death. — See Bayle, i. p. 751, note L, and the monograph by M. Rebitté, 1846, p. 147.   /lxxxi/

[1] Thomas Linacre (? 1460-1524), the founder of the Royal College of Physicians, had for some time been engaged in translating treatises of Galen into Latin. His version of the six books *De sanitate tuenda* was first printed at Paris by Guillaume Rubé in 1517. — See Johnson's *Life of Linacre,* 1835, p. 208.   /lxxxi/

[2] In the Latin a nice distinction is drawn between the two constructions of *donare: donare aliquid alicui,* and *donare aliquem aliqua re.* As Valla points out, the latter has more the notion of supplying a deficiency, or giving a 'consolation prize,' as in the well-known line of Vergil:
> Nemo ex hoc numero mihi non donatus abibit. [None of this number shall go away without a gift from me.]

The former more expresses a voluntary or complimentary gift. See the *De linguae Latinae elegantia,* 1529, leaf 87 vers.   /lxxxi/

originals into Latin. So well has the task been performed, that if all that author's works (which I consider worth all other medical lore put /lxxxi/ together) be in time translated, the want of a knowledge of Greek is not likely to be seriously felt by our schools of medicine.

I have hastily skimmed over that work, as it stands in Linacre's papers (for the courteous loan of which, for so long a time, I am very greatly indebted to you) with the result that I deem myself much benefited by the perusal. But I promise myself still greater profit when the book itself, on the publication of which at the presses of this city you are now busily engaged, shall have appeared in print.

While I thought myself already under a sufficient obligation to you on this account, here you have presented to me More's *Utopia,* as an appendix or supplement to your former kindness. He is a man of the keenest discernment, of a pleasant disposition, well versed in knowledge of the world. I have had the book by me in the country, where my time was taken up with running about and giving directions to workpeople (for you know something, and have heard more, of my having been occupied for more than a twelvemonth on business connected with my country-house); and was so impressed by reading it, as I learnt and studied the manners and customs of the Utopians, that I well-nigh forgot, nay, even abandoned, the management of my family affairs. For I perceived that all the theory and /lxxxii/ practice of domestic economy, all care whatever for increasing one's income, was mere waste of time.

And yet, as all see and are aware, the whole race of mankind is goaded on by this very thing, as if some gadfly were bred within them to sting them. The result is that we must needs confess the object of nearly all legal and civil qualification and training to be this: that with jealous and watchful cunning, as each one has a neighbour with whom he is connected by ties of citizenship, or even at times of relationship, he should be ever conveying or abstracting something from him; should pare away, repudiate, squeeze, chouse, chisel, cozen, extort, pillage, purloin, thieve, filch, rob[1], and — partly with the connivance, partly with the sanction of the laws — be ever plundering and appropriating.

This goes on all the more in countries where the civil and canon law, as they are called, have greater authority in the two courts. For it is evident that their customs and institutions are pervaded by the principle, that those are to be deemed the high-priests of Law and Equity, who are skilled in *caveats* — or *capiats,* rather; men who hawk at their unwary fellow-citizens; artists in formulas, that is, in gudgeon-traps; adepts in concocted /lxxxiii/ law; getters up of cases; jurisconsults of a controverted, perverted, inverted *jus.* These are the only fit persons to give opinions as to what is fair and good; nay, what is far more, to settle with plenary power what each one is to be allowed to have, and what not to have, and the extent and limit of his tenure. How deluded must public opinion be to have determined matters thus[1]!

---

[1] If it is impossible to impart elegance to such a string of expletives, I must plead that they are only a close reproduction of the Latin.   /xxxiii/

[1] With these denunciations of the law as then administered may be compared the not less severe strictures of Dean Colet in his *Exposition of Romans* (edited with the *Letters to Radulphus,* 1876), p. 162; and in his *Lectures on Corinthians,* pp. xviii, 45. Both he and Budé had probably in their minds the language of Cicero, *De Oratore,* i. 55.   /lxxxiv/

The truth is that most of us, blind with the thick rheum of ignorance in our eyes, suppose that each one's cause, as a rule, is *just*, in proportion to its accordance with the requirements of the *law*, or to the way in which he has based his claim on the *law*. Whereas, were we agreed to demand our rights in accordance with the rule of truth, and what the simple Gospel prescribes, the dullest would understand, and the most senseless admit, if we put it to them, that, in the decrees of the canonists, the divine law differs as much from the human; and, in our civil laws and royal enactments, true equity differs as much from law; as the principles laid down by Christ, the founder of human society, and the usages of His disciples, /lxxxiv/ differ from the decrees and enactments of those who think the *summum bonum* and perfection of happiness to lie in the moneybags of a Croesus or a Midas. So that, if you chose to define Justice now-a-days, in the way that early writers liked to do, as the power who assigns to each his due[1], you would either find her non-existent in public, or, if I may use such a comparison, you would have to admit that she was a kind of kitchen stewardess: and this, alike whether you regard the character of our present rulers, or the disposition of fellow-citizens and fellow-countrymen one towards another.

Perhaps indeed it may be argued, that the law I speak of has been derived from that inherent, world-old justice called *natural* law[2]; which teaches that the stronger a man is, the more he should possess; and, the more he possesses, the more eminent among his countrymen he ought to be: with the result that now we see it an accepted principle in the Law of Nations, that persons who are unable to help their fellows by any art or practice worth mentioning, if only they are adepts in those complicated knots and stringent bonds, by which men's pro- /lxxxv/ perties are tied up (things accounted a mixture of Gordian knots and charlatanry, with nothing very wonderful about them, by the ignorant multitude, and by scholars living, for the sake of recreation or of investigating the truth, at a distance from the Courts), — that these persons, I say, should have an income equal to that of a thousand of their countrymen, nay, even of a whole state, and sometimes more than that; and that they should then be greeted with the honourable titles of wealthy men, thrifty men, makers of splendid fortunes. Such in truth is the age in which we live; such our manners and customs; such our national character. These have pronounced it lawful for a man's credit and influence to be high, in proportion to the way in which he has been the architect of his own fortunes and of those of his heirs: an influence, in fact, which goes on increasing, according as their descendants in turn, to the remotest generation, vie in heaping up with fine additions the property gained by their ancestors; which amounts to saying, according as they have ousted more and more extensively their connections, kindred, and even their blood relations.

But the founder and regulator of all property, Jesus Christ, left among His followers a Pythagorean communion and love; and ratified it by a

---

[1] 'Quae animi affectio, suum cuique tribuens, . . . iusticia dicitur,' [This disposition of the soul, assigning to each man his own, . . . is called justice,] Cicero *de Fin.* v. 23. /lxxxv/

[2] 'The good old rule' of Wordsworth:
    'the simple plan,
That they should take, who have the power,
  And they should keep, who can.' /lxxxv/

plain example, when Ananias was condemned to death for breaking this law of communion. By laying down /lxxxvi/ this principle, Christ seems to me to have abolished, at any rate among his followers, all the voluminous quibbles of the civil law, and still more of the later canon law; which latter we see at the present day holding the highest position in juris-prudence, and controlling our destiny.

As for the island of Utopia, which I hear is also called *Udepotia*[1], it is said (if we are to believe the story), by what must be owned a singular good fortune, to have adopted Christian usages both in public and in private; to have imbibed the wisdom thereto belonging; and to have kept it un-defiled to this very day. The reason is, that it holds with firm grip to three divine institutions: — namely, the absolute equality, or, if you prefer to call it so, the civil communication[2], of all things good and bad among fellow-citizens; a settled and unwavering love of peace and quietness; and a contempt for gold and silver. Three things these, which overturn, one may say, all fraud, all imposture, cheating, roguery, and unprincipled deception. Would that Providence, on its own behalf[3], would cause these /lxxxvii/ three principles of Utopian law to be fixed in the minds of all men by the rivets of a strong and settled conviction. We should soon see pride, covetousness, insane competition, and almost all other deadly weapons of our adversary the Devil, fall powerless; we should see the interminable array of law-books, [the work of][1] so many excellent and solid understandings, that occupy men till the very day of their death, consigned to bookworms, as mere hollow and empty things, or else given up to make wrapping-paper for shops.

Good heavens! what holiness of the Utopians has had the power of earning such a blessing from above, that greed and covetousness have for so many ages failed to enter, either by force or stealth, into that island alone? that they have failed to drive out from it, by wanton effrontery, justice and honour?

Would that great Heaven in its goodness had dealt so kindly with the countries which keep, and would not part with, the appellation they bear, derived from His most holy name! Of a truth, greed, which perverts and sinks down so many minds, otherwise noble and elevated, would be gone from hence once for /lxxxviii/ all, and the golden age of Saturn would return. In Utopia one might verily suppose that there is a risk of Aratus and the early poets having been mistaken in their opinion, when they made Justice depart from earth, and placed her in the Zodiac[1]. For, if

---

[1] As much as to say *Nunquamia*, as well as *Nusquamia; Kennaquhan*, as well as *Kennaquhair*. — On the meanings which the name *Utopia* can be made to bear, see the Introduction [in Lupton's *Utopia*], p. xl.   /lxxxvii/

[2] I do not feel sure what Budé exactly meant by *ciuilitas*, but have taken it to signify the title to share, as citizens, in the common property.   /lxxxvii/

[3] Lat. *suo nomine:* unless the reading should be *suo numine*.   /lxxxvii/

[1] If *detinentia* in the Latin be correct, this is the only way in which I can understand the passage. But it seems more likely that *detinentium* was originally written: — 'law books, that keep so many excellent and solid understandings occupied on them, till the very day of death.' /lxxxviii/

[1]   'Sic justa in populos mox Virginis inculpatae
        Exarsere odia, et caelum pernicibus intrat
        Diua alis.'

[The righteous hatred of a blameless maiden flared forth among the peoples and on swift

we are to believe Hythloday, she must needs have stayed behind in that island, and not yet made her way to heaven.

But in truth I have ascertained by full inquiry, that Utopia lies outside the bounds of the known world. It is in fact one of the Fortunate Isles, perhaps very close to the Elysian Fields; for More himself testifies that Hythloday has not yet stated its position definitely. It is itself divided into a number of cities, but all uniting or confederating into one state, named Hagnopolis[2]; a state contented with its own customs, its own goods, blest with innocence, leading a kind of heavenly life, on a lower level indeed than heaven, but above the defilements of this world we know[3], which amid the endless pursuits of mankind, as empty and vain as they are /lxxxix/ keen and eager, is being hurried in a swollen and eddying tide to the cataract.

It is to Thomas More, then, that we owe our knowledge of this island. It is he who, in our generation, has made public this model of a happy life and rule for leading it, the discovery, as he tells us, of Hythloday: for he ascribes all to him. For while Hythloday has built the Utopians their state, and established for them their rites and customs; while, in so doing, he has borrowed from them and brought home for us the representation of a happy life; it is beyond question More, who has set off by his literary style the subject of that island and its customs. He it is who has perfected, as by rule and square, the City of the Hagnopolitans itself, adding all those touches by which grace and beauty and weight accrue to the noble work; even though in executing that work he has claimed for himself only a common mason's share. We see that it has been a matter of conscientious scruple with him, not to assume too important a part in the work, lest Hythloday should have just cause for complaint, on the ground of More having plucked the first flowers of that fame, which would have been left for him, if he had himself ever decided to give an account of his adventures to the world. He was afraid, of course, that Hythloday, who was residing of his own choice in the island of /xc/ Udepotia, might some day come in person upon the scene, and be vexed and aggrieved at this unkindness on his part, in leaving him the glory of this discovery with the best flowers plucked off. To be of this persuasion is the part of good men and wise.

Now while More is one who of himself carries weight, and has great authority to rest upon, I am led to place unreserved confidence in him by the testimony of Peter Giles of Antwerp. Though I have never made his acquaintance in person — apart from recommendations of his learning and character that have reached me — I love him on account of his being the intimate friend of the illustrious Erasmus, who has deserved so well of letters of every kind, whether sacred or profane; with whom personally I have long corresponded and formed ties of friendship.

---

wings she has long since entered heaven.]

Festi Avieni *Aratea Phaenomena.*

The illusions to Astraea are common in the poets.   /lxxxix/

[2] As Budé had suggested that the island was also called *Udepotia,* he here takes the further liberty of calling the imaginary state *Hagnopolis,* 'Holy City,' or 'City of the Saints.' Compare the last words of the passage quoted above, p. xxxvi, n. 3, and what was said before about More's lectures on the *Civitas Dei,* p. xlix.   /lxxxix/

[3] See Colet's *Lectures on I Cor.,* p. 30.   /lxxxix/

Farewell, my dear Lupset. Greet for me, at the first opportunity, either by word of mouth or by letter, Linacre, that pillar of the British name in all that concerns good learning; one who is now, as I hope, not more yours than ours. He is one /xci/ of the few whose good opinion I should be very glad, if possible, to gain. When he was himself known to be staying here, he gained in the highest degree the good opinion of me and of Jehan Ruelle, my friend and the sharer in my studies[1]. And his singular learning and careful industry I should be the first to look up to and strive to copy.

Greet More also once and again for me, either by message, as I said before, or by word of mouth. As I think and often repeat, Minerva has long entered his name on her selectest album; and I love and revere him in the highest degree for what he has written about this isle of the New World, Utopia.

In his history our age and those which succeed it will have a nursery, so to speak, of polite and useful institutions; from which men may borrow customs, and introduce and adapt them each to his own state. Farewell.

From Paris, the 31st of July[2]. /xcii/

---

[1] Joannes Ruellius is mentioned in a letter of Erasmus, dated Antwerp, 1517, as a physician who, like Linacre, had had the good fortune to learn Greek in early life. *Epist.* ed. 1642, col. 629. He published in 1536 a treatise *De natura stirpium,* printed at Paris by Colinaeus, in folio; 'a magnificent book,' as it is called by Greswell: *View of the Parisian Greek Press,* i. 91 n.   /xcii/

[2] No year is given; but it must have been 1517.   /xcii/

Jerome Busleyden

To Thomas More

Greeting.[1]

It was not enough, my accomplished friend More, that you formerly spent all your care, labour and study upon the interests and advantage of individuals; but you must bestow them (such is your kindness and generosity) on the community at large. You thought that this benefit of yours, whatever it might be, deserved the greater indulgence, courted the greater favour, and aimed at the higher renown, on this very account, that it was likely to profit the more, the more widely it was diffused and the more there were to share it. To confer this benefit has always been your object on other occasions, and of late you have, /cccxiii/ with singular good fortune, been most successful in attaining it: I mean, in that 'afternoon's talk,' which you have reduced to writing and published, about the right and good constitution, that all must long for, of the Utopian commonwealth.

In your happy description of that fair institution, we nowhere miss either the highest learning or consummate knowledge of the world. Both those qualities are blended together in the work, meeting on such equal terms that neither yields to the other, but both contend on an equality for the palm. The truth is, you are the able possessor of such varied learning, and on the other hand of so wide and exact a knowledge of the world, that, whatever you write, you assert from full experience, and, whatever assertion you have decided to make, you write most learnedly. A felicity this as rare as it is admirable! What makes it rarer is that it withholds itself from the many, and only imparts itself to the few;—to such above all as have the candour to wish, the knowledge to understand, the credit which will qualify, and the influence which will enable them to consult the common interest as dutifully, justly, and providently as you now plainly do. For, deeming yourself born not for yourself alone, but for the whole /cccxiv/ world, you have thought fit by this fair service to make the whole world itself beholden to you.

And this result you would not have been able to effect so well and rightly by any other means, as by delineating for rational beings themselves an ideal commonwealth, a pattern and finished model of conduct, than which there has never been seen in the world one more wholesome in its institution, or more perfect, or to be thought more desirable. For it

Letter of Jerome Busleyden to Thomas More, in *The "Utopia" of Sir Thomas More,* edited and translated by J. H. Lupton. Oxford: Oxford University Press, 1895, pp. cccxiii-cccxix.

[1] This letter, which was not translated by Robynson, came before the *Utopia,* in the edition of 1516, but in that of 1518 was placed after it, as here.·. . .   /cccxiii/   [Jerome Busleyden, a Luxembourger, was an eminent humanist and a counsellor of Charles, the young King of the Netherlands. He was a canon of Brussels and also of Mechlin, where he maintained a splendid house, more than once alluded to by More. Like Colet at Oxford, and with the same opposition, he established a foundation at Louvain for teaching the three learned languages—Hebrew, Greek, and Latin. His will, containing the bequest for this purpose, was dated June 22, 1517. He died on the 26th of August in the same year—*Editor's note.*]

far surpasses and leaves a long way behind the many famous states, that we have heard so much about, of Sparta and Athens and Rome. Had these been inaugurated under the same favourable conditions, with the same institutions, laws, enactments and rules of life to control them as this commonwealth of yours, they would not, we may be sure, have by this time been lying in ruins, levelled with the ground, and now alas! obliterated beyond all hope of renewal. On the contrary, they would have been still unfallen, still fortunate and prosperous, leading a happy existence, mistresses of the world meanwhile, and dividing a widespread empire by land and sea.

Of these commonwealths you compassionated the un- /cccxv/ happy lot. And so you wished to save other states in like manner, which now hold the supreme power, from undergoing a like vicissitude, by your picture of a perfect state; one which directed its chief energies not so much to framing laws as to appointing the most approved magistrates. (And with good reason: for otherwise, without them, even the best laws, if we take Plato's[1] word for it, would all be counted dead.) Magistrates these, above all, after whose likeness, pattern of uprightness, ensample of conduct, and mirror of justice, the whole state and right course of any perfect commonwealth whatever ought to be modelled; wherein should unite, above all things, prudence in the rulers, courage in the soldiers, temperance in the private individuals, and justice in all[2].

And since the commonwealth you make so famous is manifestly formed, in fairest manner, of these principles, it is no wonder if on this account it comes not only as an object of fear to many, but also of reverence to all nations, and one for all generations to tell of; the more so, /cccxvi/ that in it all competition for ownership is taken away, and no one has any private property at all. For the rest, all men have all things in common, with a view to the commonwealth itself; so that every matter, every action, however unimportant, whether public or private, instead of being directed to the greed of many or the caprice of a few, has sole reference to the upholding of one uniform justice, equality and communion. When that is made the entire object of every action, there must needs be a clearance of all that serves as matter and fuel and feeder of intrigue, of luxury, envy, and wrong; to which mankind are hurried on, even at times against their will, either by the possession of private property, or by the burning thirst of gain, and that most pitiable of all things, ambition, to their own great and immeasurable loss. For it is from these things that there often suddenly arise divisions of feeling, taking up of arms, and wars worse than civil; whereby not only is the flourishing state of wealthy republics utterly overthrown, but the renown they won in other days, the triumphs celebrated, the splendid trophies, the rich spoils so often won from conquered enemies, are all utterly effaced.

---

[1] See the *De Legibus*, Lib. vi. (§751, B, C).   /cccxvi/

[2] This is a brief summary of the Fourth Book of the *Republic*, the object of which is to show that the *wisdom* of the ideal State will reside in the Guardians or Magistrates, the *courage* in the Soldiers or Auxiliaries, and the political *temperance* in the general body of citizens. *Justice*, like a common bond, keeps all classes in their place. See the Introduction [in Lupton's *Utopia*], p. lii.   /cccxvi/

If on these matters the words I write should chance to be less convincing than I desire, these will at any rate /cccxvii/ be ready at hand the most sufficient witnesses for me to refer you to: I mean, the many great cities formerly laid waste, the states destroyed[1], the republics overthrown, the villages burnt and consumed. As scarce any relics or traces of their great calamity are to be seen at this day, so neither are their names preserved by any history, however ancient it be, and however far back its records extend.

These memorable disasters, devastations, overthrows, and other calamities of war our states, whatever they be, will easily succeed in escaping, if they only adapt themselves exactly to the one pattern of the Utopian commonwealth, and do not deviate a hair's-breadth from it. By so acting alone, they will at length most fully recognize by the result how greatly they have profited by this service you have rendered them; especially since by its acquisition they have learnt to preserve their own state in safety, unharmed, and victorious. It follows that their debt to you, their present deliverer, will be no less than is the just due of those, who have saved — I do not say some one member of a state, but the whole state itself. /cccxviii/

Meanwhile farewell. Go on and prosper, ever devising, carrying out and perfecting something, the bestowal of which on your country may give it long continuance and yourself immortality. Farewell, learned and courteous More, glory of your island, and ornament of this world of ours.

From my house at Mechlin[1], 1516. /cccxix/

---

[1] This is a reiteration of what More had said about the Carthaginians and others [Lupton's *Utopia*], p. 49.   /cccxviii/

[1] The splendour of Busleyden's house at Mechlin seems to have impressed More. See his epigrams upon it, and on the collections of coins, and the like, to be found there (*Epigrammata*, ed. 1638, pp. 131, 133). In his letter to Erasmus, written shortly after his return from Flanders, he dwells on the same subject.   /cccxix/

Cornelius Graphey

Cornelius Graphey[1] to the reader.

Wilt thou knowe what wonders straunge be in the
    lande[2] that late was founde?
Wilte thou learne thy life to leade, by diuers wayes
    that godly be?
Wilt thou of vertue and of vice vnderstande the very
    grounde?
Wilt thou see this wretched world, how ful it is of
    vanitie?
Then read, and marke, and beare in mind, for thy be-
    houfe, as thou maie best
All thinges that in this present worke, that worthie
    clerke sir Thomas More,
With witte diuine ful learnedly, vnto the worlde hath
    plaine exprest,
In whom London well glory maye, for wisedome and
    for godly lore.

Cornelivs Graphevs ad lectorem.

Vis noua monstra, nouo dudum nunc orbe reperto?
    Viuendi uaria uis ratione modos?
Vis qui uirtutum fontes, uis unde malorum
    Principia? et quantum rebus inane latet?
Haec lege, quae uario Morus dedit ille colore,
    Morus Londinae nobilitatis honos.

BASILEAE APVD IOANNEM FROBE
NIVM MENSE MARTIO[3].
AN. M. D. XVIII.

/cccxxii/

Laudatory Poem, in *The "Utopia" of Sir Thomas More,* edited and translated by J. H. Lupton.
Oxford: Oxford University Press, 1895, p. 322.

  [1] A full account of Cornelius Grapheus (Schreiber) of Alst is given in the Appendix to vol. I.
of Ullmann's *Reformers before the Reformation,* tr. by Menzies, 1855, pp. 397-416. Grapheus died
Dec. 19, 1558, having survived his friend Erasmus twenty-two years. In 1521 he came under the
grasp of a severe penal law enacted against heresy in the Netherlands by Charles V, and after
being imprisoned in Brussels for a considerable time, he recanted and was released, March 25,
1522. Erasmus always retained a kindly feeling for him, and left him a legacy in his will.
/cccxxii/

  [2] The immediate reference is to Utopia; but probably in the Latin, *nouo orbe,* there is a suggestion of the wider range of discoveries in the New World.   /cccxxii/

  [3] For the date, see the Introduction [in Lupton's *Utopia*], p. lxx.   /cccxxii/

Twentieth-
Century
Opinion

Robert Bolt

The bit of English history which is the background to this play is pretty well known. Henry VIII, who started with everything and squandered it all, who had the physical and mental fortitude to endure a lifetime of gratified greeds, the monstrous baby whom none dared gainsay, is one of the most popular figures in the whole procession. We recognize in him an archetype, one of the champions of our baser nature, and are in him vicariously indulged.

Against him stood the whole edifice of medieval religion, founded on piety, but by then as moneyed, elaborate, heaped high and inflexible as those abbey churches which Henry brought down with such a satisfying and disgraceful crash.

The collision came about like this: While yet a Prince, Henry did not expect to become a King, for he had an elder brother, Arthur. A marriage was made between this Arthur and a Spanish Princess, Catherine, but Arthur presently died. The Royal Houses of Spain and England wished to repair the connection, and the obvious way to do it was to marry the young widow to Henry, now heir to Arthur's place. But Spain and England were Christian monarchies and Christian law forbade a man to marry his brother's widow.

To be a Christian was to be a Churchman and there was only one Church (though plagued with many heresies) and the Pope was its head. At the request of Christian Spain and Christian England the Pope dispensed with the Christian law forbidding a man to marry his brother's widow, and when in due course Prince Henry ascended the English throne as Henry VIII, Catherine was his Queen.

For some years the marriage was successful; they respected /vii/ and liked one another, and Henry took his pleasures elsewhere but lightly. However, at length he wished to divorce her.

The motives for such a wish are presumably as confused, inaccessible and helpless in a King as any other man, but here are three which make sense: Catherine had grown increasingly plain and intensely religious; Henry had fallen in love with Anne Boleyn; the Spanish alliance had become unpopular. None of these absolutely necessitated a divorce but there was a fourth that did. Catherine had not been able to provide Henry with a male child and was now presumed barren. There was a daughter, but competent statesmen were unanimous that a Queen on the throne of England was unthinkable. Anne and Henry were confident that between them they could produce a son; but if that son was to be Henry's heir, Anne would have to be Henry's wife.

The Pope was once again approached, this time by England only, and asked to declare the marriage with Catherine null, on the grounds that it contravened the Christian law which forbade marriage with a brother's widow. But England's insistence that the marriage had been null was now balanced by Spain's insistence that it hadn't. And at that moment Spain was

From the Preface, *A Man for All Seasons*. New York: Random House, Inc., 1962, pp. vii-xx.

well placed to influence the Pope's deliberations; Rome, where the Pope lived, had been very thoroughly sacked and occupied by Spanish troops. In addition one imagines a natural disinclination on the part of the Pope to have his powers turned on and off like a tap. At all events, after much ceremonious prevarication, while Henry waited with a rising temper, it became clear that so far as the Pope was concerned, the marriage with Catherine would stand.

To the ferment of a lover and the anxieties of a sovereign Henry now added a bad conscience; and a serious matter it was, for him and those about him./viii/

The Bible, he found, was perfectly clear on such marriages as he had made with Catherine; they were forbidden. And the threatened penalty was exactly what had befallen him, the failure of male heirs. He was in a state of sin. He had been thrust into a state of sin by his father with the active help of the Pope. And the Pope now proposed to keep him in a state of sin. The man who would do that, it began to seem to Henry, had small claim to being the Vicar of God.

And indeed, on looking into the thing really closely, Henry found — what various voices had urged for centuries off and on — that the supposed Pope was no more than an ordinary bishop, the Bishop of Rome. This made everything clear and everything possible. If the Pope was not a Pope at all but merely a bishop among bishops, then his special powers as Pope did not exist. In particular, of course, he had no power to dispense with God's rulings as revealed in Leviticus 18, but equally important, he had no power to appoint other bishops; and here an ancient quarrel stirred.

For if the Pope had not the power to appoint bishops, then who did have, if not the King himself — King by the Grace of God? Henry's ancestors, all those other Henries, had been absolutely right; the Bishops of Rome, without a shadow of legality, had succeeded over the centuries in setting up a rival reign within the reign, a sort of long-drawn usurpation. The very idea of it used to throw him into terrible rages. It should go on no longer.

He looked about for a good bishop to appoint to Canterbury, a bishop with no ambitions to modify God's ruling on deceased brothers' wives, yet sufficiently spirited to grant a divorce to his sovereign without consulting the Bishop of Rome. The man was to hand in Thomas Cranmer; Catherine was divorced, /ix/ Anne married, and the Established Church of England was off on its singular way.

That, very roughly indeed, is the political, or theological, or politico-theological background to the play. But what of the social, or economic, or socio-economic, which we now think more important?

The economy was very progressive, the religion was very reactionary. We say therefore that the collision was inevitable, setting Henry aside as a colorful accident. With Henry presumably we set aside as accidents Catherine and Wolsey and Anne and More and Cranmer and Cromwell and the Lord Mayor of London and the man who cleaned his windows; setting indeed everyone aside as an accident, we say that the collision was inevitable. But that, on reflection, seems only to repeat that it happened.

What is of interest is the way it happened, the way it was lived. For lived such collisions are. "Religion" and "economy" are abstractions which describe the way men live. Because men work we may speak of an economy, not the other way round. Because men worship we may speak of a religion, not the other way round. And when an economy collides with a religion it is living men who collide, nothing else (they collide with one another and within themselves).

Perhaps few people would disagree with that, put like that, and in theory. But in practice our theoreticians seem more and more to work the other way round, to derive the worker *from* his economy, the thinker *from* his culture, and we to derive even ourselves from our society and our location in it. When we ask ourselves "What am I?" we may answer "I am a Man" but are conscious that it's a silly answer because we don't know what kind of thing that might be; and feeling the answer silly we feel it's probably a silly question. We can't help asking it, however, for natural curiosity makes us ask it all the time of /x/ everyone else, and it would seem artificial to make ourselves the sole exception, would indeed envelop the mental image of our self in a unique silence and thus raise the question in a particularly disturbing way. So we answer of ourselves as we should of any other: "This man here is a qualified surveyor, employed but with a view to partnership; this car he is driving has six cylinders and is almost new; he's doing all right; his opinions . . ." and so on, describing ourselves to ourselves in terms more appropriate to somebody seen through a window. We think of ourselves in the Third Person.

To put it another way, more briefly; we no longer have, as past societies have had, any picture of individual Man (Stoic Philosopher, Christian Religious, Rational Gentleman) by which to recognize ourselves and against which to measure ourselves; we are anything. But if anything, then nothing, and it is not everyone who can live with that, though it is our true present position. Hence our willingness to locate ourselves from something that is certainly larger than ourselves, the society that contains us.

But society can only have as much idea as we have what we are about, for it has only our brains to think with. And the individual who tries to plot his position by reference to our society finds no fixed points, but only the vaunted absence of them, "freedom" and "opportunity"; freedom for what, opportunity to do what, is nowhere indicated. The only positive he is given is "get and spend" ("get and spend—if you can" from the Right, "get and spend—you deserve it" from the Left) and he did not need society to tell him that. In other words we are thrown back by our society upon ourselves at our lowest, that is at our least satisfactory to ourselves. Which of course sends us flying back to society with all the force of rebound.

Socially, we fly from the idea of an individual to the profes- /xi/ sional describers, the classifiers, the men with the categories and a quick ear for the latest subdivision, who flourish among us like priests. Individually, we do what we can to describe and classify ourselves and so assure ourselves that from the outside at least we do have a definite outline. Both socially and individually it is with us as it is with our cities—an accelerating flight to the periphery, leaving a center which is empty when the hours of business are over.

That is an ambitious style of thinking, and pride cometh before a fall, but it was with some such ideas in mind that I started on this play. Or else they developed as I wrote it. Or else I have developed them in defense of it now that it is written. It is not easy to know what a play is "about" until it is finished, and by then what it is "about" is incorporated in it irreversibly and is no more to be separated from it than the shape of a statue is to be separated from the marble. Writing a play is thinking, not thinking about thinking; more like a dream than a scheme—except that it lasts six months or more, and that one is responsible for it.

At any rate, Thomas More, as I wrote about him, became for me a man with an adamantine sense of his own self. He knew where he began and left off, what area of himself he could yield to the encroachments of his enemies, and what to the encroachments of those he loved. It was a substantial area in both cases, for he had a proper sense of fear and was a busy lover. Since he was a clever man and a great lawyer he was able to retire from those areas in wonderfully good order, but at length he was asked to retreat from that final area where he located his self. And there this supple, humorous, unassuming and sophisticated person set like metal, was overtaken by an absolutely primitive rigor, and could no more be budged than a cliff. /xii/

This account of him developed as I wrote: what first attracted me was a person who could not be accused of any incapacity for life, who indeed seized life in great variety and almost greedy quantities, who nevertheless found something in himself without which life was valueless and when that was denied him was able to grasp his death. For there can be no doubt, given the circumstances, that he did it himself. If, on any day up to that of his execution, he had been willing to give public approval to Henry's marriage with Anne Boleyn, he could have gone on living. Of course the marriage was associated with other things—the attack on the abbeys, the whole Reformation policy—to which More was violently opposed, but I think he could have found his way round those; he showed every sign of doing so. Unfortunately his approval of the marriage was asked for in a form that required him to state that he believed what he didn't believe, and required him to state it on oath.

This brings me to something for which I feel the need to explain, perhaps apologize. More was a very orthodox Catholic and for him an oath was something perfectly specific; it was an invitation to God, an invitation God would not refuse, to act as a witness, and to judge; the consequence of perjury was damnation, for More another perfectly specific concept. So for More the issue was simple (though remembering the outcome it can hardly have been easy). But I am not a Catholic nor even in the meaningful sense of the word a Christian. So by what right do I appropriate a Christian saint to my purposes? Or to put it the other way, why do I take as my hero a man who brings about his own death because he can't put his hand on an old black book and tell an ordinary lie?

For this reason: A man takes an oath only when he wants to commit himself quite exceptionally to the statement, when /xiii/ he wants to make an identity between the truth of it and his own virtue; he offers himself as a guarantee. And it works. There is a special kind of shrug for a perjurer; we feel that the man has no self to commit, no guarantee to offer. Of course it's much less effective now that for most of us the actual words of the oath are not much more than impressive mumbo-jumbo than it was when they made obvious sense; we would prefer most men to guarantee their statements with, say, cash rather than with themselves. We feel — we know — the self to be an equivocal commodity. There are fewer and fewer things which, as they say, we "cannot bring ourselves" to do. We can find almost no limits for ourselves other than the physical, which, being physical, are not optional. Perhaps this is why we have fallen back so widely on physical torture as a means of bringing pressure to bear on one another. But though few of us have anything in ourselves like an immortal soul which we regard as absolutely inviolable, yet most of us still feel something which we should prefer, on the whole, not to violate. Most men feel when they swear an oath (the marriage vow for example) that they have invested something. And from this it's possible to guess what an oath must be to a man for whom it is not merely a time-honored and understood ritual but also a definite contract. It may be that a clear sense of the self can *only* crystallize round something transcendental in which case, our prospects look poor, for we are rightly committed to the rational. I think the paramount gift our thinkers, artists, and for all I know, our men of science, should labor to get for us is a sense of selfhood without resort to magic. Albert Camus is a writer I admire in this connection.

Anyway, the above must serve as my explanation and apology for treating Thomas More, a Christian saint, as a hero of selfhood./xiv/

Another thing that attracted me to this amazing man was his splendid social adjustment. So far from being one of society's sore teeth he was, like the hero of Camus' *La Chute*, almost indecently successful. He was respectably, not nobly, born, in the merchant class, the progressive class of the epoch, distinguished himself first as a scholar, then as a lawyer, was made an Ambassador, finally Lord Chancellor. A visitors' book at his house in Chelsea would have looked like a sixteenth-century *Who's Who:* Holbein, Erasmus, Colet, everybody. He corresponded with the greatest minds in Europe as the representative and acknowledged champion of the New Learning in England. He was a friend of the King, who would send for More when his social appetites took a turn in that direction and once walked round the Chelsea garden with his arm round More's neck. ("If my head would win him a castle in France, it should not fail to fall," said More.) He adored and was adored by his own large family. He parted with more than most men when he parted with his life, for he accepted and enjoyed his social context.

One sees that there is no necessary contradiction here; it is society after all which proffers an oath and with it the opportunity for perjury. But why did a man so utterly absorbed in his society, at one particular point disastrously part company from it? How indeed was it possible — unless there was some sudden aberration? But that explanation won't do, because he continued to the end to make familiar and confident use of society's weapons, tact, favor, and, above all, the letter of the law.

For More again the answer to this question would be perfectly simple (though again not easy); the English Kingdom, his immediate society, was subservient to the larger society of the Church of Christ, founded by Christ, extending over Past /xv/ and Future, ruled from Heaven. There are still some for whom that is perfectly simple, but for most it can only be a metaphor. I took it as a metaphor for that larger context which we all inhabit, the terrifying cosmos. Terrifying because no laws, no sanctions, no *mores* obtain there; it is either empty or occupied by God and Devil nakedly at war. The sensible man will seek to live his life without dealings with this larger environment, treating it as a fine spectacle on a clear night, or a subject for innocent curiosity. At the most he will allow himself an agreeable *frisson* when he contemplates his own relation to the cosmos, but he will not try to live in it; he will gratefully accept the shelter of his society. This was certainly More's intention.

If "society" is the name we give to human behavior when it is patterned and orderly, then the Law (extending from empirical traffic regulations, through the mutating laws of property, and on to the great taboos like incest and patricide) is the very pattern of society. More's trust in the law was his trust in his society; his desperate sheltering beneath the forms of the law was his determination to remain within the shelter of society. Cromwell's contemptuous shattering of the forms of law by an unconcealed act of perjury showed how fragile for any individual is that shelter. Legal or illegal had no further meaning, the social references had been removed. More was offered, to be sure, the chance of slipping back into the society which had thrust him out into the warring cosmos, but even in that solitude he found himself able to repeat, or continue, the decision he had made while he still enjoyed the common shelter. /xvi/

Karl Kautsky

As a Humanist and a politician, More was in the front rank of his contemporaries, as a Socialist he was far ahead of them all. His political, religious, and Humanist writings are to-day only read by a small number of historians. Had he not written *Utopia* his name would scarcely be better known to-day than that of the friend who shared his fate, Bishop Fisher of Rochester. His socialism made him immortal.

Whence originated this socialism?

Unlike the historians of the idealistic school, we do not believe in a Holy Spirit which illumines minds and fills them with ideas, to which the political and economic development adapts itself. We rather start from the assumption that the contradictions and antagonisms which the economic development creates in society stimulate thought and provoke investigations by men who are favourably situated to prosecute such researches, so that they may understand what is going on before their eyes and remove the suffering which contemporary conditions entail. In this way arise political and social ideas which influence contemporary thought, or at least, particular /159/ classes, in the degree that they respond to the actual conditions, and which are correct so far as they coincide with the interests of the aspiring classes.

So it comes about that certain ideas are only operative under certain conditions, that ideas which at one time encounter indifference and even scorn are taken up with enthusiasm, and often without strict verification, a few decades later. Idealist historians are unable to explain why this is so; they are therefore obliged in the last resort to seek refuge in God, in a mystery, like all idealist philosophers; it is the "time spirit" which decides whether or not an idea shall achieve social validity.

The materialist conception of history alone explains the influence of particular ideas. It is not concerned to deny that every age has its particular ideas which condition it, and that these ideas form the dynamics of social development. It does not, however, stop at this point, but proceeds to investigate the forces which set the machinery in motion, and these it finds in the material conditions.

It is clear that ideas must be fermenting for some time before they can exercise any influence on the masses. There is a tendency to reproach the masses with running after novelties, whereas the truth is that they cling most obstinately to the old. The antagonism of the new economic conditions to the transmitted conditions and the ideas which accord therewith must be fairly pronounced before it penetrates to the mind of the masses. Where the acumen of the investigator perceives unbridgable antagonisms of classes, the average man sees only accidental personal disputes; where the investigator sees social evils which could only be removed by social transformations, the average man consoles himself with the hope that times are only temporarily bad and will soon improve. We are not speaking

"The Roots of More's Socialism," *Thomas More and His Utopia*, translated by H. J. Stenning. London: A. & C. Black, Ltd., 1927, pp. 159-171.

/160/ of the members of classes on the decline, most of whom will not face facts, but have in mind the nascent classes, whose interests it is to see, but who cannot see until they bump right up against the new conditions. Their ideas also were conditioned by the newly developing material conditions, but these conditions were not yet sharply defined enough to render the aspiring classes accessible to these ideas.

But a thinker who takes his stand on the material conditions may be a whole epoch in advance of his time, if he perceives a newly evolving mode of production and its social consequences not only sooner than most of his contemporaries, but straining far into the future, also glimpses the more rational mode of production into which it will develop.

Thomas More is one of the few who have been capable of this bold intellectual leap; at a time when the capitalist mode of production was in its infancy, he mastered its essential features so thoroughly that the alternative mode of production which he elaborated and contrasted with it as a remedy for its evils, contained several of the most important ingredients of Modern Socialism. The drift of his speculations, of course, escaped his contemporaries, and can only be properly appreciated by us to-day. Despite the immense economic and technical transformations of the last three hundred years, we find in *Utopia* a number of tendencies which are still operative in the Socialist Movement of our time.

Our first enquiry pertains to the causes of such an extraordinary phenomenon. If we are not to resort to spiritism and clairvoyance, there must have been a peculiar chain of circumstances which inclined More alone in his age towards socialist theories — Münzer's socialism was of a character quite different from More's, and cannot therefore be taken into account. /161/

Despite the fact that, for obvious reasons, none of More's biographers has dealt with this question and that More himself gives us but few hints, we think we are able to indicate at least some of these causes, partly personal, partly of a local nature, which in conjunction with the general situation as we have sketched it in the first part, explain why Socialism found a theoretical expression earlier than Capitalism.

These circumstances are, put shortly, More's personal character, his philosophical training, his activity in practical affairs, and the economic situation of England.

More's personal character may indeed be regarded as one of the causes of his Socialism. Erasmus tells us how amiable, helpful, and full of sympathy with the poor and oppressed More was: he called him the protector of all the poor.

Only in the northern countries of Western Europe were the material conditions in the sixteenth century favourable to the formation of such a disinterested character. In the mercantile republics of Italy, as in the Courts of the Romance monarchies, egotism, the grand feature of the new mode of production, reigned absolutely; it reigned openly, boldly, full of revolutionary defiance. It was a vast egotism, quite different from the cowardly, mendacious, despicable egotism of to-day, which hides itself behind conventional hypocrisy.

Generally speaking, in the towns of England and Germany, entirely different economic conditions prevailed from those in the Italian towns, and to a lesser degree in the towns of France and Spain. Agriculture, together with the Mark constitution, still formed to a great extent the basis even of the urban mode of production; the separation of the country from the town was nowhere completely defined.

"As late as the year 1589, the Duke of Bavaria recog- /162/ nised that the burghers of Munich could not exist without commons. Tillage of the soil must then have been a chief support of the citizens" (L. L. v. Maurer).

At the commencement of the sixteenth century the primitive agrarian communism still existed in England. It had survived under cover of feudalism, and only then began to yield place to another system of agriculture. The features which corresponded to primitive communism still existed, especially among the lower population, and we meet them in More only slightly glossed over with the Humanistic and courtier traits and the self-censure which the conditions imposed upon him. In his serenity, tenacity, unyieldingness, selflessness, and helpfulness we see the impress of all the characteristics of communistic "Merry England."

But sympathy with the poor does not make one a socialist, although without that sympathy no one is likely to become a socialist. In order that socialist sentiments and ideas should grow out of this interest, it must be conjoined with a special economic situation, the existence of a working proletariat as a permanent mass phenomenon, and on the other hand profound economic insight.

The existence of a proletariat of vagabonds creates benevolence and induces almsgiving, but does not produce a socialism of the modern variety.

Now in More's time England was much favoured with respect to the economic development, much more so than, for example, Germany. In respect of the opportunity to appreciate it More's position was almost unique in the northern countries. The only persons who had then learnt to think scientifically and methodically, to generalise, and who were, therefore, capable of formulating a theoretical socialism, were the Humanists. Now in the northern countries Humanism was an exotic growth, in which no class had a special interest. While the /163/ Humanists in Italy were busily engaged in active affairs, and therefore gave expression to the economic and political tendencies of their time and country, the great majority of German Humanists were merely schoolmasters with no glimmering of practical affairs, who, instead of delving into the past for weapons in the struggles of the present, stood aloof from those struggles and retired to their studies, in order to live wholly in the past.

Germany's development did not tend to close the gap between science and life. On the contrary, the rudeness, the barbarism, the boorishness into which Germany sank to an increasing extent after the sixteenth century, and from which she did not emerge until the beginning of the eighteenth century, rendered the maintenance of science in Germany possible only by its being completely divorced from active life.

The fundamental cause of Germany's decay resided in the alteration of the trade routes after the end of the fifteenth century, which not only impeded the economic development in Germany, but transformed it for some time into economic retrogression.

The discoveries of the Portuguese in the second half of the fifteenth century opened a sea route to India. At the same time the old communications with the East through Asia Minor and Egypt were interrupted by the invasions of the Turks, while the caravan routes from Central Asia had previously been closed in consequence of local upheavals.

This paralysed not only the trade of the Mediterranean seaboard, but also that of the towns on the great German waterways, which, besides being the intermediaries of the trade between Italy and the North, traded with the East on their own account by other routes—via Trapezunt and the Black Sea as well as the land route over Russia. The /164/ total effect of these changes was to sever the arteries of the German towns, especially of the Hansa towns on the Baltic and the towns in Southern Germany, Nuremberg, Augsburg, etc.

The towns on the Rhine and on the estuaries of the North Sea suffered less, but the trade which they supported was insignificant and its direction had changed. It flowed not from East to West, from South to North, but contrariwise.

Antwerp became for the sixteenth century what Constantinople had been in the fourteenth century and what London was to become in the eighteenth century: the centre of world trade, the focus of the treasures of the East, to which the Americas were now added, whence they were poured out over the whole of Europe.

The proximity of Antwerp inevitably exercised the most stimulating effect upon the commerce of England, and especially of London. And even in More's time England strove to acquire overseas possessions, although as yet without any great success. England's commerce increased as Germany's declined.

Out of mercantile the beginnings of industrial capital were already beginning to develop. Englishmen began to manufacture wool in their own country after the Flemish example, and even in the time of Henry VIII. complaints were heard of the decay of independent handicraft in wool-combing. In Richard III.'s time, Italian merchants in England were accused (An Act touching the merchants of Italy) of buying up large quantities of wool and employing the weavers to prepare it.

But in the England of More the beginnings of the capitalist mode of production in agriculture were much more perceptible than these nuclei of industrial capital. It is one of England's most remarkable peculiarities that /165/ capitalism developed there earlier in agriculture than in industry.

The causes of this have already been indicated: they are to be traced to the quality of English wool, which made it a much-sought-after raw material for woollen manufactures.

Next to wool, timber and fuel were important agricultural products in England, in view of the growth of the towns, as was also barley for the Flemish breweries. The demand for wool grew in the degree that manufactures on the one hand, and the means of transport on the other, developed. At the outset English wool found its chief market in the Netherlands, but at the end of the fifteenth century it was being exported both to Italy and to Sweden. Among other things, this may be inferred from two commercial treaties which Henry VII. concluded with Denmark and Florence in 1490.

As the market grew, the merchants and great landowners of England redoubled their efforts to extend wool production. The landowners found the simplest way of doing this was to claim for themselves the common lands which the peasants had a right to use. Thus the peasant was more and more deprived of the opportunity of keeping cattle, his entire business fell into disorder, and financial ruin overtook him. Then the great landowner's land hunger grew more quickly than the peasant was "freed" from the soil. All kinds of expedients were adopted. Not merely individual peasants, but sometimes the inhabitants of entire villages and even small townships were expelled, to make room for sheep.

So long as the landlords themselves farmed their estates, or, as happened for a short period, leased portions of them to tenants, to whom they advanced the necessary agricultural plant, cattle, etc., the expansion of their property was always limited by the plant and stock which the land- /166/ lord possessed. There was no point in extending his property unless he was able at the same time to add to his plant and stock. This limit melted away and the land hunger of the great landowners knew no bounds with the arrival of the capitalist farmer, who used his own capital to employ wage workers to cultivate the land which he leased. This class arose in England in the last third of the fifteenth century. It rapidly increased in the sixteenth century, in consequence of the unexampled profits which it then made, and which not only accelerated the accumulation of capital, but also attracted capitalists from the towns.

The rise of profits is to be especially attributed to the depreciation of gold and silver which was caused by the immense transfers of the precious metals from America to Europe; the effect of this monetary depreciation may well have been accentuated by the currency debasement of princes.

In the course of the sixteenth century the prices of agricultural products rose by 200 to 300 per cent. in consequence of the currency depreciation. Rents, on the other hand, were slow in rising, as the leases ran for long terms, and did not keep pace with the prices of agricultural products. Therefore they fell actually if not nominally.

The farmers' profits grew at the expense of rents.

This not only increased the number of farmers and the amount of their capital, but also formed a fresh incentive for the large landowners to extend their estates, in order to make good their losses in this way.

The consequence was a rapid impoverishment of the small peasants. A concurrent phenomenon was the dispersal of the feudal bands of retainers, to which we have made reference in the first part.

The retainers were in any case a burden for the working people. Where they remained in existence, they were a /167/ burden on the peasants who were obliged to support them. Where they were broken up, they became a scourge to the wage earners, by swelling the ranks of the unemployed.

The fourteenth and fifteenth centuries were the Golden Age for the peasants and wage workers of England.

At the end of this epoch they were both suddenly plunged into deepest poverty. The number of workless swelled to terrible dimensions. The most gruesome punishments were not, of course, calculated either to diminish their numbers or to restrain them from crime: punishment for crime was uncertain, but sure was the punishment for abstention from crime: starvation.

Not much better than the situation of the workless was that of the propertyless workers, who then began to form a numerous class in agriculture. What parliamentary legislation had only incompletely achieved in the preceding two centuries was easily attained in the sixteenth century by the oppressive weight of the reserve army of the workless. Real wages diminished, and labour time was extended.

Food prices rose by 300 per cent., wages only by 150 per cent. From More's time onwards began that steady decay of the English workers in town and country, whose position reached its lowest level in the last quarter of the eighteenth and the first quarter of the nineteenth century, after which it improved, at least for certain sections, owing to trade union organisation.

Wages fell along with rents, profits grew, and so did capitalism.

When capitalism first invades industry and then turns to agriculture, it seems at the outset to wear a benevolent aspect. It must aim at a constant extending of the market, of production, while the importation of labour-power proceeds but slowly. In its early stages, such an industry is always complaining of the lack of labour- /168/ power. Capitalists must outbid handicraftsmen and peasants in order to entice away from them their journeymen and bondsmen: wages rise.

In this way capitalism began in many countries; it was hailed as a blessing. Not so in England, where it first invaded and revolutionised agriculture. Improvements in methods of cultivation made many workers superfluous. Capitalism in agriculture meant the direct setting-free of workers. In England this process of setting-free proceeded in its severest forms, at a time when industry was developing but slowly and required only small supplies of labour-power; least of all, the ignorant country labourer.

And hand in hand with the separation of the workers from the land, from their means of production, a rapid concentration of landed property into a few hands was going on.

Nowhere else in Europe, therefore, were the unfavourable reactions of the capitalist mode of production upon the working classes so immediately obvious as in England; nowhere did the unhappy workers clamour so urgently for assistance.

That such an economic situation should cause a man of More's character to reflect and to cast about for means of alleviating the intolerable conditions is what we should expect.

More was not the only person who sought for and propounded such expedients. From numerous writings of that time, from numerous Acts of Parliament we may perceive how deep was the impression made by the economic revolution then proceeding, and how generally the shabby practices of the landlords and their tenants were condemned.

But none of those who put forward remedies had a wider outlook, to none of them came the conviction that the /169/ sufferings incident to the new mode of production could only be ended by a transition to another and higher mode of production; none of them, save More, was a Socialist.

A theory of Socialism could only arise within the realm of Humanism. As a Humanist, More learned to think methodically and to generalise. As a Humanist he was enabled to look beyond the horizon of his time and his country: in the writings of classical antiquity he became acquainted with social conditions different from those of his own time. Plato's ideal of an aristocratic-communist community must have prompted him to imagine social conditions which, being the opposite of those existing, were free from their concomitant poverty. Plato's authority must have encouraged him to regard such a community as more than a mere figment of the imagination, and to set it up as a goal which humanity should strive to attain.

In so far was Humanism favourable to More's development. But the situation in England was, in a scientific respect, similar to that in Germany: English Humanism remained an imported, exotic growth, without roots in the national life, a mere academic affair. Had More been a mere Humanist, he would hardly have attained to Socialism. We know, however, that More's father, much to the regret of Erasmus and his other Humanist friends, soon tore him away from his studies, in order to put him to the study of law and then to launch him on a practical career. We know in what close relationship More stood to the London merchants, how he was entrusted with the care of their interests on every important occasion. The majority of the positions which More filled impelled him to deal with economic questions; the fact that he was appointed to these posts also proves that he was regarded as an expert in economic matters. /170/

We know that he was a popular advocate, that in 1509 he was appointed Under-Sheriff, in which position he had sufficient opportunity to gain an insight into the economic life of the people. We have also mentioned several missions of which he was a member, for the conduct of commercial negotiations. The first was to Bruges in 1515. In the same year Parliament appointed him a Commissioner of Sewers. His second mission was to Calais in 1517, in order to compose disputes between English and French merchants. In 1520 we find him on a mission to Bruges, to settle disputes between English merchants and the Hansa. Then he became Treasurer, and, in 1523, Speaker in the Commons, both positions presupposing experience in financial matters, and shortly afterwards Chancellor of the Duchy of Lancaster: truly, if anybody had an opportunity to become acquainted with the economic life of his time, it was More. And he became acquainted with it from the most modern standpoint that was then possible, from that of the English merchant, for whom world trade was then opening up. In our view, this close connection of More with mercantile capital cannot be too strongly emphasised. To this we attribute the fact that More thought on modern lines, that his Socialism was of a modern kind.

We believe that we have disclosed the most essential roots of More's Socialism: his amiable character in harmony with primitive communism;

the economic situation of England, which brought into sharp relief the disadvantageous consequences of capitalism for the working class; the fortunate union of classical philosophy with activity in practical affairs — all these circumstances combined must have induced in a mind so acute, so fearless, so truth-loving as More's an ideal which may be regarded as a foregleam of Modern Socialism. /171/

Vyacheslav Volgin[1]

February 7 marked the 475th anniversary of the birth of Sir Thomas More. Humanist, prominent statesman, and author of the first socialist utopia, Thomas More was one of the most interesting men of the eventful sixteenth century.

Few political or social writings ever produced exerted so profound and lasting influence as More's "De optimo reipublicae statu," more widely known as "Utopia." It was from this little book that a whole trend of social thought—the trend known as utopian socialism—took its beginning.

Living at the time when he did, More could not go beyond mental projection of an imaginary ideal society (which is so characteristic of utopian socialism). In sixteenth century society he could not, of course, discover a force capable of removing the social contradictions which he noted and condemned. For socialism as a science the time was not yet ripe. But for its period, "Utopia" is a work amazing in its depth and discernment.

The First Book of "Utopia" contains a description, quoted by Marx in "Capital," of the dispossession of the English peasant which was then taking place. This description differs from the many that have come down from More's contemporaries in its vivid forcefulness and in the boldness of the conclusions More draws. He is not content to seek particular remedies for this particular evil. No, he delves down deeper, to the general, underlying cause both of this and of the other social evils. That cause is the rule of private property, the private ownership of goods. More's remarks on this subject, with which the First Book concludes, are the focal point of the whole work. They summarize his whole critique of the society he lived in, and are the foundation on which his description of an ideal society is built.

Where possessions are private, More says, there can be no justice and the public weal cannot prosper. All riches there, no matter how abundant, always fall into the hands of a few and the rest are doomed to want and poverty. For a just and equitable order of things, private property must be entirely abolished. And in the Second Book of "Utopia" he depicts such a just order, on some imaginary island, an order free of the evils that private property brings with it.

The Utopian community More describes is a harmonious economic whole. All land in Utopia is a public possession. If there is a surplus of labour in some place, the commonwealth moves it to where it is needed, and from places that have an excess of some product it sends that product to places lacking it, so that there may be a proper balance in all things. It is the commonwealth, too, that carries on trade with other nations.

The prime economic unit in Utopia is the family. Each family follows

"Sir Thomas More," *News, A Review of World Events*, XXXIX (February 15, 1953), 14-15.
1. Vyacheslav Volgin, Vice-President of the U.S.S.R. Academy of Sciences, is a prominent public figure and leading Soviet historian who has been especially interested in the history of socialist ideas. The *Utopia* has been known in Russian translation since 1789, and there have been at least three translations in the twentieth century.—*Editor's note.*

some particular craft. But its work is supervised by public officers, and its entire product is delivered to the commonwealth.

This system extends, with a few exceptions, to everyone. Every citizen is trained to some craft, and throughout the time that he is capable of working, he is employed chiefly in that craft. Working the land is not regarded as one of the crafts and is done by everybody in turn, in two-year terms. When the citizen's two years are over, he returns to the town and again takes up his craft. Everything produced, both on the land and in the crafts, belongs to the commonwealth, which provides citizens with all they require. The head of the family goes to the public store-houses and markets and there receives what he and his family have need of.

More realizes, of course, that such distribution — according to needs — is only possible given abundance of goods. This abundance, however, he does not make contingent upon expansion of the productive forces through technical progress but upon the elimination of idle parasites, who were so numerous in the European societies he knew and criticized. He tells us /14/ whom he regards as parasites: first of all, the lords, nobles, and priests; their retinue of servants, the multitude of beggars; all persons engaged in producing luxuries; and also the women, who, he says, are employed very irrationally or not employed at all. In Utopia only two groups of able-bodied citizens are exempt from manual labor: public officers (for the duration of their term of service) and men of learning.

In "Utopia" the principle of community is presented chiefly as production in common. More is not opposed to communal consumption; in fact, he clearly thinks it preferable. At the same time, his approach to the matter is a very broad-minded and realistic one. We find in Utopia common eating halls, and the great majority of citizens take their meals there. But those who do not wish to do so are supplied with provisions in the public markets. Individual feeding does not, in More's opinion, endanger the community principle, and he accordingly allows it. A possessive attitude towards house and garden plot, on the other hand, does appear to him likely to undermine communal principles. And so in Utopia people change houses and gardens every ten years, by drawing of lots.

One must also remark upon one other feature of More's social theory. There were quite a number of movements in the later Middle Ages which proclaimed community of possessions as their principle. But all these movements were religious in character. They preached the principle of community as "the law of God." More divested the principle of this religious integument, he proclaimed it on the grounds of reason. The Utopian order is to him the best because it is the most rational and the most conducive to man's well-being on earth. Man has been ordained by God to order his life according to the laws of nature. His soul has been ordained to felicity. It is madness, More says, to follow sharp and painful virtue and banish the pleasure of life. Nature prescribes a life of joy as the end and object of all men's actions. But for the ordering of a joyful life, reason and nature bid men to aid and assist each other. It is on these wholesome principles that the ethics and laws of the Utopians are based.

It is indeed amazing to think that a work like this could have appeared in the early sixteenth century. But then More was a man of exceptionally wide intellectual vision. Besides a fine classical education, he had a profound knowledge of contemporary writings. He was well acquainted not only with the "Republic" of Plato, but with Amerigo Vespucci's and Peter Martyr's accounts of the life of the American and West-Indian natives, who held their land and dwellings in common and made no distinctions between "mine" and "thine." At the same time, he was keenly alive to social developments in the world around him, and was affected most by the misery wrought by the enclosures. Under the impact of the stirrings of the dispossessed, he proved able to draw up a complete design for an ideal society free of the evils of his time. All those centuries ago, when the bourgeois order was just coming into being, More subjected its principles to penetrating criticism and proclaimed in their stead the principles of social equality and community. He must indeed be acknowledged the father of utopian socialism and one of its greatest exponents. /15/

R. W. Chambers

The Meaning of UTOPIA

An ex-Cabinet minister is still alive who dates his political career from the accidental purchase of a copy of *Utopia* at a second-hand bookstall. One of his colleagues in the Cabinet has written of *Utopia,* that no treatise is better calculated to nourish the heart of a Radical. *Utopia* has become a text-book of Socialist propaganda. It did more to make William Morris a Socialist than ever Karl Marx did. All this testifies to its abiding power; yet we must never think of More as writing it for Nineteenth-Century Radicals or Twentieth-Century Socialists. Even he could not do that.

The first step to an appreciation of *Utopia* is to understand how it must have struck a scholar in the early Sixteenth Century. That is a difficult task, yet not an impossible one; and if we would understand More himself, it is a task which we must undertake.

We shall then find, I think, that few books have been more misunderstood than *Utopia.* It has given the English language a word 'Utopian' to signify something visionary and unpractical. Yet the remarkable thing about *Utopia* is the extent to which it adumbrates social and political reforms which have either been actually carried into practice, or which have come to be regarded as very practical politics. Utopia is depicted as a sternly righteous and puritanical State, where few of us would feel quite happy; yet we go on using the word 'Utopia' to signify an easy-going paradise, whose only fault is that it is too happy and ideal to be realized. *Utopia* is the first of a series which we have christened 'Ideal Commonwealths'. Some of these, for example William Morris' *News from Nowhere,* really *are* ideal. /125/ They are 'Utopian' in the current sense, that is to say, they are quite unpractical fancies of what this world might be like if the dreamer could shatter it to bits, and then remould it nearer to the heart's desire. For instance, in *News from Nowhere* we might be sure that the Divine Worship of the citizens would be Morris' ideal. If he gives them no Divine Worship, that also tells its tale. Now, More does not make his Utopians Christian. So modern scholars have argued: 'Utopia is an ideal commonwealth; *argal* More thought the vague deism of his Utopians more ideal than the popular religious beliefs of his time.'

Such argument might be reasonable if *Utopia* were a modern 'Ideal Commonwealth'. But we must never forget that More's education fell not in the Nineteenth but in the Fifteenth Century. To a man educated in that century, the distinction was obvious between the virtues which might be taught by human reason alone, and the further virtues taught by Catholic orthodoxy. It was part of the medieval system to divide the virtues into the Four Cardinal Virtues (to which the heathen might attain) and the Three Christian Virtues. The Four Cardinal Virtues—Wisdom, Fortitude, Temperance, and Justice—are the foundation of Plato's com-

From *Thomas More.* New York: Harcourt, Brace and Company, 1935, pp. 125-144.

monwealths, as outlined in the *Republic* and the *Laws*.[1] These virtues were taken into the medieval system — part of the immense debt it owes to Greek philosophy. The Three Christian Virtues — Faith, Hope, and Charity — come of course from St. Paul's *First Epistle to the Corinthians.* Four and Three make Seven — the Perfect Number, which was extremely comforting. The perfect Christian character must comprise all seven. But the four heathen virtues were sufficient to ensure that a man or a State might be a model of conduct in secular matters. In Dante's *Divine Comedy* Virgil represents Philosophy, Reason, Human Wisdom. He is able to rescue Dante from the dark wood (although he was one of those who had not the three sacred virtues) because he knew and followed the four other virtues without fault. So Virgil can guide Dante till he meets Beatrice, but can go no further.

For a pattern of a State, Dante turns to Heathen Rome or to Heathen Greece. And it is not because of his deep learning that Dante does this. Our great English medieval poet, William /126/ Langland, the author of *Piers Plowman,* had but a commonplace education, but his system is similar. *Do Well* is the virtue of secular life, and the examples of it are the great non-Christian philosophers and rulers: Aristotle, Solomon, Socrates, Trajan. *Do Better* and *Do Best* represent forms of Christian virtues. And so More's friend, Busleiden, in his introductory letter to *Utopia,* tells us that the perfect commonwealth must unite 'Wisdom in the ruler, Fortitude in the soldiers, Temperance in private individuals, and Justice in all.'*

In basing his *Utopia* upon these four heathen virtues, More is following medieval tradition; further, he is following his great examples, Plato's *Republic* and *Laws;* but, above all, he makes his satire upon contemporary European abuses more pointed. The virtues of Heathen Utopia show up by contrast the vices of Christian Europe. But the Four Cardinal Virtues are subsidiary to, not a substitute for, the Christian virtues. More has done his best to make this clear. It is not his fault if he has been misunderstood, as the following example will show.

Most of us would agree with Dame Alice in deploring More's extreme austerities. We have seen that, years before *Utopia* was written, she had complained to More's confessor about that shirt of hair. It was no good. It may have been some ten years after *Utopia* was written that, as Roper tells us, More's daughter-in-law, young Anne Cresacre, noticed it:

> My sister More, in the summer as he sat at supper, singly in his doublet and hose, wearing thereupon a plain shirt, without ruff or collar, chancing to spy, began to laugh at it. My wife [Margaret Roper] not ignorant of his manner, perceiving the same, privily told him of it; and he, being sorry that she saw it, presently amended it. He used also sometimes to punish his body with whips, the cords knotted, which was known only to my wife, whom for her secrecy above all other he specially trusted, causing her, as need required, to wash the same shirt of hair.[1]

---

[1] *Republic,* Book IV; *Laws,* Book XII.   /126/
* See page 88 — *Editor's note.*
[1] Roper, p. 49.   /127/

Now, despite all this, we are told that the Utopians condemn bodily austerities as 'a point of extreme madness, and a token of a man cruelly minded toward himself'.

More's biographers and commentators have been puzzled. /127/ Yet the very next sentence of *Utopia* explains the puzzle. The Utopians have only reason to guide them, and they believe that *by man's reason* nothing can be found truer than their view, '*unless any godlier be inspired into man from Heaven*'. The same point is made by More later. There *are* orders of ascetics in *Utopia*: if the ascetics grounded their action on reason the Utopians would mock them; but as they base it on religion, the Utopians honour them and regard them as holy.[1]

We find More, a dozen years later, urging against the Reformers this same doctrine which lies at the root of *Utopia*: 'That Reason is servant to Faith, not enemy.' More argues against the Lutherans that Reason, Philosophy, and even Poetry have their part to play: the Lutherans, who would cast away all learning except the Bible are, says More, 'in a mad mind', and he quotes St. Jerome to prove that pagan Philosophy and Poetry have their use for Christians. By 'Poetry' More of course means any work of the imagination: his Protestant critics deride *Utopia* as 'poetry', and More himself as a 'poet'. When a Sixteenth-Century Catholic depicts a pagan state founded on Reason and Philosophy, he is not depicting his ultimate ideal. Erasmus tells us that More's object was 'to show whence spring the evils of States, with special reference to the English State, with which he was most familiar'. The underlying thought of *Utopia* always is, *With nothing save Reason to guide them, the Utopians do this; and yet we Christian Englishmen, we Christian Europeans . . . !*

Just as More scored a point against the wickedness of Christian Europe, by making his philosophers heathen, so Jonathan Swift scored a point against the wickedness of mankind by representing *his* philosophers, the Houyhnhnms, as having the bodies of horses. Yet we do not call Swift inconsistent, because he did not live on a diet of oats, or, like poor Gulliver, fall into the voice and manner of horses in speaking. Swift did not mean that all horses are better than all men. He meant that some men are worse than horses. More did not mean that Heathendom is better than Christianity. He meant that some Christians are worse than heathen.

Dante and Langland and innumerable medieval writers had /128/ said the same before him. The conviction that life might be nobly lived on the basis of the four heathen cardinal virtues was one which the Catholic Middle Ages had inherited from Greek philosophy.

So, naturally, More is interested in the problem which for half a lifetime tormented Dante and Langland; what will be the fate, in the next world, of the just heathen, who are an example to us in the affairs of this world? More's answer is tentative, but he quotes with approval the 'comfortable saying' of Master Nicholas de Lyra, the Franciscan, Dante's younger contemporary. Nicholas de Lyra argued that, though a much fuller faith is demanded from Christians, it suffices for the heathen to have believed 'that God is, and that He is the rewarder of them that seek Him'; these are, says de Lyra, 'two points such as every man may attain

---

[1] *Utopia*, ed. Lupton, pp. 210, 282 [see pp. 44, 61].   /128/

by natural reason, holpen forth with such grace as God keepeth from no man'.

And More quoted this,[1] not in his alleged 'emancipated' youth, but in his last book, the *Treatise upon the Passion,* written in the Tower, when he had dismissed all worldly affairs, and was awaiting martyrdom 'for the faith of the Catholic Church'.

What, then, is the attitude of *Utopia* as to these two articles, which represent, in More's view, the orthodoxy to which a heathen may attain? King Utopus tolerated all varieties of belief and disbelief, save on these two points; he forbade, 'earnestly and straitly' that any man should disbelieve in either (1) Divine Providence, or (2) a future life in which, as the Utopians believed, the just would be rewarded by God's presence.

So far was this simple creed from appearing lax to More's friends, that the marginal note (written either by Erasmus or by Peter Giles) contrasts the Utopian faith in immortality with the laxity and doubts of many Christians: '*The immortality of the soul, concerning which not a few, though Christians, to-day doubt or dispute.*' But in Utopia, the man who disbelieves either of these articles is not counted as a citizen, or even as a man; he is excluded from all office, and despised, as being necessarily of a base and vile nature. To suffer lifelong public contumely, in a land where all life is lived in public, and where, save as a /129/ citizen, a man has and is nothing, is a punishment which many would feel to be worse than death. Yet the sceptic may not, publicly, argue in his own defence. Then comes the sentence which has been so often quoted, out of its context. In the old translation it runs, 'Howbeit they put him to no punishment'. Of course, More did not write such nonsense. What he really says is, 'They do not put him to any bodily punishment'—so long, that is, as he humbly submits to the disgrace and to the silence which his heresies involve. The charge against More of inconsistency rests upon refusing to notice his distinction between liberty to hold an opinion, and liberty to preach that opinion; between a man being in More's phrase 'a heretic alone by himself' and being 'a seditious heretic'.

Bishop Creighton, to prove that More in later life 'put his principles aside', quotes the passage which tells how King Utopus, when settling the Utopian constitution, found many religions prevalent in the land, and ordained that they should all be tolerated. Creighton then omits the passage about Utopus disgracing and muzzling those who held the opinions he thought pernicious. But this passage is vital; for, in the light of it, we find that Utopus did *not* tolerate the preaching of all views, but only of those which he, in his wisdom, thought tolerable. Then Creighton begins to quote again. Even those who held most noxious opinions 'were put to no punishment'. They are put to no bodily punishment, so long as they will submit to being disfranchised, despised, and silenced.

But, as the watchman says to Dogberry, 'How if they will not?'

We can tell what would happen *then*, when we remember that, even in the discussion of such opinions as the State allows, any violent or seditious speech is punished in Utopia by banishment or bondage. And, in Utopia, if a man condemned to bondage jibs at his punishment, he is slain out of

---

[1] *Works*, 1557. p. 1287-8.   /129/

hand like a wild beast. Suppose that two sceptics, who did not believe the soul of man to be immortal, had discussed, in private, in Utopia, how they could get the law repealed which silenced and disfranchised them. They would have incurred the penalty imposed on those who plot against the fundamental laws of Utopia. And, even for the highest magistrates, that penalty is death. /130/

Still, within these narrow limits, the Utopian has liberty of conscience. He may not spread among the common people a belief which the State thinks harmful, nor may he discuss the most innocent opinions in a way likely to cause sedition and dissension. He may not, in private, discuss any affair of State. But, if he submits to these restrictions, he is left alone; he is not to be terrorized into saying that he believes what he does not believe.

It may be a low ideal of liberty which allows, to a man who holds views disapproved by the authorities, freedom of thought only on condition that he does not claim freedom of speech. But that *is* the liberty Utopia allows. I shall try, later, to show how far More stuck to that ideal.

UTOPIA *and the problems of 1516*

But we merely confuse the issues if we use our modern, question-begging terminology, and contrast More's alleged 'emancipated youth' with his orthodox old age. If we try to judge it in relation to the early Sixteenth Century, we shall find that *Utopia* is by no means 'emancipated'; it is rather a protest against undue 'emancipation'.

Utopia is, in part, a protest against the New Statesmanship: against the new idea of the autocratic prince to whom everything is allowed. I do not say that it is an impartial protest. The evil counsellors, who are represented in the First Book of *Utopia* egging the prince to despotism, might have replied that their ideal was not necessarily base or sycophantic. Patriots have sometimes seen in tyranny the only force strong enough to make their country great; reformers have sometimes seen in it the only force strong enough to carry through the reformation they desire. But *Utopia* is hostile to it.

Again, *Utopia* is, in part, a protest against the New Economics: the enclosures of the great landowners, breaking down old law and custom, destroying the old common-field agriculture. Here again, we must not suppose that *Utopia* gives us the full story. There was much more in the problem of enclosures than the greed of the great landlord, 'the very plague of his native country'.[1] The up-to-date farmer was also in favour of sweep- /131/ ing away all traces of the older communal husbandry. Thomas Tusser, a humble but practical agriculturist, says:

> Where all things in common do rest,
> Yet what doth it stand ye in stead?

Now, in contrast to this changing world, More depicts a state where 'all things in common do rest', and where there is no place for the grabbing

---

[1] *Utopia*, ed. Lupton, p. 53 [see p. 8].   /131/

superman. More's theoretical *Utopia,* looking back to Plato's *Republic* and to corporate life in the Middle Ages, probably seemed to some contemporaries the reverse of 'progressive'. Cardinal Pole has told of a conversation he had in his youth with Thomas Cromwell. Cromwell ridiculed the *Republic* of Plato, which, after so many centuries, has led to nothing. *He* had a book on statesmanship in manuscript, by a practical modern writer, based on experience. The book, which Cromwell offered to lend to Pole, was *The Prince* of Nicholas Machiavelli.[1]

It is noteworthy that the two most potent books on the State written in the Sixteenth Century were written within so few years of each other. Parts of *Utopia* read like a commentary on parts of *The Prince,* as Johnson's *Rasselas* reads like a commentary on Voltaire's *Candide,* though we know that in neither case can the English writer have read his continental predecessor. There is a reason for the coincidence; before *The Prince* was written, ideas used in *The Prince* had been gaining ground. They were the 'progressive' ideas, and we may regard *Utopia* as a 'reaction' against them.[2] Over and over again, in Book I of *Utopia,* Raphael Hythlodaye imagines himself as counselling a prince, telling him what he ought to do, against those who are telling him what he *can* do; and always Raphael admits that these ideas of justice which he has brought from Utopia are opposed to all that the most up-to-date statesmen of Europe are thinking and doing.

And so, from the point of view of the new age of Machiavellian statesmanship and commercial exploitation, *Utopia* is old- /132/ fashioned. The King is to 'live of his own', in medieval wise, and to turn a deaf ear to the counsellors who would make him all-powerful. The big landlords are to have mercy on their tenants, and not to allow them to be sacrificed to economic progress, and the law of supply and demand in the wool market.

And the outlook of *Utopia* on the ecclesiastical problems of 1516 is also conservative and orthodox. Among the most pressing problems of church government was that of the immunity of the clergy; among the most pressing problems of ,doctrine, the immortality of the soul; beyond all these was the problem of monasticism.

Most urgent in England, at this date, was the question of clerical immunity. If a cleric committed felony, was he to be hanged like a mere layman, or was he to be left to the gentler reproof of the ecclesiastical courts? The question had been fought out between Henry II and Becket — a battle of giants: the murder of Becket had caused a revulsion of feeling which left the victory on the ecclesiastical side. But now the problem was being raised again: the first rumblings of a storm which was to burst in fury twenty years later. Whilst More was planning *Utopia,* London had been in a ferment over the question whether clerks in minor orders were to enjoy immunity. The problem, of course, was not limited to England. It had just been declared in the Lateran Council that laymen had no

---

[1] *Epistolarum,* Pars I, Brescia, 1744, pp. 135-7. An attempt has been made to argue that Pole mistook the book, and that Cromwell really meant to lend him *The Courtier of Castiglione.* (Van Dyke, *Renaissance Portraits,* p. 401.) The argument is unconvincing.   /132/

[2] I had written this before reading Hermann Oncken's lecture on the *Utopia* (1922), but I am glad to find that I have the support of his authority: *Sitzungsberichte der Heidelberger Akademie, Phil.-Hist. Klasse* (1922), 2, p. 12.   /132/

jurisdiction over the clergy,[1] but there were many reasons why discussion was peculiarly acute in London throughout the whole of 1515.

Very characteristically, More sticks to the medieval principle, whilst stripping it of its abuses. Priests in Utopia who commit any offence suffer no temporal punishment; they are left only to God and themselves: 'For they think it not lawful to touch him with man's hand, be he never so vicious, who after so singular a sort was dedicate and consecrate to God, as a holy offering.' But inconveniences do not result to the State, because in Utopia priests are so few, and so carefully chosen: 'of exceeding holiness, and therefore', More grimly says, 'very few'. /133/

Now, if we read *Utopia* as a modern skit, we may think that this discussion of clerical immunity was introduced merely as an opening for the 'satirical observation' that priests of exceeding holiness are very few. That, for example, was how Benjamin Jowett took More's words.[1] They seemed to him to show More's 'detestation of priests', and therefore 'curiously disagree' with More's life. There is no disagreement. A dozen years later, in his defence of the Church, we find More insisting on selecting priests carefully, and limiting the number. But if, alike in England and in *Utopia,* the laymen fitted to be made priests are few, that is a reflection, not on the clergy, but on us, the laity: 'for of us', says More, 'they be made'. And he quotes a saying he heard Colet make, many years before, that the clergy will always be one degree better than the laity.[2]

The feeling in London had been embittered by the case of Richard Hunne. Hunne was a prosperous Merchant Taylor of high character, who had a quarrel with the clergy. He was accused of heresy, and whilst in the bishop's prison, awaiting trial, he was found hanged. Had he added the crime of suicide to the crime of heresy? Or had the clergy added the crime of murder to that of false-witness? More was certain that it was a case of suicide. He discussed the matter at length many years after. But popular feeling accused the bishop's officials of murder. Bishop FitzJames of London declared that the Londoners were so set in favour of heresy that a London jury would condemn a clerk 'though he were as innocent as Abel'. Bishop FitzJames was given to exaggerated language, but, allowing for that, it is clear that there was a good deal of anticlerical feeling in London at the time. It is all the more noteworthy that so loyal a Londoner as our under-Sheriff should represent the inviolability of the clergy as a sound principle, prescribed by the law of reason which governs Utopia.

We must never forget then that in Utopia the despotic supremacy of the State is balanced by the inviolability of a priesthood entirely exempt from State control.

Another leading problem of controversy was the immortality of the soul. Did philosophy and human reason, apart from revelation, teach such immortality? There were philosophers /134/ who said 'No'; and, three years before *Utopia* was published, this matter also had come before the Lateran Council.[1] Teachers of philosophy were enjoined to point out how Christian philosophy corrected the views of the heathen on

---

[1] 5 May, 1514.   /133/
[1] *Dialogues of Plato*, 1875, III, p. 189.   /134/
[2] *Dialogue, Works*, 1557, pp. 225-8.   /134/
[1] 19 Dec. 1513: *Concilium Lateranense V, Sessio viii*. See *Conciliorum Omnium tomus XXXIV*, Paris, 1644, pp. 333-5, 557.   /135/

immortality; they were to refute these heathen errors, and steps were taken to ensure that the student *in sacris ordinibus constitutus* should not spend more than five years upon philosophy and poetry, before diluting them with the safer studies of theology and pontifical law.

Now, let us try and look at *Utopia* from the point of view of 1516. Here is a heathen community, whose religion is founded on philosophy and natural reason. Yet, so far from doubting the immortality of the soul, they base their whole polity upon it. No disbeliever in immortality may be a citizen of Utopia. In life, and in death, every true Utopian has a firm trust in the communion of saints.

So that, in the eyes of More's friends, Erasmus or Peter Giles, *Utopia* is a striking defence of a vital tenet of the Christian faith. More will not tolerate the ambiguous formula: 'As an orthodox Catholic I believe in immortality; as a philosopher I doubt.' Reason and philosophy teach the Utopian to affirm that he is somehow in touch with the souls of the noble dead, mighty overseers whose presence encourages him to do his duty the more courageously.

Thus here we find More in *Utopia* opposing the scepticism of his age, precisely as we have seen him opposing its Machiavellian statecraft. And so thoroughly is *Utopia* a book of the hour, that here again More seems to be making a comment on a book which he had never seen. For it was in the very same November of 1516, in which Peter Giles was writing the dedicatory epistle of *Utopia,* that the professor of Philosophy at Bologna, Pomponazzi, published his famous treatise on the Immortality of the Soul. Pomponazzi submitted to the Church in all matters of faith, but, as a philosopher, he stubbornly upheld his doubt as to the doctrine of immortality.[2]

Therefore More's *Utopia,* among other things, is a contribu- /135/ tion to this current controversy. More attacks the enemy in their philosophical camp, and makes his heathen Utopians into unexpected allies of the Catholic faith with regard to this great dogma—and, as we shall see later, with regard to other things as well.

But the imminent problem was monasticism. There was an incompatibility between the declining spirit of the monastic common life, and the rising commercialism of the grasping 'new rich'. Within a quarter of a century commercialism was to destroy monasticism in England. More stands, as it were, at the crossways, and asks, 'Why not destroy commercialism? Is not the spirit of the common life really better worth preserving?" It is significant that *the religious houses are the one European institution which the Utopians are said to approve.* And with reason, for in Utopia, though the rule of celibacy is necessarily absent, the monastic idea is at work. The Utopian State is as sumptuous as many a religious house was. But the Utopian, like the monk or friar, may possess nothing. Everyone in Utopia must wear the common habit (in a letter to Erasmus we shall find More calling it Franciscan).[1] There are four varieties, for men and women, married and unmarried. 'The cloaks of the Utopians are all of one

---

[2] The *Tractatus de immortalitate animae* is dated Bologna, 6 Nov. 1516; *Utopia* is dated Antwerp, 1 Nov. 1516.   /135/
[1] Allen, II, No. 499.   /136/

colour, and that is the natural colour of the wool.' Their hours of work, of recreation, the very games they may play, are all regulated. There are no foolish and pernicious games like dice. Instead, the Utopians have two games, one of which is intended to teach mathematics, and the other to teach morals. The Utopians eat in refectories, beginning every dinner and supper by reading something pertaining to good manners and virtue. Talk at table is initiated and directed by the elders, who graciously encourage the younger married people to join in the discussion, by turning it into a kind of oral examination. As for the men below twenty-two and the girls below eighteen: they serve, or else stand by, in marvellous silence, watching their elders eat and talk.

In much of this, More is perhaps joking; it was his way to utter his jests with such a solemn face as to puzzle his own household.[2] But, underneath More's fun, was a creed as stern as that of Dante, just as, underneath his gold chain, was the /136/ shirt of hair. And, quite certainly, the ideal of *Utopia* is discipline, not liberty. It is influenced by some of the most severe disciplines the world has ever known. Through Plato's *Republic* it goes back to the barrack life of a Spartan warrior through More's own experience to the life of a Charterhouse monk. And the discipline of Utopia is enforced rigidly, even ferociously. If the Utopian attempts to break the laws of his native land, there is the penalty of bondage, and, if that fails, of death. We have seen that even to speak of State affairs; except at the licensed place and hour, is punishable in Utopia with death, lest permission to discuss politics might lead to revolution. Has any State, at any time, carried terrorism quite so far?

Many framers of ideal commonwealths have shirked the question of compulsion, by imagining their citizens to have all become moral overnight. More does not choose this easy way. He recognizes that there will be a minority, to whom higher motives do not appeal. For them, there is penal servitude; if that fails, death.

But no great State can be founded on terrorism. For the mass of its citizens, Utopia is founded on religious enthusiasm. Faith in God, and in the immortal destiny of the human soul, supplies the driving power which is to quench human passion and human greed.[1] Based on religion, Utopia is supported by a belief in the dignity of manual labour. Even rulers and magistrates, although legally exempt, share in this work as an example to others.[2] So a six-hours' day suffices, and the rest of the time is free for those intellectual and artistic pursuits in which, to the Utopians, pleasure consists.[3] But religion is the basis of all.

Now a monk of to-day, Dom Ursmer Berlière, of the Abbey of Maredsous, has pointed out how at the beginning of the Middle Ages, monasticism, as St. Benedict shaped it, gave a pattern to the State. St. Benedict's monastery 'was a little State, which could serve as a model for the new Christian society which was arising from the fusion of the conquered and conquering races—a little State which had for its basis,

---

[2] Cresacre More, 1726, p. 179; cf. *Works*, 1557, p. 127.   /136/
[1] [Chambers' *Thomas More*,] pp. 274-5.   /137/
[2] [*Ibid.*,] p. 147.   /137/
[3] [*Ibid.*,] *passim*, especially pp. 152, 206.   /137/

religion; for its support, the honour given to work; for its crown a new /137/ intellectual and artistic culture'.[1] The writer was not thinking of *Utopia*. I do not know if he had ever read it. But, at the end of the Middle Ages, we find More depicting a State founded on just these things: the common life, based on religion; honour given to manual labour; intellectual and artistic culture. However far these things might sometimes be from monastic practice, the writer of *Utopia* could never have approved of the destruction of monasticism; he looked for its reform.

And, just as the customs of Utopia have their bearing on the urgent questions of the time, so has the framework of the book — the story of the travels and circumnavigation of Raphael Hythlodaye. We have only to look at a globe — a flat Mercator's map conceals the fact — to see how the destiny of England had been shaped by the discovery of the New World. England, till More's day remote from the centre of things, and unable to employ very profitably the skill of her mariners, was now found to be peculiarly well placed. The farther from the Equator, the shorter the way round the world. A similar favourable situation had enabled the Norsemen to discover America five centuries before, though they could not exploit their discovery. But now Englishmen were bound to seek for a north-west passage to Japan, China, and India. True, America blocked their way. But this only meant that they found something even better than they sought. And so, under an Italian captain, resident in Bristol, Bristol men in a Bristol ship first discovered the mainland of America, with authority to set up the royal banners of Henry VII in 'any village, town, castle, island or mainland of them newly found', and to import into England free of customs any merchandise they might get there. If every man had his due, America would be called Cabota; and Henry VII, rather than a modern peer, would be hailed as the first Crusader for Empire Free Trade. But Cabot had a bad press, or rather no press at all; the new art of printing spread the fame of a later explorer, Amerigo Vespucci; so Amerigo became godfather of the new continent, and, as we have seen, it was *his* travels, 'now in print and abroad in every man's hands', which inspired Thomas More. /138/

Yet recent research has shown that More had also domestic inspiration.

More was about nineteen when John Cabot discovered the mainland of America. During the rest of the reign of Henry VII transatlantic exploration was kept before men's eyes. The 'Company Adventurers into the New Found Lands' were busy at Bristol. About 1502, three specimen savages, clothed in skins and eating raw flesh, were presented to the King. Two years later, two of them were still to be seen about the Palace at Westminster, clothed and looking like Englishmen. More had probably seen them, and wondered what thoughts lay behind their inscrutable faces. In 1505 'wild cats and popinjays of the Newfound Island' were brought to the King at Richmond. In the last year of the reign of Henry VII, Sebastian Cabot went in search of the North-West Passage. It seems clear that he penetrated the strait later known by the name of Hudson, and found it opening into the immense expanse which we call Hudson Bay. Such an anticipation by Cabot, in 1509, of later Elizabethan and

---

[1] *L'ordre monastique des origines au XIIe. siècle*, 2ᵉ. edit., 1921, p. 45.   /138/

even Stuart exploration seems almost incredible. Yet 'if he was lying, he had the devil's own luck. For we know now that the facts are substantially as he represented them'.[1] Cabot naturally assumed that Hudson Bay was what we call the Pacific, and consequently that he had discovered the North-West Passage. He returned to England with the glorious secret to find Henry VII dead, and Henry VIII and Wolsey obsessed with their continental schemes. After three years of disappointment, Sebastian left England and entered the Spanish service. He lived nearly fifty years longer without ever having an opportunity of finding that his magnificent discovery was only a dead end. For him, perhaps it was as well that he was not destined to be numbered among the 'frozen pilots' upon whose funeral the Arctic stars have looked down. But the cessation of North American exploration meant that for England valuable experience was lost, the work of Henry VII was undone, and England was 'beaten back from the seas into the dusty vortex of European politics'.[2]

Yet there were still Englishmen who understood the /139/ importance of transatlantic adventure, and Professor A. W. Reed's researches into the circle of Thomas More has brought to light the story of the first attempt at the colonization of North America by England. Six months after the publication of *Utopia,* More's brother-in-law, John Rastell, set off on the *Barbara* of Greenwich on a voyage of discovery to the New Found Lands. That not merely exploration, but the establishment of some kind of settlement was in his mind, follows from the fact that he took 'tools for masons and carpenters, and other engines that he had prepared for the New Lands'. John Rastell expected to be away for three years, during which he had arranged by prepayment that Judge John More should keep his wife and servants. Judge More seems to have taken a large share in guaranteeing the venture. The expedition turned back, owing to an organized mutiny, which apparently had the approval of the Earl of Surrey, the Lord High Admiral, who was opposed to sending any part of the fleet across the Atlantic when it might be needed in the Channel. Spirited interference in continental politics did not allow of valuable fighting ships being sent on voyages of exploration, likely to last three years.

Now every reader of *Utopia* must be struck by the weight there placed on colonization. The Utopians hate war: 'War they do detest and abhor; and contrary to the custom almost of all other nations, they count nothing so much against glory, as glory gotten in war'.[1] But to secure colonies for an overflowing population, they consider that even war is justified 'by the law of nature'. 'For they count this the most just cause of war, when any people holdeth a piece of ground void and vacant, to no good nor profitable use, keeping others from the use and possession of it.'[2]

All this sounds so imperialistic that some foreign critics have seen in Thomas More one further typical perfidious Englishman, who (with a Machiavellism more subtle than that of Machiavelli himself) propounded

---

[1] J. A. Williamson, *The Voyages of the Cabots,* 1929, p. 241.   /139/
[2] Callender, *The Naval side of British History,* p. 47.   /139/
[1] *Utopia,* ed. Lupton, p. 243 [see p. 51].   /140/
[2] The same, p. 155 [see p. 30].   /140/

exactly such pretexts for expansion as would be useful to the British Empire of future centuries, and who yet, with characteristic English hypocrisy, pretended to be fighting for morality all the time.

But, when More emphasizes that the Utopians only go to /140/ war for reasons which concern the welfare of their citizens or of their allies, he is wishing to get in a side blow at the state of Europe in 1516, and the censure wars waged at the whim of, and for the personal aggrandizement of, autocrats like Francis I, or Henry, or Wolsey. I admit that the reasons for warfare approved by the Utopians, if made into a code, and applied to history from the Seventeenth Century to the present day, would load the dice heavily in favour of the British Empire; for they are adapted to a great colonizing island State, such as Utopia is supposed to be, and such as Britain later became. But could More, with all his foresight, have foreseen all this?

One recent German historian[1] has suggested that More, when he makes the Utopians claim the right as a populous nation to colonize empty spaces, may have been thinking of English settlements in North America. Another[2] argues that these theories of the natural right of colonization are no part of the original description of Utopia, already written in 1515; they do not harmonize with it, he thinks, but are a later addition made in 1516. And it must be admitted that this is acute criticism, for these German historians were quite unaware of Professor Reed's discovery; it had not been published when they wrote. And it is certain that John Rastell was not thinking merely of the North-West Passage to the Indies. He describes his object at some length. He wants *colonization:* that Englishmen should make 'first building and habitation' in the lands Cabot had discovered; that the king should have his 'dominion extending into so far a ground', that the heathen should be evangelized. The trade Rastell thinks of is not in oriental spices, gold or jewels, but in the products of the North American coast—timber, pitch, tar, and above all fish. But, he complains, the French are getting there before us: 'yearly of fish there they [the French] lade above an hundred sail'.[3]

The moment was favourable. Of course Englishmen could only at their peril trespass in the Spanish Indies; but there was nothing to hinder them from exploiting the claim which the /141/ wise Henry VII had staked out in the North. The Spaniards had enough to do in the warm water, without venturing among the ice-floes. Charles V could not, and would not, quarrel with England over a claim which was of no use to him. Indeed he would not quarrel with England over much more important matters; for he had his life-long feud with Francis of France, and if Henry had sided with Francis they could together have closed the English Channel against him, and cut off his dominions in the Netherlands from his dominions in Spain. So the way for exploration in North America lay open to England. But Henry and Wolsey, absorbed in winning 'ungracious dogholes' in France, had none of the curiosity about Atlantic

[1] Hermann Oncken in *Sitzungsberichte der Heidelberger Akademie, Phil.-Hist. Klasse,* 1922. /141/

[2] Ernst Tröltsch, *Christian Thought, its history and application,* London, 1923, pp. 145 etc. /141/

[3] See Rastell's *New Interlude of the Four Elements.*   /141/

adventure which More and Rastell felt. Later, in 1521, Henry showed a transient interest in the New Found Land. It has been suggested that this was due to More, then rising in the king's favour, and discussing with him Geometry and Astronomy (and probably Cosmography). But the French war of 1522 stopped this, as it stopped other useful schemes. Expeditions did indeed set out in 1527 and 1536. The explorers found Portuguese, Breton and Norman vessels before them in the New World, but did nothing useful themselves. North American exploration was left to Jacques Cartier and the French.

Although we need not follow More's German critics in making him the father of British Imperialism, the discovery of Rastell's venture does prove that this criticism has a certain element of truth. Colonization and transatlantic adventure meant much to the writer of *Utopia*.

Yet there is nothing so sinister about it as these German critics have argued. The Utopians only settle where there is 'much waste and un-occupied ground', and they admit to full citizenship any of the natives who care to join them. It would have been well if all Sixteenth-Century colonization had been equally humane. And More's words cannot be twisted into a plea for a monopoly of colonial rights for England; if he is staking out a claim, it is for the common body of Christendom. For *Utopia* is a work of our common Western European civilization, dedicated to subjects of Charles V, Giles and Busleiden, the Latin text published in six great European cities before it was ever published in England, and translated into German, /142/ Italian, and French before, in 1551, the English translation appeared.

We can only understand *Utopia* if we remember the Europe for which it was written; at home John Rastell preaching exploration to the More household; abroad the travels of Vespucci in every man's hands; Vespucci, who had found folk holding property in common, and not esteeming gold, pearls, or jewels. (It is important to remember that the Inca empire of Peru, which in more than one detail had a likeness to Utopia, was not known till some fourteen years later; Cortes had not yet conquered Mexico.)

The problem of poverty and unemployment (destined in England to be aggravated by the Dissolution of the Monasteries) was already a European one. Ten years after *Utopia*, More's friend Vives wrote a tract on it. At the root of More's interest in colonization lies his pity for the unemployed labourers:

'Poor silly wretched souls; away they trudge out of their known and accustomed houses; all their household stuff, being suddenly thrust out, they be constrained to sell it for a thing of naught. And when they have, wandering about, soon spent that, what can they do but steal, and then be hanged, or else go about abegging. Whom no man will set awork, though they never so willingly offer themselves thereto.'

But the fact that *Utopia* belongs to its age does not mean that it is the less epoch-making. Some things which may now seem commonplaces to us were less so then. It may seem quite natural to us that in Utopia there should be no class distinctions. It was less obvious to a scholar of the Renaissance. Plato's Commonwealths had been based on class distinction. In the *Laws* the citizens fall into four classes. In the *Republic,* also, there are classes, although so much attention is given to the warrior class, and their common life, that we almost forget the others. Plato is emphatic that every man should have one job only, and he does not waste words on his artisans, except to urge that they must be experts in their own business, and must stick to it. The Middle Ages inherited the same idea of the State: plough-men and artisans to labour, clerks to pray and study, knights to fight. But the Utopian citizen does all three things; /143/ he labours with his hands, studies in his spare hours, and, though he hates warfare, is, at need, a soldier.

It is noteworthy that, despite his admiration for Greek life and thought, More did not build Utopia after the Hellenic pattern. His free citizens are not a privileged class dependent on slave labour, nor are his bondmen a distinct class. Bondage in Utopia is penal servitude — a humane substitute for the death penalty. The repentant bondman is restored to freedom, the incorrigible bondman is slain.[1] But the citizens themselves are all workers.

Finally the outstanding feature of *Utopia* is implied in the great sentence with which Raphael ends his story:

> When I consider all these commonwealths which nowadays anywhere do flourish, so God help me, I can perceive nothing but a conspiracy of rich men, procuring their own commodities under the name and title of the commonwealth.[2]

The Middle Ages had often been charitable to the poor, and More's age had inherited vast charitable endowments. More altogether approved of these endowments, and, later, we shall find him defending them against the fanaticism of reformers who wished to hand them over to a conspiracy of rich men procuring their own commodities under the title of the commonwealth. But More's claim for *justice* goes far beyond medieval admonitions to charity. Its publication throughout Europe by the printing press marks an epoch. /144/

---

[1] *Utopia*, p. 230 [see p. 48].   /144/
[2] The same, p. 303 [see p. 66].   /144/

Richard O'Sullivan

"The study of English law is quite incompatible with true learning" (it is Erasmus speaking) "but those who succeed in it are held in the highest esteem by the English people". "Although", he continues, "the mind of Thomas More which was fitted for better things naturally dreaded legal studies, still albeit he gave much time to letters he became so skilled in law that no one of those who concentrated entirely on it had a better practice".

In the introduction to *Utopia* we are given a sketch of St. Thomas More's daily life during his busy years at the Bar. "Whiles I doo dayelie bestow my time aboute lawe matters: some to pleade, some to heare, some as an arbitratoure, with myne awarde to determine, some as an umpier or a Judge, with my sentence finally to discusse. Whiles I go one waye to see and visit my frende; another way about myne owne privat affaires; whiles I spend almost al the day abrode amonges others, and the residue at home among myne owne; I leave to myself, I meane to my booke no time. For when I am come home, I muste commen with my wife, chatte with my children, and talk wyth my servauntes. All the whiche thinges I reckon and accompte amonge businesses, forasmuche as they muste of necessitie be done; and done must they nedes be, onelesse a man wyll be straunger in his owne house. And in any wyse a man muste so fashyon and order hys conditions, and so appoint and dispose him selfe, that he be merie, jocunde, and pleasaunt amonge them, whom eyther nature hathe provided, or chaunce hath made, or he hym selfe hath chosen to be the felowes, and copanyons of hys life; so that with to muche gentle behavioure and familiaritie, he do not marre them, and by to muche sufferaunce of his servauntes make them his maysters. Amonge these thynges now rehearsed, stealeth awaye the daye, the moneth, the yeare. When do I write then? And all this while have I spoken no worde of slepe, neyther yet of meate, which emong a great /46/ number doth wast no lesse tyme than doeth slepe, wherein almoste halfe the life tyme of man crepeth awaye. I therefore do wynne and get onely that tyme whiche I steale from slepe and meate. Whiche tyme because it is very litle, and yet somewhat it is, therefore have I at the laste finished Utopia, and have sent it to you, frende Peter, to reade and peruse."

In a well-known letter of Erasmus we have a glimpse of the family life at Chelsea:

> More has built near London upon the Thames, a modest yet commodious mansion. There he lives, surrounded by his numerous family, including his wife, his son, and his son's wife, his three daughters and their husbands, with eleven grandchildren. There is not any man living so affectionate to his children as he, and he loveth his old wife as if she were a girl of fifteen. Such is the excellence of his disposition that, whatever happeneth could not be helped, he is as cheerful and well-pleased as though the best thing possible had been done. In More's

house you would say that Plato's academy was revived again, only, whereas in the academy the discussion turned upon geometry and the power of numbers, the home at Chelsea is a veritable school or university of Christian learning. In it none, man or woman, but readeth or studieth the liberal arts, yet is their chief care piety. There is never seen any idle; the head of the house governs it, not by lofty carriage and oft rebukes, but by gentleness and lovable manners . . . nor is mirth wanting as a savour therewithal.

The lines on which St. Thomas desired his children to be educated are laid down in a letter he wrote to their Tutor, one William Gunnett:

"I have often begged not you only but all my friends, to warn my children to avoid the precipices of pride and haughtiness and to walk in the pleasant meadows of modesty; not to be dazzled at the sight of gold; not to lament that they do not possess what they erroneously admire in others, not to think more of themselves for gaudy trappings nor less for the want of them; neither to deform the beauty that nature has given them by neglect; nor to try to heighten it by artifice; to put virtue in the first place, learning in the second, and in their studies to esteem the most whatever may teach them /47/ piety towards God, charity to all and Christian humility in themselves.

"Nor do I think that the harvest will be much affected whether it is a man or woman who sows the field. They both have the same human nature which reason differentiates from that of the beasts; both therefore are equally suited for those studies by which reason is cultivated and becomes fruitful like ploughed land on which the seed of good lessons has been sown. If it be true that the soil of a woman's brain be bad and more apt to bear bracken than corn, by which saying many keep women from study, I think on the contrary that a woman's wit is on that account all the more diligently to be cultivated, that nature's defect may be redressed by industry. They will thus learn what end they should propose to themselves in their studies and what is the fruit of their endeavour namely the witness of God and a good conscience.

"I do desire that you, my dear Gunnell, would sing this song to them, and repeat it and beat it into their heads, that vain glory is a detestable thing, and that there is nothing more sublime than the humble modesty so often praised by Christ; and this your prudent charity will so enforce as to teach virtue rather than to reprove vice, and make them love good advice instead of hating it.

"And thus you will bring about that my children, who are dear to me by nature, and still more dear to me by learning and virtue, will become most dear by their advance in knowledge and good conduct. Adieu."— *From the Court on the Vigil of Pentecost.*

These letters of More and Erasmus show forth the ideas that guided the thought of life of St. Thomas More in relation to the family and the education of children and the equality of the sexes, in work and learning. Those ideas reappear in *Utopia,* which for all its debt to Plato differs from his ideal Commonwealth precisely in the position that is given to the family. "Whereas Plato with his stringent measures sacrifices family life to what he believes to be the welfare of the State; More with the same end in view fosters an intimate family life for /48/ the benefit of the Commonwealth." Indeed the description of family life in Utopia has more than a remote resemblance to the picture that is drawn by Erasmus of the household of Chelsea. "First the city consisted of families. The families most commonly be made of kinredes, their women when they be married at a lawful age go into their husbands houses. But the male children and all their male offspring continue still in their own family and be governed of the eldest and auncientiest father unless he dote for age, for then the next to him in age is placed in his room." None of the cities had more than six thousand families and no family could have less than ten or more than sixteen persons, the natural differences in number being adjusted by the transfer of children from one family to another. Obedience was the bond of peace. "Wives serve their husbands, children their parents and always the younger serve the older."

It is true that the marriage tie might be dissolved in Utopia for adultery or "the intolerable wayward morals of either party"; though it is to be observed that parties guilty of a breach of the marriage obligation were punished "with most grievous bondage". Utopia, then, is not conceived as a Christian State. It is the land of natural reason without the illumination of faith. It is founded on the four cardinal virtues, wisdom, fortitude, temperance and justice. In the introductory letter we are told that the perfect Commonwealth must unite wisdom in the ruler, fortitude in the soldiers, temperance in private individuals, and justice in all. These same virtues are the foundation of the Commonwealth of Plato as outlined in the *Republic* and the *Laws*. In the Christian State they were perfected by the three theological virtues of faith, hope and charity; but Utopia, as we have seen, was not conceived as a Christian State.

It is a non-Christian State founded on reason and nature, unperfected by faith and grace. Erasmus tells us that the object of More in writing *Utopia* was to show whence spring the evils of society, with special reference to the English State with which he was most familiar. "The underlying thought always is; with /49/ nothing save reason to guide them the Utopians have reached this measure of perfection; and yet we Christian Europeans . . ."*

It is none the less of supreme importance to observe that the Commonwealth of Utopia is founded not only on reason but also on religion. In his *Treatise on the Passion,* which was written while he was in the Tower awaiting death, More cites a passage from Nicholas Lyra, which says that though a much fuller faith is demanded from a Christian it suffices for a heathen to believe "that God is, and He is the reward of those who seek Him". These are, he says, two points such as every man may attain by natural reason, "holpen forth with such grace as God keepeth from no man". The citizens of Utopia (or the most and wisest part of them) believed in the existence of "a certain godly power, unknown, incomprehensible, immutable, inexplicable, far above the capacity and reach of man's wit, dispersed throughout all the world, not in bigness but in

---

* See *Thomas More,* by Professor R. W. Chambers, p. 128 [see p. 111].   /50/

virtue and power. Him they call the Father of all". King Utopus, though he was convinced that there was one religion alone which was true and all others superstitious and vain, yet did he well foresee "that the truth of its own power would at last issue out and come to light". And so he gave to every man free liberty and choice to believe what he would, "saving only that he earnestly and straitly charged them that no man should conceive *so vile and base an opinion of the dignity of man's nature,* as to think that souls die and perish with the body; or that the world runneth at all adventures governed by no divine providence".

The citizens of Utopia were thus under obligation to believe in the existence of God and in the immortality of the soul. "Him that is of a contrary opinion they count not in the number of *men* but as one that hath debased the high nature of his soul to the vileness of brute beast bodies; much less in the number of their *citizens,* whose laws and ordinances if it were not for fear he would no wise esteem. Wherefore (we are told) he that is thus minded, is deprived of all honours, excluded from all offices, and removed from all administration of the /50/ Commonweal. And thus he is of all sorts despised as being necessarily of a base and vile nature."

In thus insisting on the ability of man by the light of natural reason to reach a valid conclusion as to the existence of God, and in making this belief a condition of citizenship in his ideal Commonwealth, More anticipated in a way the decree of the Vatican Council in 1870 which declares: "If any man shall say that the existence of the One and True God Our Creator and Lord may not be certainly known by the light of natural reason, acting on the evidence of created things, let him be anathema."

In his strong affirmation of the worth of natural reason, which he says, against Luther, is "servant to faith, not enemy", St. Thomas More was reiterating one of the leading principles of the philosophy of Aquinas: Faith is the perfection of reason, and Grace is the perfection of nature. He was also, I think, following the tradition of the English Common Law, of which we know he was a master. In all the books and articles that have been written about More, there appears to be a singular and uniform failure to attach any value to his life and training in the law and to his knowledge of legal science. Truly considered, law is the greatest of the social sciences, and rightly administered law, that is to say justice, is the greatest of the social services; "the strongest and the surest bond of the Commonwealth" as we read in *Utopia.** Now More, as a practising lawyer and a reader of law at the Inns of Court, must have been familiar with the text-books and records of the English law, and with the philosophy they embody. He would know the yearbooks and the great texts of Glanvill and Bracton and Fortescue. He was familiar with the concepts of freedom and of order with which these men (and their masters in philosophy and theology) had given life and energy to the Common Law and had given shape to the Constitution which is part of the Common Law.

---

* Cf. the Master of the English Common Law: Henry of Bracton – "Ad hoc autem creatus est rex et electus *ut justitiam facit universis.* . . . Non est enim Rex ubi dominatur voluntas et non lex." [For this reason a king is created and chosen, as he accomplishes justice for all. . . . He is indeed not the King when his will and not the law rules.]   /51/

And here it is proper to observe that at the end of the Anglo-Saxon period of English history, that is at the /51/ time of the Norman Conquest, the mass of the English people were slaves or serfs or villeins or otherwise of unfree condition. "The cotter the gebur the plowman the cowherd the shepherd the goat-herd [we are told] were most times serfs attached to the soil and sold with the soil. They were [it is said] the most valuable part of the stock of a farm and their pedigrees were carefully preserved." Upon that state of things came the creative energy of the Common Law. "Every man is by nature free. *Libertas* [says Bracton] *est naturalis facultas* ejus quod cuique facere libet nisi quod vi aut jure pro-hibetur."*

The whole theory and operation of the Common Law with its concept of freedom not as a political privilege but as a natural faculty proper to man as man ran thus towards the establishment of society on the basis of free citizenship. "The time has come", says Maitland, writing of the legal Renaissance of the twelfth and thirteenth centuries, "when men of one sort, free and lawful men, can be treated as men of the common, the ordinary, we may perhaps say the normal sort, while men of all other sorts enjoy privileges or are subject to disabilities which can be called exceptional". In Utopia as in medieval England, in contrast with the classical civilization of Greece and Rome, the ordinary, the natural man, is a free citizen. Only those who have been convicted of heinous offences are reduced, by way of punishment, to the state of bondage.

Again, in England and in Utopia, the free and lawful man is, in the theory of the law, innocent of crime, honest in his dealings, efficient in his work; a worthy fellow, living in a relation of friendship with his fellow men.† /52/ He corresponds with Aquinas' conception of the natural man as stated in the *Contra Gentiles:* "it is natural to man to love his like; so that every man is in a sense to every man a familiar and a friend". As with men, so with nations. Says the writer of *Utopia:* "Touching Leagues which in other places between country and country be so oft concluded, broken and renewed, they [the Utopians] never make none with any nation. . . . What purpose do they serve? they ask. As though nature had not set sufficient love between man and man. And who so regardeth not nature, think you he will abide in words?" And again: "No man ought to be counted an enemy who hath done no injury. *The fellowship of nature is a*

---

* [Liberty is (man's) natural capacity to do what pleases him except what is prohibited by force or by law.] The passage proceeds: "Sed secundum hoc videtur quod servi sunt liberi nam et ipsi liberam facultatem habent nisi vi aut jure prohibeantur . . . licet enim servi secundum efficientiam liberi tamen quoad jus gentium servi sunt, quoad jus vero naturale liberi. Et in hac parte jus civile vel gentium detrahit juri naturali." [But according to this view one sees that slaves are freemen for even they thenselves, if they are not prevented by force or by the law, have a capacity for freedom, for although they are slaves in effect, yet they are free; as far as the law of nations is concerned they are slaves, but as far as natural law is concerned, they are free men. And in this respect the law of nations draws away from the natural law.] The sentence given in the text is taken from the Roman jurist Florentinus.   /52/

† "De quolibet homine presumitur quod sit bonus homo donec probatur in contrarium" [Concerning my man, it is presumed that he is a good man until the contrary is proved.]: so Bracton.

In the manifesto of Jack Cade (1450) we read: "Item we wyll that all men knowe we blame not all the lordys, ne all tho that is about ye kyngs person ne all jentyllman ne yomen ne allmen of lawe, ne all bysshopes, ne all prestys, but all such as may be fownde gylty by just and trew enquery and by the law."   /52/

strong league; and men be better and more surely knit together by friendship and benevolence than by leagues and covenants, by hearty affection of mind than by words".

Like Aquinas, More is thus, in the language of Professor Elliot Smith, "a champion of the good character of natural man". "Deus, qui humanae substantiae dignitatem mirabiliter condidisti . . ."[1]

The Catholic emphasis on the dignity of our rational nature and of our human personality* leads directly to the affirmation of the principle of private property. The argument is put by Pope Leo XIII in the Encyclical *Rerum Novarum.* "Every man has by nature the right to possess property as his own. This is one of the chief points of distinction between man and the animal creation, for the brute has no power of self-direction, but is governed by two main instincts which keep his powers on the alert, impel him to develop them in a fitting manner, and stimulate and determine him to action without any power of choice. . . . With man it is wholly different. It is the mind or reason which is the predominant element in us who are human creatures. It is this which renders a human being human and distinguishes him essentially from the brute. And on this very account — that man alone among the animal creation is endowed with reason — it must be within his right to possess things not merely for temporary and /53/ momentary use, as other living things do, but to have and to hold them in stable and permanent possession; he must have not only things that perish in the use but those also which, though they have been reduced into use, continue for further use in course of time." The most profound reason for allowing the institution of property is thus directly drawn from the rational nature of human personality* and from the personal character of work. To deny to man the right to own is ultimately to deny personal liberty and the rational basis of personality.

St. Thomas More has often been said to have been a Communist. In the sense in which it is intended, nothing could be farther from the truth. In the action of his life, for himself and for the members of his family, he affirmed the principle of private property. In his essay on "The Four Last Things", the grimmest of his writings, he says, "It is not a sin to have riches, but to love riches". In the epitaph he wrote for his own tomb, he says that he was "to thieves and murderers grievous". In *Utopia,* moreover, he puts *in his own name* the argument against Communism which is defended by Hythlodaye. And it is an invariable rule of interpretation of his writings, that the opinions he advances in his own name are always his own opinions.

Again, the arguments he uses in favour of private property are in substance the arguments that are used by St. Thomas Aquinas in the *Summa Theologica* and by Pope Leo XIII in *Rerum Novarum.* It may be of interest to set the arguments in historical order:

---

1. O God, thou who hast created in a wondrous fashion the dignity of the human substance. . . . Opening prayer of the Ordinary of the Offertory in the Roman Catholic liturgy of the Mass — *Editor's note.*

* Persona: id quod perfectissimum est in tota natura. [Person: that which is most perfect in all nature.]   /53/

* Cp. *Summa. Theol.,* 2a. 2ae., Q. 66, Art. I: "Sic habet homo naturale dominium exteriorum rerum quia per rationem et voluntatem potest uti rebus exterioribus ad suam utilitatem quasi propter se factis." [Thus natural man has dominion over external things because by reason and will he can use external things for his service as if made for him.]   /54/

AQUINAS: Property is necessary to man for three reasons. *First,* because every man is more careful to procure what is for himself alone than that which is common to many or to all; since each one would shirk the labour and leave to another that which concerns. the community, as happens where there is a great number of servants. *Secondly,* because human affairs are conducted in more orderly fashion if each man is charged with /54/ taking care of some particular thing himself, whereas there would be confusion if everyone had to look after any one thing indeterminately. *Thirdly,* because a more peaceful state is ensured to man if each one is contented with his own. Hence it is to be observed that quarrels arise more frequently where there is no division of the things possessed.

MORE: I am of a contrary opinion (quod I) for me thinketh that men shal never there live wealthelye, where all thinges be commen. For howe can there be abundance of gooddes or of any thing, where every man withdraweth his hande from labour? Whome the reward of his owne gaines driveth not to worke, but the hope that he hath in other mens travayles maketh him slowthfull. Then when they be pricked with povertye, and yet no man can by any lawe or right defend that for his owne, which he hath gotten with the labour of his owne handes, shall not there of necessity be continual sedition and bloodshed? Specially the authority and reverence of magistrates being taken away, which, what place it may have, with such men among whom there is no difference I cannot devise.

LEO XIII: Men always work harder and more readily when they work on that which belongs to them, nay, they learn to love the very soil that yields in response to the labours of their hands not only food to eat, but an abundance of good things for themselves and those that are dear to them. . . . The practice of all the ages has consecrated the principle of private ownership as being pre-eminently in conformity with human nature and as conducing in the most unmistakable manner to the peace and tranquillity of human existence. . . . Socialism would throw open the door to envy, to mutual invective, and to discord; the sources of wealth themselves would run dry, for no one would have any interest in exerting his talents or his industry; and the ideal equality about which they entertain pleasant dreams would be in reality the levelling down of all to a like condition of misery and degradation.

In the Social Philosophy of St. Thomas More, the State or Commonwealth is thus conceived as an aggre- /55/ gation of families, consisting of men and women conscious of the dignity (and of the demand) of their human personality, obliged by virtue of their rational nature to pursue Truth and Justice and to worship God, and entitled, as part of their prerogative as reasonable beings, to possess things of their own and to maintain a position of economic independence within the State. The ideal is thus a wide diffusion of property in the hands of free citizens in a self-governing community.

According to the author of *Utopia* it is not good for individual citizens or for the Commonwealth that goods or property should be allowed to accumulate in the hands of a few rich men, "whom no need forceth to sell before they lust and they lust not before they may sell as dear as they lust". "Suffer not these rich men to buy up all, to ingrosse and to forestall and with their monopoly to keep the market alone as please them. Let not so many be brought up in idleness, let husbandry and tillage be restored, let cloth working be renewed that there may be honest labour for the idle sort to pass their time profitably which hitherto either poverty hath caused to be thieves or else now be either vagabonds or idle and shortly will be thieves."

Hateful to More is the worship of the rich: "They much more marvel at and detest the madness of them which to those rich men, in whose debt and danger they be not, do give almost divine honours for none other consideration but because they be rich".

And most hateful is the State or Commonwealth in which under the cloak of constitutional forms the rich are allowed effectively to rule: "Therefore when I consider and weigh in my mind all these Commonwealths which nowadays anywhere do flourish, so God help me, I can perceive nothing but a certain conspiracy of rich men procuring their own commodities under the name and title of the Commonwealth. They invent and devise all means and crafts, first to keep safely, without fear of lessening that which they have unjustly gathered together, and next how to hire and abuse the work and labour of the poor for as little money as maybe. These devices when the rich men have decreed to be kept and /56/ observed under colour of the Commonalty, that is to say, also of the poor people, then they be made laws".

These lines again are reminiscent of a famous passage in the Encyclical *Rerum Novarum:* "It has come to pass that working-men have been surrendered, isolated and helpless, to the hard-heartedness of employers, and the greed of unchecked competition. . . . To this must be added that the hiring of labour and the conduct of trade are concentrated in the hands of comparatively few; so that a small number of very rich men have been able to lay upon the teeming masses of the labouring poor a yoke that is little better than slavery".

It is not difficult, then, to understand the popular judgement of More which is reflected in the Elizabethan play of which Shakespeare was at any rate joint author: he was "the best friend the poor e'er had". It is easy also to understand the interest that the officials of the Marx Engels Museum at Moscow have in the writings of Thomas More, and the pains they took some years ago to obtain copies of some of his rare works that were reprinted in a little periodical by the Reparatrice nuns at Chelsea: which caused Professor R. W. Chambers to burst into poetry:

When the Bolsh has blown the bourgeois up with gunnery
And stained his hands in Capitalist gore
He pines for correspondence with a nunnery
On the merits of the Blessed Thomas More.

In the opinion of St. Thomas More, then, laws must not be framed or administered in the interests of one class, be it Capitalist or Proletarian, but in the interests of the common good. He has no patience with the argument "that the King's Government, though it would, can do nothing unjustly: on the principle forsooth that all that men have, yea also the men themselves, be the King's. And that every man hath so much of his own as the King's gentleness hath not taken from him. And that it shall be most for the State advantage that the subjects have very little or nothing in their possession, as whose safeguard doth herein consist that the people do not wax wanton and wealthy through /57/ riches and liberty because where these things be, there men be not wont patiently to obey hard unjust and unlawful commandments; while on the other hand need and poverty do hold down and keep under stout courage and make men patient perforce, taking from them bold and rebelling stomachs".

"Here again", says More, "I should rise up and boldly affirm that all these counsels be to the King dishonour and reproach, for his honour and safety are maintained and upheld more by the wealth and riches of his people than by his own treasures: I should declare that the Commonalty choose the King for their own sake and not for his sake; to the intent that through his labour and study they might all live wealthily, safe from wrong and injury; and that therefore the King ought to take more care for the welfare of the people than for his own welfare, even as the office and duty of a shepherd is, as shepherd, to feed his sheep rather than himself". It is thus the duty of a King (and the King's Government) so to behave that he (or they) shall be feared by evil men and loved by good men. Conversely it is the duty of good citizens (and a duty that St. Thomas More practised in life) to co-operate with the King and his Ministers even if there be little hope that good may come of it.

"If evil opinions and intentions cannot be utterly and quite plucked out of their hearts, if you cannot even as you would remedy vices which use and custom hath confirmed: yet for this cause you must not leave and for-sake the Commonwealth; you must not abandon the ship in a tempest because you cannot rule the winds and the sea. No, nor must you not labour to drive into their heads new and strange ideas which you know well will not be acceptable to men of clean contrary opinions. But you must with crafty wile and subtle thought study and endeavour yourself as much as in you lieth to handle the matter wittily and handsomely, and that which you cannot turn to good, so to order it that it be not very bad. For it is not possible for all things to be well unless all men be good. Which I think will not be for a good many years yet."

From these and other passages it is manifest that in /58/ his political, as in his social, philosophy More was always not only a good Englishman but also a good European, that he belonged to the tradition of Christian Europe as well as to the tradition of English Common Law. *Utopia* is in truth a conservative work; it is a protest alike against the New States-manship of Machiavellian princes and the New Economics of the En-closures. The essence of Henry's revolution was to sweep aside one of the two sets of rulers, ecclesiastical and civil, who in theory had governed Christendom. One medieval ideal had been that the temporal and spiritual Powers should guide and check each other. And this system of dual control seemed so much a matter of course that although the Utopians were heathens they reflect the medieval theory of two parallel authorities, civil magistrates and priests; though of the priests we are told that "they were men of exceeding holiness and therefore very few". Henry's revolution left the King supreme. The day came when he was empowered by statute to define *ex Cathedra* from the English throne the religious truths that every Englishman must believe on pain of death. It was natural for a reformer like Tyndale to write: "The King is, in this world, without law; and may at his lust do right or wrong and shall give account but to God only". It was equally natural that Henry should say of Tyndale's book, "This book is for me and all Kings to read", and it was equally natural that an English lawyer and the author of *Utopia* should disapprove Tyndale and his book, seeing that the dual authority, ecclesiastical and civil, and the limitations of the Royal Power were part of the fundamental constitution of Utopia — and of England. "The King", said Bracton in the thirteenth century, "is under God and the law."

"The Common Law", men said, "is the highest inheritance of the King by which he and all his subjects shall be ruled."

"England", said Sir John Fortescue in the fifteenth century (expressly adopting the distinction that is made by St. Thomas Aquinas in the *de Regimine Principum* and elsewhere), "England is a constitutional and not an absolute monarchy: *regimen politicum sed non regimen /59/ regale.*" "The King of England cannot alter the laws without the consent of his subjects nor burden them with new impositions against their will." At his trial, St. Thomas More carried the matter a step further and, in support of his argument that an English Act conferring on an English King supremacy in matters ecclesiastical was invalid, stated (*inter alia*) that "This Realm being but one member and small part of the Church might not make a particular law disagreeable with the general law of Christ's Universal Catholic Church, no more than the City of London being but one poor member in respect of the whole Realm might make a law against an Act of Parliament binding the whole Realm".

In truth, as Professor Chambers says in his admirable work on Thomas More,* from *Utopia* to the scaffold More stands "for the common cause as against the private commodity of any single man or any single kingdom". He will not accept the New Statesmanship which regards the nations as wholly independent, "Gladiators in the European Arena", and which enabled one nation to look with complacency and almost with satisfaction at the prospect of another being destroyed by the Turkish enemy. "Christendom", said More in a famous sentence, "Christendom is one Corps, one body."

For More, as time goes on, peace becomes the passion of his life: peace between princes and peace in the Church, without which Europe could expect nothing but generations of warfare. In a memorable conversation with his son-in-law at Chelsea, he said to Roper: "Now would to our Lord, son Roper, upon condition that certain things were well established in Christendom, I were put into a sack and here presently cast into the Thames."

"What great things be those, sir, that should move you so to wish?"

"In faith, son, they be these: first is that where the most part of Christian Princes be at mortal war, they were all at a universal peace. And the

* In this article I have drawn freely from Professor Chambers' work and make full and due acknowledgement.   /60/

second that where /60/ the Church of Christ is at this present sore afflicted with many errors and heresies, it were settled in a perfect uniformity of religion."

Of the Reformation he had said in another place, anticipating the wars of religion and the thirty years' war: "After that it were once come to that point and the world once ruffled and fallen in a wildness, how long would it be and what heaps of heavy mischief would there fall ere the way were founded to set the world in order and peace again."

As it chanced, in the year in which More resigned his office of Chancellor, there ascended the chair of moral theology in the University of Salamanca one Franciscus de Vittoria who was, on the Catholic basis of the dignity of human nature and of the friendship and the fellowship of Everyman with Everyman, to lay the first foundations of a true system of international law. Some four hundred years later in the year 1934 there was published at the Oxford University Press, under the auspices of the Carnegie Endowment for International Peace, and edited by Professor James Brown Scott, President of the American Institute of International Law, a volume entitled *The Spanish Origin of International Law,* which had for its thesis "that there was a Spanish school of International Law in the sixteenth century, within forty years after the discovery of America; that the founder of this school was Franciscus de Vittoria, prima Professor of theology in the University of Salamanca; that his two *Relectiones, De Indis* and *De Fure Belli,* set forth his law of nations, which was to become international law not merely of Christendom but of the world at large."

> This book [says Professor James Brown Scott] presents a not unworthy thesis. It attributes to the discovery of America the expansion of international law until it has become a universal rule of conduct. It proclaims an international community composed of all the nations, the vast majority being the small powers whose defence is righteousness, justice, and the moral standard. It gives to the great expounders of the modern law of nations, who have been silent for centuries, a voice and a control in the development of the science which they founded. Vittoria could analyse the conditions of his day, feeling the necessity for the /61/ community larger than Christendom, and foreseeing the international community of the future. His assertion that the righting of the wrong of a particular State should not be done if it involved a greater injury to the community at large, was the view of a statesman as well as a theologian. And his conception of the community of nations, co-extensive with humanity and existing as a result of the mere co-existence of States, without a Treaty or convention, is the hope of the future.

There was, as we know, an English master of legal and political science who before Vittoria (to whom he was indeed united in faith and charity) had developed in the *Utopia* the conception of a community of nations "co-extensive with humanity and existing as a result of the mere co-existence of States, without Treaty or Convention", which Professor

James Brown Scott tells us is "the hope of the future". *"The fellowship of nature is a strong league* and men can be better and more surely knit together by friendship and benevolence than by Leagues and Covenants, by hearty affection of minds than by words." /62/

Russell Ames

Throughout more than four hundred years a book called *Utopia*, written in 1515-1516 by an Englishman named Thomas More, has been read by thousands of people in dozens of countries—usually, it seems, with fascination and enthusiasm. Since then, ever more widely, the word "Utopian" has been used to describe man's happiest plans for the reconstruction of society and, ever more cynically, to imply the futility of such plans. Fortunately for the race, history has a way of realizing the impossible, the cynics are in time proved wrong, and it is the scientific dreamers like Thomas More rather than the "practical men of common sense" who are found to have grasped reality.

Perhaps it is a hopeful fighting instinct in man, a social refinement of an instinct for self-preservation, that maintains interest in books like More's *Utopia*. Certainly the Utopian idea is a pervasive and powerful one, a lever to lift mountains if the idea rests on reality. We may guess that one-half of human mental life is devoted to Utopianism, to the imaginative construction of desirable circumstances, and not all of this is escapism.

But these generalities cannot explain why More's *Utopia* has had such a wide and continued audience when thousands of similar books have died. Nor can literary graces explain it: few now read the original Latin, and the Elizabethan translation by Robynson, though it has a charm of its own, makes rather awkward reading for the modern audience. It seems that the explanation must lie, largely, in the content of the work—in its scope, its breadth and depth, its humanity, its truthful reflection of life—in those qualities which permit great rather than good literature to triumph over translation, even poor translation.

Utopia is divided into two parts. The first is a vigorous attack on social evils of the time, especially in England—on /3/ misrule by the rich, oppression of the poor, diplomatic intrigue, ruinous war, excessive taxation, and a cruel legal system. The second part is a description of an imaginary communist society on the island of Utopia (literally, "Nowhere"). Both parts are presented by More as if they are the opinions and observations of a humanist traveler, Hythlodaye (literally, "a distributor of nonsense").

The "Utopian" second part seems to dominate the mind whenever *Utopia* is mentioned. Often the book is called an idyllic fantasy or a humanist *jeu d'esprit*. Yet nothing was ever less idyllic or playful than the bitter criticism which comprises the first part of *Utopia*, which may be called a "Looking-glass" for princes, for rich men, and for England. The two parts hold the keys to one another. It is important to remember that the picture of Utopia was written first and the topical satire later, as if More, fearing that his purpose in creating an imaginary society might not be understood, described exactly those evils he wished to correct.

Either part of *Utopia* is a somewhat larger achievement than most men

"Introduction," *Citizen Thomas More and His Utopia*. Princeton: Princeton University Press, 1949, pp. 3-21.

aim at in a book. Throughout the history of civilization there has been God's plenty of social pamphleteering and of truly fantastic Utopia-writing. It is a larger mind which has welded the two together in a higher realism. According to a social rather than a formal aesthetic, great writing gives us not only the rich patterns of life as it is but some glimpses of how it *must* be one day when man will control nature and himself.

More stands at the threshold of modern culture as one of the originators of substantial imaginative prose, of analytical realism in the form of the novel. *Utopia* portrays aristocratic culture, with its poetic romances, in the hard light of bourgeois prose. The pretensions of feudalism — superior "blood," luxury, magnificence, "justice" in law and property — are measured by reason and nature, are given *social* rather than mystical explanation. A true realism, however, like Shakespeare's or More's, is not stunted /4/ by literalism and expresses the poetry of life. This we find especially in the second part, "Utopia," of More's book, where social man is seen perfecting himself. It should be noted, though, that the first part, the "Looking-glass," contains some little Utopias, and that the second indirectly portrays much of English and European life.

The description of Utopia by itself may be considered one or more of a great many different things: 1. A fantastic escape from unpleasant reality. 2. A blueprint for a better society which More thought men might soon establish. 3. A better society which might exist in some far-off time. 4. A better society which More desired but did not believe possible. 5. A reconstruction of medieval social virtues. 6. A revival of primitive Christian communism. 7. A speculative portrait of rumored American societies, like that of the Incas. 8. A strictly rational philosophic construction, minus Christianity, for the purposes of moral instruction. 9. A pleasant fable written by a humanist for the amusement of himself and his scholarly friends. 10. A fruit of classical studies, following Plato's *Republic*. 11. An early plan for British imperialism. 12. A Christian humanist account of a scholar's paradise, where philosophers are kings and the church is purified. 13. A society constructed as the direct opposite to England for the purpose of disguising social criticism. 14. A description of a desirable and possible organization of city republics.

Long as it is, the above list could be longer. Each interpretation has some truth in it, though all can hardly be equally true. Most commonly advanced have been the eighth, ninth, tenth, and twelfth. The last two are close to the interpretation offered by the present study, in which the Utopian society is considered a protective disguise for the satire and the danger-ously progressive projects of a humanist reformer and middle-class English citizen. The first part of *Utopia* is negative. The second part is positive, recommending, indirectly, a program of democratic reform /5/ in which a republican principle of city federation overshadows aristo-cratic and monarchical principles.

The present study of *Utopia* concerns itself, in considerable detail, with establishing More's place in the middle class, the character of that class in England particularly, and its relation to other classes. There is no assump-tion, however, that More's class affiliation or personal economic interests directly determined what he wrote in *Utopia:* if that were the way of it, any successful English burgher might have written *Utopia* and many of them would have done it. Nor is it argued that the book has social or aesthetic value simply because it expressed the interests of a progressive class. It has value because More's special qualities and experiences enabled him to give a rich, clear-headed, and humane description of social process.

The social relations of More's time and his class position did, however, set the necessary framework within which such thought as his could develop. And therefore, the main thesis of the present study may be broadly stated thus: *Utopia* is not an accident of individual genius but a product of capitalism's attack on feudalism, a part of middle-class and humanist criticism of a decaying social order. From this it follows that whatever More may have derived from Plato, Augustine, and Thomas Aquinas, he is more significant to us as a precursor of Diderot, Jefferson, and Sun Yat Sen. Though it is true that the *Utopia* is somewhat anti-capitalist, both from an idealist-medieval and an embryonic-socialist point of view, the core of the book is republican, bourgeois, and demo-cratic — the result of More's experience as a man of business, as a politician, and as an Erasmian reformer.

This approach is neither entirely original nor exhaustive. It is unoriginal in that Karl Kautsky has shown how Utopia speaks for the London mer-chants, and Frederic Seebohm has related More to humanist reform. Their work, neglected by twentieth century scholarship, is revived, ex-/6/ panded, and documented in this study. The approach is not ex-haustive because it involves little discussion of religious or literary in-fluences, and treats of More not as a grammarian but as a reformer, not as a saint but as a London citizen.

Most studies of More and his famous book have concentrated on his religion or on his communism in the abstract, without much regard for his business life or for politics and economics. These have, however, been given attention in some works on More and, more frequently, in studies of Erasmus which serve to illuminate More's life.*

More's humanist activities have been slighted by English writers, and this has been discussed by Delcourt and Nelson.† His commercial and political activities have received even less attention.‡ This is a significant omission, for /7/ there is substantial truth in Preserved Smith's asser-

---

* Among these studies are: Frederic Seebohm, *The Oxford Reformers,* Everyman's Library, 1914; Karl Kautsky, *Thomas More and His Utopia,* 1890; R. W. Chambers, *Thomas More,* 1936; A. Renaudet, "Erasme économiste," in *Mélanges offerts à Abel Lefranc,* 1936, and *Etudes Eras-miennes,* 1939; Marie Delcourt, "Recherches sur Thomas More," *Humanisme et Renaissance,* 1936, and "Le Pouvoir du Roi dans L'Utopie," in *Mélanges offerts à Abel Lefranc;* Frederick Baumann, "Sir Thomas More," *Journal of Modern History,* 1932; Preserved Smith, *Erasmus,* 1923; William Nelson, "Thomas More, Grammarian and Orator," *PMLA,* 1943.   /7/
† "Recherches sur Thomas More" and "Thomas More, Grammarian and Orator."   /7/
‡ Consideration of More's business life and comments on the political-economic meaning of *Utopia* can be found in Kautsky, Seebohm, Baumann, and Nelson as cited; in Michael Freund, "Zur Deutung der Utopia des Thomas Morus," *Historische Zeitschrift,* CXLII. 254-278; in Hermann Oncken, "Die Utopia des Thomas Morus und das Machtproblem," *Sitzungsberichte der Heidelberger Akademie,* Philos.-histor. Klasse II, 1922; in J. H. Lupton, introduction and notes to *Utopia,* 1895.
Kautsky's book on More has been translated into English but is little known; Seebohm's *Oxford Reformers* is widely available in the Everyman's Library edition. Baumann's suggestions are contained in a review article. Nelson shows the relation of some newly published facts about More's connection with the Mercers' Company to his work as a humanist. Oncken and Freund are chiefly concerned with the *Utopia* as a germ of British imperialism. R. W. Chambers,

tion, concerning More and his *Utopia,* that "the sources of its inspiration were neither Plato's *Republic* nor the writings of Roman and Christian
publicists, but his own experiences as lawyer, judge, and government
officer."*

More's *Utopia* expresses the various reforming purposes of the statesman, the lawyer, the merchant, the humanist, and the man of religion.
These purposes were, of course, intertwined and overlapping as well as
distinguishable. The middle class, in its inconsistent and only partly
conscious campaign against feudalism, had the merchants as its chief
economic power and the humanists as its ideological shock troops — with
More active in both groups. The *Utopia,* incorporating many views acceptable to the London merchants, presented a program of social reform,
and was, first of all, a humanist tract. Its form and spirit owed much to
classical literature and to religious tradition, but its substance was contemporary and secular.

The hypothesis may be very seriously projected that the *Utopia* in every
detail had a practical meaning in More's day. This is not to say that More
was urging his contemporaries immediately to institute in their societies
every practice of the Utopians. The hypothesis implies, rather, that those
Utopian practices which were fantastic consistently indicated a practical
line of conduct which would be understood by sympathetic readers.

R. W. Chambers, in the most notable of recent books on More, shows
that many Utopian customs and ordinances directly reflect More's
opinions of current problems, particularly religious problems. Chambers
believes, however, that More often makes his Utopians do things which are
not approved because the Utopians follow reason rather /8/ than the
imperatives of the Christian religion. It is more accurate to say that
even when the Utopians depart from practices acceptable to Christianity, they do so in such a way as to indicate how a sixteenth century
European should behave. Chambers feels that "The underlying thought
of *Utopia* always is, *With nothing save Reason to guide them, the Utopians
do this; and yet we Christian Englishmen, we Christian Europeans . . . !*"[1]
This is certainly part of the meaning of Utopia; but it may be better
phrased thus: *The Utopians, guided by Reason and also by their basically
sound religion, have almost achieved a truly Christian ideal which they live by
while we Christians do not.* In short, though More was limited by the necessities of keeping his fiction logical, consistent, and an adequate disguise
for his attacks and proposals, he makes every effort within this framework
to teach social and religious truth. The Utopians "joine unto the reasons
of Philosophye certeyne principles taken oute of religion: wythoute the
whyche . . . they thynke reason of it selfe weake and unperfecte."[2]
The Utopians have more than reason to guide them, and are quite con-

referring to London Aldermanic and Common Council records and to the *Letters and Papers
. . . of the Reign of Henry VIII,* gives many details of More's professional employment in
"Historical Notes" to Nicholas Harpsfield's *Life and Death of Sir Thomas*   /7/   *More,*
Knight, E.E.T.S., 1932. W. H. Hutton has given the most complete account of More's political
activities (*Sir Thomas More,* 1900.)

A very complete bibliography on everything concerning More has been compiled by Frank
and Majie Padberg Sullivan: *Moreana 1478-1945,* Rockhurst College, 1946.   /8/
* *Erasmus,* 1923, p. 20.   /8/
1. The numerical footnotes are printed at the end of this article — *Editor's note.*

scious of the fact; their only real difference from Europeans is that they actually follow reason, which leads them closer and closer to Christian religion and to ideal Christian behavior.*

The hypothesis outlined above suggests the following type of analysis. Utopian children confess their misdeeds to their parents.[3] This does not mean that More advises English children to stop confessing to priests. It means two quite different things: first, the Utopians, though not in contact with Christianity, by reason and natural religion found their way to confession, and this proves that the confessional as ordained by the church is both a godly and a rational institution; secondly, the Utopian practice suggests that a virtuous Utopian parent is a better confessor than a corrupt European priest, and that the latter had better reform himself. Thus, the institution of confession /9/ is upheld, and at the same time reform is advocated. Similarly, when we see that in *Utopia* many religions are permitted, we should not assume that More advocates the dismemberment of European Christianity and the institution of many new religions. More does mean, however, in these years before Luther appeared on his horizon, that true faith will peacefully conquer false ideas, that bigoted repressions may halt that revival of true religion which Colet and Erasmus were attempting, and that it is unchristian for Portuguese gold-hunters to drive Indians into church with the sword. More's general discussion of religion in Utopia is meant to prove, not the superiority of agnosticism to Christianity, but that Christianity has nothing to fear from peace, freedom, and rational criticism.

The meaning of More's apparent advocacy of communism — a question more closely related to the main interest of this study — can be understood through a similar type of analysis. It is improbable, though possible, that More was a practical advocate of communism in England, however much he *may* have been drawn to the theory of it. The lesson of Utopian communism is, however, that economic conditions are the cause of social evils and that the English ruling classes will not make themselves happier and wealthier by overworking, dispossessing, hanging, or failing to employ the poor, or even by exhorting the poor with pious phrases to a better life. In such futile ways they will only impoverish their country. Instead, they must revive husbandry and cloth-working, improve law and government, and extend trade. Most critics of *Utopia* have spent so much time trying to prove either that communism won't work, or that More was not a communist, that they have ignored the immediate and practical significance of his economic criticism.

Many other aspects of the *Utopia* need detailed rather than abstract attention. More the lawyer, as well as More the saint, the humanist, and the statesman, wrote the book. His actual practice as a lawyer clearly led him to the severest criticism of legal trickery and injustice. His legal studies, however, probably gave him part of his social ideals. The /10/ Roman law, to which he had some attachment as a member of a society of Roman lawyers, did support the claims of absolute monarchy, but it also, in the Justinian code, proposed a harmonious commonwealth

---

* Budé wrote that the Utopians "have adopted Christian usages both in public and in private." (Lupton's edition of *Utopia*, lxxxvii.) [See p. 84.]   /9/

of nations[4] which was an ideal of More's both in Utopia and in England. John Rastell, More's brother-in-law, in his preface to a *Book of Assizes* which he printed in 1513, praises the function of good laws as a curb upon greed: "Wealth, power and glory are . . . in themselves evil things, since they cannot be achieved except at the cost of impoverishment, subjection and humiliation. They cannot, for that reason, constitute the commonweal."[5]

Similarly, the influence of primitive Christian communism on *Utopia* has not been emphasized, though *Utopia* itself emphasizes it.[6] The direct effect of the Gospels must have been strong. Even more important was the republican, and more or less radical economic character of northern humanism. From this, which is not the main subject of the present study, probably flows the major influence on *Utopia*.

That the first book refers in a general way to contemporary social evils is, of course, obvious to all readers. That the whole work refers frequently to specific events with which More was often personally acquainted, is not so well known.

Some of the more obvious examples can show how specific these references were. Hythlodaye, telling why he will not take service as an adviser to princes, asked More how the king of France would respond if advised to govern his own land well and give up foreign invasion, and More admitted that the king would not be pleased with the advice.[7] This is no general, classical attack on war but a definite reference to the invasion of Italy by Francis I in the preceding year (1515) which culminated in the victory of Marignano in September. Clearly the advice against invasion applied equally well to Henry VIII's invasions of France (1512-1514). Hythlodaye's description of the way /11/ kings are advised to get money[8] perfectly describes the recent practices of Henry VII: juggling the value of currency, feigning war and taxing for it, reviving old laws to collect new fines, establishing new regulations to sell exemption from them. Particularly, the attack on the revival of old Crown privileges points to Henry VII's collection of dues for the knighting of his dead son Arthur, which More resisted in the parliament of 1504. It was noted above that shafts directed against Francis I also struck Henry VIII: similarly criticism of Henry VII applied in part to Henry VIII. Both the French and the Utopian practice of bribing and corrupting enemy populations suggested the intrigues of Henry VIII and his minister Dacre, who sowed treason among the Scotch lords. It is reasonable to assume that every item of criticism in *Utopia* recalled to well-informed readers precise events in current history, many of which may not be easy to identify today.

More's connections with the merchants of London, with the Court, and with humanists, kept him familiar also with more remote continental affairs and even with some African, Asian, and American conditions. Reports at this time from Sir Robert Wingfield, English ambassador to the Emperor Maximilian, are rich in references to the politics of eastern Europe, the Turkish threat, and Italian conditions. The direct attack on international intrigues in the first book of *Utopia*,[9] as well as the ironic attack in the second book,[10] were unusually apropos in these two years (1515-1516) when the book was being written. International relations were peculiarly unstable. Peace had just come in 1514 after England's successful wars against France. In 1515 France invaded Italy and won an unexpected victory which sharply changed the balance of forces. The new peace following was of the most fluid character, and the diplomatic correspondence of the time shows that all cats were ready to jump in any direction at any moment.

The influence of foreign events and conditions on /12/ Utopia has hardly been mentioned by its students, though Chambers discusses the problem of the unity of Christendom against the Turk, and points out, concerning More's embassy of 1515, that "Everywhere in *Utopia* we can trace the influence of these [Flemish] foreign scholars and foreign men of affairs, as well as of the civilization of the noble Flemish cities."[11] This was probably the most important continental influence, for More did not travel much elsewhere. It is noted by J. H. Lupton, who contrasts London with the towns of Flanders.[12]

Also important among the influences on *Utopia* were ideals of city and gild life, and a popular English devotion to the common weal. It is surprising that Kautsky, a socialist, neglects these, though he pays general tribute to the liberty-loving sentiments of the English and emphasizes his belief that More, in peculiar English conditions, differed from other humanists in his concern for the people. The youthful radicalism of John Rastell, More's brother-in-law, and his ideal of the commonwealth expressed in legal theory,[13] the common weal advocated by economists like Clement Armstrong[14] — all these, mentioned below, are native parallels to *Utopia,* and express its practical content, rather than its literary form as Plato's *Republic* does.

To summarize the problem of the general character of *Utopia:* rather abstract polemics over religion and communism, divorced from the detailed events of More's experience, have obscured *Utopia's* nature as an effort at practical social reform. The obscurity has been lighted up by Chambers, Seebohm, and Kautsky more than by other writers.

The two best books on More, those by Kautsky and Chambers, may now be given a general criticism. This is none too grateful a task, for the critic's sword is very likely to develop a reverse edge when he also attempts an interpretation of More and his *Utopia.* More's experience was so rich and varied, the society in which he lived so fast /13/ changing and contradictory in nature, his book so disguised in meaning, so many-sided, constructed on so many levels of reference, that almost any foolish speculation concerning *Utopia* is likely to have a little truth in it, and almost any well-founded hypothesis is bound to be incomplete and somewhat one-sided. A few claims and excuses can be made for the present study. It does not pretend to exhaust the subject: it does not concentrate on that aspect of *Utopia* which the present writer considers central — its nature as a pamphlet written to promote humanistic, Erasmian social reform. Secondly, this writer is quite certain that he has felt little or no compulsion to dress More in his own political and religious clothing. Lastly, this study consciously employs throughout the weakest of all forms of argument — analogy. The *Utopia* being itself the best evidence of what More was thinking when he wrote it, at the same time hiding much of his thought within many levels of meaning, interpretation must proceed by probability, by hopeful comparisons.

Kautsky's study, *Thomas More and His Utopia,* is the only one which gives full attention to the book as an expression of the views of the English middle class, particularly of the London merchants. It is a brilliant work but, unfortunately, little read. Kautsky, in much of his general historical view and in his detailed analysis of *Utopia,* is sound and flexible. Occasionally, however, his generalizations are loose and his applications of them mechanical. On a number of important points new materials and more concrete analysis suggest changes of emphasis, and even reversal of his interpretation.

Most of the faulty generalizations in Kautsky's work are rooted in what this study holds to be a mistaken view of the stage in historical development which England had reached in the early sixteenth century. Kautsky maintains that "In More's time capitalism was just beginning to gain the upper hand over the industry and agriculture of Eng- /14/ land. Its domination had not lasted long enough to effect a technical revolution. . . ."[15] It will be seen in Chapter I below that this description would probably apply better to the eighteenth century, better certainly to the end of the sixteenth century than to its beginning. Capitalism was yet a long way from *dominating* English society, but Kautsky's belief that it was doing so leads him to see the central conflict of the time as that between capitalism and the workers of England,[16] rather than between feudalism and capitalism.

Perhaps, as we all tend to do, Kautsky has transferred his own dominant interest in his own time into the life of the past. Whatever the reason for it, his idea that capitalism was dominant and feudalism completely broken[17] causes him to view princely absolutism as almost identical in interests with capital,[18] the humanists as universally supporters of monarchy insofar as they had any political views,[19] the English nobility as completely subservient to the Crown,[20] the London citizens as the chief props of Tudor absolutism and the only rival of its power,[21] etc.

By claiming that the great landowners were at least temporarily helpless —as a result of the Wars of the Roses[22]— Kautsky tends, perhaps unconsciously, to consider the Tudor monarchy a great power in and of itself rather than a fulcrum for pressures, though occasionally he notes the rather feeble influence of various groups on government.[23]

Only one group is said to have had any substantial influence. "In More's time," Kautsky writes, "the citizens of London were a power for which the English kings had more respect than for the Church, the nobles, the peasants, and the country towns," the masters of London were "the actual masters of the country," and the "merchants possessed the greatest power in London."[24] When we add Kautsky's implication that More was the leading representative of the London merchants,[25] More appears almost as the uncrowned king of England.

Of course, Kautsky does not mean to imply just this. He /15/ notes that though "the middle classes could not be bribed or intimidated . . . their representatives could; while the king could have members of Parliament who displeased him executed for high treason."[26] Also, he calls the London citizens "the decisive power in the realm *next to* [italics mine] the monarchy."[27] And he does, finally, in a roundabout way, suggest that the nobility had decisive power, saying that "in More's time the English nobility and clergy were the submissive servants of the monarchy, to which they imparted an absolute power such as it then possessed in no other country of Europe."[28] Aside from questions of its accuracy in detail, this statement is a paradox lodged at the very center of our problem. A class capable of imparting absolute power cannot, in any logic, actually be feeble and servile. If the English nobility made the Crown more powerful than London, then the nobles were the ruling class, even if not a very strong one, and were as a group, in the last analysis, the masters rather than the servants of monarchy.

However wrong or right Kautsky may be, he has been alone in discussing such fundamental questions as a prelude to interpretation of *Utopia,* and the meaning of *Utopia* waits on our answer to the question of the precise character of European, especially English, society at the time the book was written. For this reason a brief general description of "late feudalism" in the stage of absolute monarchy, as it existed about the year 1515, will be given in Chapter I.

If it is held that the period of absolute monarchy has generally been, almost to its end, feudal rather than capitalist, a number of Kautsky's less sweeping generalizations also become suspect. Emphasis then shifts from merchant and humanist satisfaction with the *status quo* to emphasis upon middle class discontent with monarchy and sympathy with oppressed peasants and craftsmen. At least, this seems the proper emphasis for the "advanced" elements in the /16/ middle class, and surely, at the time he wrote *Utopia,* More expressed very advanced ideas which caused Kautsky to say: "We see how revolutionary *Utopia* was. . . ."[29]

It would be a mistake, however, to assume that Kautsky is crudely inconsistent. He is far too conscious of the actual contradictory nature of things for that, and it is difficult to suggest error in his work without ignoring some telling correction of it. Nevertheless, an attempt should be made to correct some of his interpretations — partly to call his study forcefully to the attention of students of More who may have missed it, and partly to warn them of the type of theoretical weakness they may find in it. A few examples follow.

Though Kautsky recognizes that the London citizens were in frequent opposition to the early Tudor Crown, he says that "scarcely any class in the sixteenth century regarded the monarchy as more necessary than did the merchants,"[30] and he says of capital that "order was its most important vital element."[31] Yet later he remarks that "the vital principle of capitalism is free competition . . . and therefore the abolition of caste distinctions."[32] Now it is certainly true that mercantile capitalists needed many of the freedoms which monarchial order established for them, and it is also true that the essence of later, fully developed capitalism was free competition. But to take only one side of this contradiction, then to ignore further contradictions within that side, and to draw from it the basic political views of Thomas More — he was "an opponent of every popular movement and a champion of constitutional monarchy"[33] — is doubtful logic to say the least. It will be seen below that the more merchants loved order, the more they were devoted to and parasitic upon feudalism; that the lesser nobility were more devoted to the Crown than the merchants were; and that the merchants were more jealous of their own order of monopoly within the towns than of the king's order. As for More's politics, Kautsky repeats his /17/ opinion toward the end of his book and then partially corrects it: "It is characteristic of More that he could not imagine such a community [Utopia] without a prince. It is true the latter has nothing to do except to avoid coming under suspicion of striving for absolute power."[34] That is, Utopia's prince is not a prince in the Tudor sense, or in much of any other sense. Actually, he is elected by elected representatives of the people; the people themselves nominate him; and he may be deposed legally. If this may be called a species of bourgeois prince, it is so to the point of extinction. And there is, as a matter of fact, good reason to believe that the *princeps* of Utopia is a local city official, and that that republic has no monarch at all.*

Thus, it may be argued, the theoretical trend of Kautsky's thought drives him into presumable error. Other such interpretations will be discussed in appropriate places below.

Next to Kautsky's, the most valuable modern work on More is that by R. W. Chambers.† Chambers, oddly enough, barely mentions Kautsky's book and substantially ignores everything it says, but his comments on *Utopia* are an implied refutation of Kautsky. Indeed, the two may be described as precise opposites, both in the form and content of their work. Kautsky sees More as a bourgeois, critical of rising capitalism, who could leap over an era to grasp the essentials of socialism. Chambers sees More as a bourgeois, critical of rising capitalism, who dreamed of reforming society in accord with the best elements of medieval thought and practice. Both approaches are based on substantial particles of truth, but it is the main thesis of this study that More was a bourgeois, critical of rising capitalism and especially of declining feudalism, who hoped to reform society along bourgeois-republican lines in the immediate future, and that to this aim his medieval and so- /18/ cialist ideas were subordinate. Kautsky sees the life and thought of More as contradictory in nature; Chambers sees them as a unity. The underlying social theories in Kautsky's work are clearly stated, but in Chambers' they are not. Kautsky's interest is primarily intellectual and social; Chambers' interest is mainly personal and spiritual. The one writes bald historical exposition, the other charming informative essays and episodes. Kautsky has written a social interpretation of *Utopia,* and Chambers has created a kind of symphony in which the benign character of More is the theme. The reason for these differences is, of course, the fact that life made Kautsky a socialist and Chambers a conservative but tolerant medievalist.

Since Chambers' thought has been influenced by high church and liberal-capitalist English culture, it is not surprising that he tries to reconcile what may be called liberal and authoritarian, progressive and conservative elements in More's life and thought. The reconciliations

---

* See [Ames' *Citizen Thomas More and His Utopia*], pp. 86-87.   /18/
† *Thomas More*, 1936.   /18/

made are quite plausible, for Chambers' book is scholarly and very skill-
fully written, and it is hard to resist the charm of his modesty, his
generosity to opponents, and his fine idealism.

Chambers does not recognize any conflicts among More's ideas and
attitudes, though he mentions many facts which, if made neighbors, fall
to quarreling. His purposes, however, declared and implied, demand a
harmony among the facts. What, precisely, are these purposes? His
undeclared purpose seems to be to prove that More was conservative,
medieval, in religion, politics, and economics. His declared purpose is to
depict More for non-Catholic readers "not only as a martyr . . . but also
as a great European statesman . . . [whose] farsighted outlook was
neglected amid the selfish despotisms of his age . . . [and whose] words
. . . acts and . . . sufferings were consistently, throughout life, based
upon principles which have survived him."[35] It may be noted, incidentally,
that these principles are nowhere in the book precisely described, but are
only suggested by the /19/ goodness, kindness, and tolerance which the
reader finds on each page.

Chambers sets himself a difficult task. It seems that he must prove that
More was, in all ways and times, orthodox in his Catholicism, limited by
the ideals of the past, yet spacious and prophetic in his social vision. If
Chambers had openly faced certain contradictions in his task, and had
made them a part of his hypothesis, his account of More would be at the
same time less rigid and less fragmentary and would have in it more of the
growth, flow, and struggle of real life. Erasmus said (and Chambers mentions this at the beginning of his book) that he felt incompetent to portray
Thomas More's many-sided character.

Most controversy concerning More has, however, centered on this
question of his consistency. Liberal historians have found him an unfortunate example of that perennial phenomenon—the liberal in youth
turned conservative with age—and Chambers has correctly pointed out
that this is nonsense, for More was a good thirty-eight years old when he
wrote *Utopia*. But such historians are able to point out, in their turn,
that More opposed religious coercion in *Utopia* and later, as chancellor,
not only persecuted heretics but defended such persecution in theory.
Such historians, being philosophical idealists, assume that views should
never change, regardless of changing conditions: if one is against war, he
should oppose all wars; if one is for tolerance, he should tolerate anyone
and everything. Chambers, also a philosophical idealist, also believes that
one should not change his views, and claims that More did not. It is
probable, however, that More did change his views on religious tolerance
gradually, after 1516, under the pressure of such events as the rise of
Lutheranism, the knights' and peasants' wars in Germany—with the
general decline of reformers' hopes in a period of sharpening social
crisis. Chambers seeks to show that More was neither very liberal in *Utopia*
concerning religion and politics nor big- /20/ oted and cruel in later years
when he dealt with heretics. These two purposes lead him to some rather
extraordinary evasions and confusions which merit special attention
as extreme examples of the central weakness of a valuable study.
The facts in this controversy seem clear: More did establish full toleration

of all religions in Utopia, punishing only atheists; and he did, later, not only approve but also bring about the execution of heretics. Chambers, perhaps unconsciously, has blurred and obscured these facts to the point of giving precisely the opposite *impression** — that freedom of religion did not really exist in Utopia, and that More never harmed a heretic.

That Chambers cannot successfully reconcile, in the person of More, even the best elements of feudal, capitalist, and socialist thought — and it must be admitted that More does express something of each in *Utopia* alone — should not blind us to the virtues of his work. Chambers makes some acute criticisms of those liberal historians who admire Henry VIII, and a whole generation of heartless pirate capitalists, because of their gifts to "progress" and "freedom." Certainly he was right, in part, in seeing More's social criticism as a medieval protest against a horrifying "New Order." But More was not a true feudal philosopher, such as we find today in Lin Yutang or Ghandi. The New Order he opposed was not really new but a revival, an intensification, a harsh reorganization of the Old Order — just as fascism, in our day, is a spuriously "new" organization of moribund social forces. Thus it is seen that our basic criticism of Kautsky and Chambers is the same. From opposed points of view both see the brutal aspects of rising capitalism as the object of More's critical thought. An attempt will be made in the following pages to show that More criticized decadent feudalism in the interests of the "best" aspects of rising capitalism, medieval and Renaissance. /21/

NOTES

1. Chambers, p. 128.
2. *Utopia*, p. 72. (Everyman's edition cited throughout)
3. *Utopia*, p. 108.
4. J. N. Figgis, *Studies of Political Thought from Gerson to Grotius, 1414-1625*, 1931, p. 9.
5. Reed, [*Early Tudor Drama*, 1926,] p. 207.
6. *Utopia*, p. 101.
7. *Utopia*, pp. 36-37.
8. *Utopia*, pp. 37-38.
9. *Utopia*, pp. 35-36.
10. *Utopia*, pp. 89-90.
11. Chambers, p. 120.
12. Lupton, pp. xxix-xxx.
13. *Preface to the Book of Assizes* (1513).
14. "A Treatise Concerninge the Staples and the Commodities of this Realme" (c. 1519-1535), *Tudor Economic Documents.*
15. Kautsky, p. 205.
16. Kautsky, pp. 168-69, 171.
17. Kautsky, p. 119.
18. Kautsky, p. 17.
19. Kautsky, p. 99.
20. Kautsky, pp. 115-16, 118.
21. Kautsky, p. 123.
22. Kautsky, p. 116.
23. Kautsky, pp. 120-24.
24. Kautsky, p. 121.
25. Kautsky, pp. 140, 142.
26. Kautsky, p. 124.
27. Kautsky, p. 123.

* For a full description of the confusions, see Appendix A [in *Citizen Thomas More and His Utopia*].   /21/

28. Kautsky, p. 118.
29. Kautsky, p. 242.
30. Kautsky, p. 143.
31. The same.
32. Kautsky, p. 211.
33. Kautsky, p. 206.
34. Kautsky, p. 233.
35. Chambers, p. 15.   /197/

Edward Surtz, S. J.

The wisdom of Christ, Hythloday declares toward the end of his discourse in *Utopia*, was so great that He could not be ignorant of what was best for humanity, and His goodness was so immense that He could not but ordain what was best for men. If it had not been for human pride, the Savior "would have brought all the world long ago into the laws of this weal public," the very foundation of which was communism. Needless to say, not the least of the attractive features which drew the Utopians to Christianity was the fact that Christ had been pleased to establish the common life among His followers. This common life was still in vogue among the most genuine of Christian communities, namely, the enclosures of monks and friars. Here there is more than a tinge of regret that what Christ had instituted for all should be practiced by only a few.[1]

The notion that Christ has tried to call His followers back to the communism originally instituted by God finds even stronger expression within four years or less after the publication of *Utopia* in More's letter to a monk, which appeared first in *Epistolae Aliquot Eruditorum Virorum* (1520). More writes: "God manifested great foresight when He instituted all things in common. Christ, too, manifested great foresight when He made the attempt to recall mortals again from what was private to what was common. He was fully aware, there can be no doubt, /175/ that our corrupt mortal nature does not cherish lovingly what is private without detriment to what is common." All experience verifies this last statement. Whatever a man calls his own, whether his plot of land, or his sum of money, or his family, divorces his feelings from concern with what is common. Examples which More derives from religion are the following: the emphasis on private rather than official fasts, the preference of one saint to another, the exaltation of the ceremonies of one religious order over those of another, and the glorification of monastic observances over the practices common to the whole Christian people, such as "those plebeian virtues: faith, hope, charity, fear of God, humility, and others of the same kind."[2]

Similar statements are echoed by humanists and Scholastics. In his *New Testament*, Erasmus asks why Benedictines, Augustinians, and Franciscans attribute more to a rule written by a man (Benedict, Augustine, and Francis) than Christians do to their rule, which Christ gave to all and which all have equally professed in baptism. On an even more general plane, Vives in his *Help of the Poor* insists that "all things were given to us by God, to some for the sake of the others." What liberal nature has given to be common, men maliciously make private; what she has made visible and accessible, they carry off, lock up, guard, and keep from others by doors, walls, bolts, iron, weapons, and laws. "Thus, our avarice and wickedness impose scarcity and hunger on the abundance of nature and cause poverty

"Thomas More and Communism: The Solution," *The Praise of Pleasure*. Cambridge: Harvard University Press, 1957, pp. 175-191.

1. The footnotes are printed at the end of this article — *Editor's note.*

amid the riches of God." For Alexander the Englishman in his *Destruction of Vices,* false Christians make common goods private property. This he finds especially true of so-called religious who appropriate for their own use the tithes and offerings which justly ought to be common property for distribution to the needy poor. On the testimony of experience, religious and pastors and prelates are defrauding the poor and spending such revenue on personal vices and worldly pleasure and vain pomp.[3]

The dominant attitude toward Christian communism, with the resultant stress upon what was peculiar and proper to an /176/ individual or group, was symptomatic of a general disease which was affecting the very vitals of Christendom. Instead of the pure Christianity which Christ taught in His life and in the pages of His gospel, people were living a Christian life perverted by the doctrines and authority of Aristotle or watered down by clever moralists to the low standards of contemporary life. If he could not speak of Platonic and Utopian communism and other institutions in the royal council as well as anywhere else, Hythloday feels that logically "we must among Christian people wink at the most part of all those things which Christ taught us and so straitly forbade them to be winked at that those things also which He whispered in the ears of His disciples He commanded to be proclaimed in open houses." The discrepancy between the doctrine of Christ and the conduct of Christians has been glossed by cunning preachers who practice More's advice: "that which you cannot turn to good, so . . . order it that it be not very bad." Only with the greatest reluctance do men suffer the adaptation and adjustment of their morality to the standards of Christ. In order to make the two agree in some way or other, preachers "have wrested and wried His doctrine and like a rule of lead have applied it to men's manners" (*doctrinam eius uelut regulam plumbeam accommodauerunt ad mores*). What is the result? They have succeeded in nothing, except to allow men to feel more secure in their evil-doing.[4]

The convenient accommodation of Christian morality to the low practices of the day was the object of vehement attack by persons with the welfare and reformation of the Church at heart. In the very first sermon delivered in May 1512, before the Fifth Council of the Lateran, the brilliant Egidio of Viterbo had declared that it was only right and just that men should be changed by religious observances, and not religious observances by men. Erasmus, too, almost from the time of his earliest published works, cries out against the manifest absurdity of persons who "strive to bend, not the morality of men to Christ, but Christ to the life of men." He sees a race of men reigning supreme in /177/ the world, who do not measure and regulate their religious devotion by the rule of Christ (*Christi regula*), but by their own emotional predilections. They attribute an aura of sanctity to whatever they love passionately, with the result that they flatter themselves astonishingly in regard to things which are most sinful by nature. They publish that they are wearing such and such a holy cincture. "Why? Because they want, on account of a little effort, to be taken for saints. But they have no desire to live either soberly or chastely, or to suffer injuries. Why so? Because it is too hard and too difficult."[5]

The ideological source of such unfortunate and disastrous attitudes is exposed by Gerard Lister in his notes (1515) to Erasmus' *Praise of Folly*. The lofty doctrines of Christ and the corrupt values of the world, he points out, are as compatible as fire and water. The purpose of Christ's incarnation was to pluck out depraved opinions and to implant new and unprecedented ones. Thus, Christ wanted His followers to be rich, not in worldly possessions and influence, but in the contempt of all earthly goods. He wanted His own to be powerful, not in strength of body and weapons of war, but in the contempt of death. He wanted His own, finally, to be blessed with exile, imprisonment, persecution, and death. And here Lister drives home his point: "These recent theologians of ours, however, wish to effect a union between Christ and the world, and label as Christian those things which are done by the overwhelming majority, that is to say, by the world; they admit as allowable pleasures, war, weapons, two garments, and all other worldly things, provided only they are used, as they say, with moderation."[6]

The word *moderation* is a clue to the principal complaint of the humanists. They feel that the prestige of Aristotle and the Aristotelization of theology have contributed much, although not all, to the contamination of the pure teaching of Christ and to the abasement of the high moral standards of Christ. As has been seen above, Erasmus declares that the union of Aristotle and Christ is like a mixture of fire and water. Yet Christians hardly /178/ dare to deny a single doctrine of Aristotle and go to great lengths to twist his words, even those most un-Christian, to some sort of compatibility with Christ's principles. An extremely pertinent example is the maintenance of the impossibility of a communistic Christian society — in the very face of the example of Christ and His disciples and His early Church. It is from Aristotle, not from Christ, "we have learned that the commonwealth in which all things are common cannot flourish."[7]

But Aristotle is not the only source of offense. No less to blame is human law, whether ecclesiastical or civil. In his letter to Lupset, Budé trenchantly expresses the clash between the law of church and state and the law of God and Christ as follows: "in the decrees of the canonists, the divine law differs as much from the human; and, in our civil laws and royal enactments, true equity differs as much from law; as the principles laid down by Christ . . . and the usages of His disciples, differ from the decrees and enactments of those who think the *summum bonum* and perfection of happiness to lie in the money-bags of a Croesus or a Midas." In his famous Adage 3001 (*Sweet Is War to the Uninitiated*), Erasmus concentrates on the civil, or Roman, law. On account of the civil law's appearance of justice, men twist and turn and stretch the teachings of the gospel to the utmost allowable limits in order to make it agree with the civil law. The latter permits the repulsion of force with force and the prosecution of every right by every individual; it approves of big business; it legalizes usury, provided the latter is moderate; it exalts war as a glorious thing, provided it is just. And what is a just war? A just war is defined by the civil law to be one declared by the prince, however puerile or stupid. Christ and His sacred writings receive little or no hearing. Erasmus rises to an indignant grandeur as he continues:

To sum it all up, the whole doctrine of Christ is so contaminated by the writings of pagan dialecticians, sophists, mathematicians, orators, poets, philosophers, and lawyers that the greatest part of one's life is consumed before one has time for the examination of the Sacred /179/ Books. When at length you come to them, you are bound to approach them tainted with so many worldly opinions that either you are repulsed altogether by the principles of Christ or you twist them to suit the views of those pagan authors. And this state of affairs is so far from being subjected to censure that to speak of the writings of Christ is a crime for anyone except the man who has stuffed himself, as they say, even to the ears with Aristotelian, or rather sophistical, nonsense — as if the teaching of Christ were such that it could not be as common as possible to all men, or that it could in any way agree with the wisdom of pagan philosophers.[8]

As one studies all these views of the humanists, one cannot escape the conviction that there is an underlying consistency in the attitude toward Christian communism in Hythloday's views as propounded in *Utopia*, in More's mind as revealed in his letter to a monk, and in the writings of such humanists as Budé, Lister, and Erasmus. In its most simple terms, this common attitude may be expressed as follows. God originally intended communism to be the social system best suited for human beings. Fallen man, however, divided up possessions hitherto held in common, and introduced the right of private property. When He came upon earth, Christ tried to recall at least His followers to the original arrangement made by God. This attempt is evident from His own practice and that of His apostles and disciples, as well as that of the early church in Jerusalem. Except for the triumph of the common life in certain select companies (the so-called religious orders), Christ's endeavors had but little success. His program of reform was a failure, not because He Himself was deficient in any respect, but because He required the free coöperation of His creatures. Man's wickedness (in the form of pride and avarice and other monsters, according to Hythloday) led him to frustrate Christ's plan for his happiness by way of the common life. Christians were aided in this thwarting of Christ's wise provision by the authority of Aristotle and the ingenuity of clever preachers who trimmed Christ's doctrine to suit the evil times.[9]

As far as the introduction of communism in Christian nations and contemporary conditions is concerned, it is most important /180/ to note, there is nothing here but wishful thinking. There is not a single definite statement to the effect that England, or France, or Germany should become communistic. The humanistic reformers apparently do not entertain any immediate practical hope on this score. They are content to contemplate the ideal commonwealth in all the glory of its common life, and then to come dazzled down to earth again to suggest such measures as are suggested by Hythloday himself and are suited to human weakness: the restoration of the commons, the rebuilding of farms and villages, the abolition of monopoly, the limitation of acreage legally possessed, the prohibition of the sale of offices, etc. This assertion does not overlook

Hythloday's conviction that what Christian nations need is not the temporary medicine of parliamentary statutes but the perfect cure of the common life. Yet even he proposes the communistic state as a general ideal, without urging particular countries to adopt communism as a program of practical and immediate reform. In his heart he realizes that, given the general run of Christians, his commonwealth, like the republic of Plato, will never exist in the Christian West.[10]

Does this compromise mean that humanists like More are false to their ideal? By no means. Even Christ had extended His invitation to communal poverty only to the man who ardently desired to be perfect (Matt. xix. 21). The common life for all Christians remained the ideal for the humanists, but they realized that, in order to have perfect communism, one must have perfect Christians — or, at least, Christians as perfect as those of the early church in Jerusalem who sold their possessions for distribution of the proceeds to the poor by the apostles. As long as the mass of Christians is imperfect, even though striving after perfection, private property is best, with a view to the maintenance of peace and order against those merely nominal Christians who would abuse the privileges of communism. In the midst of an imperfect world, Christ gave a blessing to the poor *in spirit* (Matt. v. 3) as well as to the heroes who chose actual poverty for His sake. The important lesson of *Utopia,* too, is that every /181/ person in England and all Europe must acquire the *spirit* of common life. This spirit manifests itself above all in a detachment of heart from wealth and rank and in a passionate attachment to the cause of justice and the poor.

But is not this critical view of More's attitude toward communism really noncommittal? Is More's real attitude shown in the program of communism espoused by Hythloday *or* in the objections to communism put in his own mouth by More? More's personal attitude is manifested absolutely and unconditionally in neither, but in both. "It all depends," More himself would say. His ideal will always remain that of a common Christian life for a whole Christian nation, but the realization of this ideal depends upon the character of its citizens, who must be as perfect in their Christianity — or as eager in their pursuit of Christian perfection — as the Utopians are in their rationality. There is basically nothing heretical, dangerous, or even offensive to pious ears (*piis auribus offensivum*) in the enunciation of this proposition. The imperfection, alas, inevitably connected with man's existence, even with his spiritual life, makes the condition attached to the ideal almost impossible of fulfillment. On the other hand, if Christians are to be taken as they actually exist, the objections offered to Hythloday's opinion by More in his own person are valid. Hythloday represents More's ideal views; he himself voices his practical judgments in his own person. In a word, if he regards communism abstractly or academically (according to the *philosophia scholastica*), More favors communism. If he looks at it in concrete circumstances as a practical statesman who knows what is in man (according to the *philosophia ciuilior*), he defends private property.[11]

More's objections to communism are fundamentally the Aristotelian objections. First, the promised abundance of all goods will not materialize

since every man will try to get out of work. He will shun labor because the prospect of personal gain is not present to spur him on and because the foolish confidence he has that other citizens will do the necessary work will make him lazy. /182/ Secondly, when consequent poverty begins to afflict the people and when no man can defend according to the law the common property given for his personal use, the result will be continual slaughter and revolt, with the stronger taking over the portion of the weaker. Hythloday the idealist, it will be noted, does not even attempt to answer these arguments, because they are unanswerable if one takes human nature as it actually exists. His only reply is indirectly to appeal to the principle that no line of argumentation is valid against an actual fact (*contra factum non valet illatio*). What is Hythloday's *fact*? Nothing else than the island of Utopia. Because of communism, "you never saw people well ordered but only there." But Utopia exists only in More's brain; so, too, the communistic Christian commonwealth exists only as an ideal in his mind and heart.[12]

But More does not surrender the thought of the realization of his communistic ideal without a shot. Toward the very end of *Utopia*, he speaks of many customs and laws of the island as being extremely absurd institutions, especially "the community of their life and living without any occupying of money" (*uita . . . uictuque communi, sine ullo pecuniae commercio*). What is the result of the existence of such communism in a nation? By this one feature, "all nobility, magnificence, worship, honor, and majesty . . . utterly be overthrown and destroyed" (*qua una re funditus euertitur omnis nobilitas, magnificentia, splendor, maiestas*). Yet nobility, magnificence, splendor, and majesty are the true embellishments and ornaments of a commonwealth in the opinion of the populace (*ut publica est opinio*). This last expression, used as it is parenthetically, embodies the most skilled and subtle irony: it is a stroke worthy of a master of rhetoric. For the whole purpose of *Utopia* has been to prove that these are *not* the qualities which should distinguish a commonwealth. The success of a commonwealth is to be measured by the well-being and happiness of its people, not by external fame and glory. The ideal commonwealth is much like that of the Polylerites: "their life is commodious rather than gallant [*splendide*] and /183/ may better be called happy or lucky than notable or famous [*nobiles aut clari*], for they be not known as much as by name, I suppose, saving only to their next neighbors and borderers." It is the mad striving for nobility and majesty, magnificence and splendor, which is bringing Christian princes and peoples to their downfall and which is causing the poor and needy to suffer unutterable hardships. If suffering and ruin are the price of glory, farewell magnificence, welcome common life![13]

But the common life must not be purchased at any price or any cost. Injustice must not be committed, for the right of private property, even if based on human law, is just insofar as it proceeds from the civil power with God-given authority. Violence must be eschewed, for the common life as lived by unwilling members is intolerable. Such reasons as these show why the doctrines of the Anabaptists "that there ought to be no rulers at all in Christendom, neither spiritual nor temporal, and that no man should have anything proper of his own, but that all lands and all goods ought by God's law to be all men's in common" savor of heresy.[14]

In his description of the errors of the Anabaptists, More links together their concept of Christian freedom and their espousal of communism. By the year that More published his work against Luther (1523), the communistic experiments of Muenzer, Pfeiffer, Rothmann, and John of Leyden had not occurred. But the concept of faith as the supreme and only law for Christians, with a resultant depreciation or denial of all human laws, had been emphasized almost from the earliest days of the Reformation. According to the exegesis of the innovators, the "freedom wherewith Christ has made us free" (Gal. iv. 31, cf. Gal. ii. 4, v. 13; 2 Cor. iii. 17; Jas. ii. 12, etc.) lay in immunity from every bond of every law, not merely in liberation from the slavery of sin (John viii. 31 sqq., Rom. vi. 17 sqq.), from the state of servile fear (Luke i. 74), or from the yoke of the extremely heavy ceremonial and judicial law of Moses (Acts xv. 10, Gal. iv. 21-31). It was the law of faith in the gospel alone which could bind the disciples /184/ of Christ. It is in his discussion of the emancipation of the Christian from human law in his attack on Luther that More in passing gives his views on private property and communism.[15]

More labels as manifestly absurd the contention of Luther in *The Babylonian Captivity of the Church* (1520) that good and prudent magistrates would administer the government much better under the guidance of nature than by the agency of laws. The reason given by More against this view is that a good magistrate is not more just in pronouncing judgment (where the chances of corruption are usually numerous) than in passing a law. In fact, More goes so far as to claim that judgment is scarcely ever rendered justly unless it is rendered in dependence on, and in agreement with, an existent law. This holds true even for private property. "[N]either the law of the gospel apportions possessions, nor reason by itself alone prescribes the ways of distinguishing one's property, unless agreement [*consensus*] is added to reason." The theoretical basis for this statement, of course, is the Scholastic doctrine, with Scotistic rather than Thomistic overtones. According to Scotus, possessions are justly labeled as private, not according to the adjudication of the natural law, but according to the dictates of reason: not reason by itself, but reason as supplemented — or implemented, to use contemporary terminology — by human law. Typically Scotistic, too, is the concept of agreement (*consensus*). For just as individuals and families agree to surrender some of their powers to a king or democratic government, so reason persuades them to a partition of lands and goods for the preservation of peace and order. This agreement or arrangement finds expression in human positive law. Divine positive law, of course, does not assign property to individuals or particular groups (except in the case of the apportionment of the Holy Land to the Hebrews), since there is no trace of such divine legislation by God in the Old Testament or by Christ in the New. This is the meaning of More's clause that "the law of the gospel does not apportion possessions."[16] /185/

To sum up briefly, More's position is that neither the natural law nor the divine positive law (say, the gospel of Christ) is the basis of private property. But human reason sees readily that private property, and not common possession, is the system best adapted to man's nature. Men therefore divide up the goods of the world according to an agreement. But what is this agreement? Nothing but a human law. More writes: "This agreement [*consensus*] is, in the common form of mutual negotiation, a public one: and this agreement, whether reached by custom or expressed in words, is a public law." If Luther does away with laws and gives the magistrates a free rein, one of two things will happen: (1) they will issue no command or prohibition, and then magistrates will be useless, or (2) they will rule according to their own natural impulses and carry out every arbitrary whim, and then the populace will not enjoy greater freedom but suffer even worse slavery. This is what will happen if "one must obey, not certain and stated laws, but wills which are uncertain and changing from day to day."[17]

Luther congratulates himself, says More, on having modified this foolish opinion in which he wishes to abolish all human laws. At the Diet of Worms (1521), the reformer answered that the law of the gospel will be alone sufficient and human laws useless at last (1) if magistrates were good and (2) if the genuine faith were preached. More continues: Luther maintains this view "as if even the best magistrates could bring about that the whole Christian people would wish to live in common, or that the wicked would refuse to steal, or [as if] any preaching of the faith could effect that no persons would ever be bad." To prove that the human law which alone is the basis for the right of property is just and obligatory upon Christians, More argues as follows:

> The law of the gospel which forbids theft is just and obliges Christians. But the human laws which punish theft and safeguard private property merely carry out the law of the gospel in regard to theft. Therefore these human laws are just and oblige Christians. /186/

In fact, the basic assumption of the argument is that the human laws which define just possession and unjust theft are the implementation of the law of the gospel, so that if they were abolished, the law of the gospel would mean nothing since no one would know what was possessed justly or taken unjustly. All this is contained in More's few words: "If the law of the gospel does not permit theft, certainly the human law which punishes theft is not useless, and the human law which alone distinguishes private possessions [*lex humana quae sola rerum proprietatem diuidit*] is obligatory upon Christians, since with the abolition of the latter law theft could not even exist." Telltale is the modifier "alone" (*sola*), for it betrays the Scotistic cast of More's mind in regard to private property. Not the natural law, but positive human enactments, are the only source of private property.

More then declares that it will do Luther no good to take refuge in the advocacy of communism in order to establish the uselessness of human laws: "[I]f he [Luther] maintains that it would be more advantageous for us to lack the law from which the private possession of goods is born and to live in a certain community of nature [*in communitate quadam naturali*], thus eliminating the object of theft, it would in no way help his cause, even if one conceded him that point; for even if people could live in common with fewer laws by far, nevertheless they could not live without any laws at all."

As examples of necessary laws in a communistic commonwealth, More instances the laws regulating labor and the laws punishing crimes, which, after all, would be rife even in that kind of life. He concludes: "Now if, in spite of the most genuine preaching of the faith (even according to the way in which the apostles kept preaching it most authentically) and in spite of the elevation of the very best magistrates everywhere to positions of authority over the Christian people, private property could stay and many people remain unjust, it is undeniable that human law is obligatory for Christians lest one man should snatch what the law has apportioned to another, and that it is not useless /187/ insofar as it punishes the offender if anyone should commit theft." The meaning of this rather obscurely phrased sentence is clear: human laws, say, on property and theft, are useful and obligatory on Christians as long as one or both of the following conditions are present: as long as the right of private property is just or/ and as long as some people are wicked. The latter, of course, will exist whether communism or private property prevails in a commonwealth.

This single page from his work against Luther gives the admirers of More's *Utopia* a much clearer picture of his real views on communism. The passage from *A Dialogue of Comfort against Tribulation* which is usually cited as presenting More's opinion is far less informative. It begins as follows: "[M]en of substance must there needs be; for else shall you have more beggars, pardie, than there be, and no man left able to relieve another." It is immediately evident from this sentence that More is dealing, not with the broad philosophical foundations of communism and property as he did in *Utopia* and in his answer to Luther, but with a particular scheme of some Protestants to "share the wealth." The plan plainly envisaged a general census of the money and land in the nation and then a fair and equal division of both among all the citizens. Practical More, of course, considers such a scheme absurd: "For this think I in my mind a very sure conclusion, that if all the money that is in this country, were tomorrow next brought together out of every man's hand, and laid all upon one heap, and then divided out unto every man alike, it would be on the morrow after worse than it was the day before. For I suppose when it were all equally thus divided among all, the best should be left little better than a beggar almost is now; and yet he that was a beggar before, all that he shall be the richer for that he should thereby receive, shall not make him much above a beggar still. . . ."[18]

In these sentences More points out the manifest unreasonableness and infeasibility of this particular plan, not of communism in general. The words prove, not that More is in favor of indi- /188/ vidual proprietary dominion, but that under these special circumstances it constitutes for him the lesser evil. What follows in the *Dialogue* is as true in communistic Utopia as in private-propertied England, because it merely advocates a division of labor. In Utopia, the one who provides a livelihood for the many is the government or the community as a whole.

Men cannot, you wot well, live here in the world, but if some one man provide a mean of living for some other many. Every man cannot have a ship of his own, nor every man be a merchant without a stock: and these things, you wot well, must needs be had; nor every man cannot have a plough by himself. And who might live by a tailor's craft, if no man were able to put a gown to make? Who by masonry? Or, who could live a carpenter, if no man were able to build neither church, nor house? Who should be makers of any manner of cloth, if there lacked men of substance to set sundry sorts a work?

All these trades have been more than adequately organized and provided for in Utopia. Consequently, what More is here disclaiming and repudiating is not the vision of a perfect commonwealth which can always exist as an ideal to be contemplated, but petty schemes for sharing the wealth. Rather than adopt any of these harebrained reforms, it is far better to continue the present system in which "surely the rich man's substance is the wellspring of the poor man's living." As long as this latter remains true, "[s]ome man that hath but two ducats in his house, were better forbear them both and leave himself not a farthing, but utterly lose all his own, than that some rich man, by whom he is weekly set a work should of his money lose the one half: for then were himself like to lack work."

It is not fair to argue, as some have done, from these sentences in the *Dialogue of Comfort* that More had no concept of anything like the communistic state of today, in which the government owns the agents of production and distributes the products of industry with a certain attempt at equality. He may have had specifically no idea of the dictatorship of the proletariat in a totalitarian state, but the very existence of the *Utopia* refutes the view that he had no picture of a communistic state in which /189/ democratic forms of election and deliberation play the major role. In the *Dialogue of Comfort*, More is writing as a statesman who is scanning closely the contemporary economic setup. His final decision is that for the present a continuation of the existing economic and social organization is best. Consequently he advises strongly against the equal distribution of all the wealth among all the citizens as absolutely ruinous. As for the Utopian system of government, men are so far from being willing or perfect enough even to discuss it that More does not hint at it even as a possibility. He has no intention of casting pearls before swine. The most that can be gathered from the *Dialogue* is that More as a statesman finds the retention of private property and private enterprise the best and the most reasonable policy under contemporary circumstances. But he would undoubtedly agree that, if human nature has remained the same through the ages, Utopian communism will always remain mainly an ideal, and private property the most practical system for the preservation of peace and order.

In his heart, More realizes that his Utopian commonwealth, like the republic of Plato, will never exist in the Christian West, unless the perfect sons of the perfect God are born to dwell therein. The ideal Christian Utopia must wait until men become ideal Christians, perhaps only in "the holy city, New Jerusalem, coming down out of heaven from God" (Apoc. xxi. 2).

By way of afterthought and conclusion, it might be useful to add that Hythloday's description and defense of the Utopian common life, although not a declamation in the strict sense of the term, partakes of the nature and properties of the genre.[19] More viewed the *Utopia* as a literary achievement, not primarily as a serious document which outlined impartially the arguments for and against communism. Here are found the exaggeration of the advantages and the minimization of the disadvantages of communism which are essentially characteristic of the declamation. Here are discovered the artful tricks which aim to provide the reader with manifold and rich pleasure. A serious purpose, as /190/ has been seen, is far from absent, but it is directed much more to the denunciation of contemporary abuses and to the depiction of a reasonable and just commonwealth than to the aggressive advocation of communism as a practical solution and plan. If More, like Erasmus, had been attacked for heterodox and radical opinions, he would have answered as his friend had done, namely, that it was not the truth of the matter (that is, the rightness and justice of communism) which was to be regarded, but the literary powers of the author. He would be little more prepared to defend seriously the adoption of a communism of property than that of a communism of women, although just as he had espoused the one in an idealistic way in his *Utopia,* so he had upheld the other in a youthful dialogue.[20] Ideas which one treated idealistically in a literary piece could be retracted and damned in practical life. The important thing was the lesson to be learned, since every true work in the Renaissance was to combine the useful with the delightful, the profitable with the pleasurable. The lesson for Christians to take from the Utopian common life was twofold: poverty in spirit, namely, the blessedness of the first beatitude (Matt. v. 3), and brotherly love, which was to be like that of the primitive Church, especially readiness to share one's goods with the poor (Acts ii. 44-45). /191/

NOTES

1. *Utopia,* pp. 269, 305-306. (Lupton edition cited throughout)
2. *Correspondence* [*The Correspondence of Sir Thomas More,* ed. E. F. Rogers (Princeton, 1947)], pp. 195-196.
3. Alexander Anglus, *Destructorium Viciorum,* pars VI, cap. xli (no pagination); Erasmus, "Paracelsis," *Novum Instrumentum,* sig. aaa 6r; Vives, "De Subventione Pauperum," *Opera,* IV, 450-451.
4. *Utopia,* pp. 100-102. In his letter to Dorp written at this time, More again refers to the leaden or Lesbian rule *(Correspondence,* p. 43). For a current explanation of the expression, see Erasmus, *Adagia,* No. 493 *(Lesbia regula),* col. 243 (cf. Adage 1436, col. 629). See also Budé, *Annotationes,* p. 2, for reference to, and explanation of, "Lesbia structura" with employment of "plumbea norma." Read the section "Of hym that dare not vtter the trouth for fere of displeasour or punysshement," in Barclay's *Ship of Fools,* II, 231 sqq.
5. Egidio of Viterbo, "Oratio Prima Synodi Lateranensis," Mansi, *Concilia,* XXXII, 669; Erasmus, "Enchiridion," *Opera,* V,   /228/   40; *Adagia,* No. 3616 *(Quod* volumus sanctum est), col. 1226. See other pertinent observations by Erasmus, "Ratio Verae Theologiae," *Opera,* V, 114, and "Explanatio Symboli," *ibid.,* V, 1136. The cincture in honor of St. Thomas Aquinas was blessed with a prayer which asked God for the gift of chastity for the wearer *(Rituale Romanum* [Mechliniae, 1926], p. 705).
6. "Moria," *Opera,* IV, 493, note.
7. *Adagia,* No. 3001 *(Dulce bellum inexpertis),* col. 1071.
8. Budé to Lupset, *Utopia,* pp. lxxxiv-lxxxv; Erasmus, *Adagia,* No. 3001 *(Dulce bellum inexpertis),* cols. 1071-1072.
9. *Utopia,* p. 306.
10. *Utopia,* pp. 57-58, 107-109.

11. *Utopia,* pp. 97-100. For analogous views, see T. E. Bridgett, *Life and Writings of Sir Thomas More,* 2nd ed. (London, 1892), p. 103; C. Hollis,. *More* [Milwaukee, 1934], pp. 71-73; M. Carmichael, "Utopia: Its Doctrine on the Common Life," *Dublin Review,* CXCI (1932), 186. Carmichael remarks: "If he [More] could write, as he has done, in praise [of the common life], in commendation, with convincing persuasiveness, and yet not believe—then the *Utopia* is an unprofitable and dangerous extravaganza" *(loc, cit.).* The simple position that More expresses his personal and real objections to compulsory state communism in *Utopia* is defended tenaciously by W. E. Campbell, *More's Utopia and His Social Teaching* (London, 1930), e.g., pp. 28-29, 140 sqq.

12. *Utopia,* pp. 109-111.

13. *Utopia,* pp. 65, 308.

14. "Confutation of Tyndale," *Works,* p. 656.

15. *Gulielmi Rossei . . . Opus . . . quo Retegit ac Refellit Insanas Lutheri Calumnias: Quibus . . . Regem Henricum . . . Scurra Turpissime Insectatur.* The work will be noted here as *In Lutherum.*

16. "In Lutherum," *Opera,* fol. 80v. On *consensus,* see C. R. S. Harris, *Duns Scotus* (Oxford, 1927), II, 346-349.

17. "In Lutherum," *Opera,* fo. 80v. All the following references to Luther in the text are to this work and page.

18. This and following references are to *A Dialogue of Comfort against Tribulation,* (London, n.d.), p. 184.

19. See above, Chapter II *ad init.*

20. Erasmus, *Opus Epistolarum Des.·Erasmi Roterodami,* eds. P. S. Allen *et. al.* (Oxford, 1906-1947), IV, 21.   /229/

David M. Bevington

Students of *Utopia* are divided in their interpretation of Thomas More's political and economic opinions. Is More himself for or against common ownership of property? Writers on the question have tended to fall into two clearly defined camps, according to mankind's innate tendency to be born into this world as "either a little Liberal, Or else a little Conservative," and the polemical conflict between the factions has assumed in the context of our uneasy modern world the proportions of ideological warfare. The revered name of Thomas More has been invoked in support of the radical socialist states of the Soviet world empire, as well as in support of the anti-Communist position of the Papacy. Both interpretations purport to be founded on a critical reading of *Utopia*.

One literary reason why *Utopia* has lent itself to such divergence of opinion is its basic genre: the dialogue. More's island community is essentially the focal point for an extended discussion on government and society between various speakers or *personae*, each a character created by the author and having his individual point of view: Peter Giles, Hythloday, and the *persona* More who may or may not represent the views of Thomas More the writer. Giles's part in the discussion is minor, but Hythloday and *persona* More present two fundamental sides to the question. Hythloday's platform is the common ownership of property, and he refuses to concede the feasibility of gradual reform in a monarchical society. The *persona* More is often forthrightly opposed to the doctrine of common ownership, and argues instead for a policy of compromise and slow change within the limitations of practical politics. Their dialogue concludes in apparent lack of reconciliation of these opposing points of view. Accordingly, the critic can choose his hero. If Thomas More speaks directly for himself through the name of More, as he does in his later dialogues against Tyndale, then Hythloday is a dangerous public enemy like Tyndale whose dogmas are explicated only to be exploded.[1] If on the other hand /496/ Thomas More uses his own name merely as a protective device in order to propound through Hythloday an essentially subversive political philosophy, then the *persona* More may be viewed as a dupe or stooge, setting up straw men to be demolished in orderly succession by the invincible progressive.[2]

"The Dialogue in *Utopia*: Two Sides to the Question," *Studies in Philology*, LVIII (July 1961), 496-509.

[1] W. E. Campbell, *More's Utopia and His Social Teaching* (London, 1930). Campbell argues further that More himself considered *Utopia* to /496/ be a minor work, a *jeu d'esprit* describing an impossible dream world, which he wrote in Latin so as not to arouse the vulgar throng who might not understand. See also H. W. Donner, *Introduction to Utopia* (London, 1945). /497/

[2] The champion of the socialist interpretation, Karl Kautsky, is certain that the opinions of Thomas More are entirely in accord with those of Hythloday. In Kautsky's view *persona* More continually shifts his argument, concedes major points, and is finally worsted in every aspect. His objections to communal property-sharing are the conventional ones—lack of incentive and lack of authority—and only set the stage for Hythloday's demonstration of the manner in which such difficulties are solved in the communal state. The fact that the real Thomas More wished to apply the socialist remedy to his own society is evidenced by his role as member of and spokesman for the rising middle class, in revolt against aristocracy and feudalism. *Thomas More and His Utopia*, trans. H. J. Stenning (New York, 1927). See also Russell Ames, *Citizen Thomas More and His Utopia* (Princeton, 1949). /497/

Between the cry of voices from both sides, the middle position of regarding *Utopia* as the impartial presentation of two points of view, as a dialogue of the mind with itself, has received less attention than it deserves.[3] The moderate stand is an unglamorous one. It does not have the ineluctable force of an idea carried to its logical absolute. Nevertheless the moderate position has much to commend itself in the writings of the eminently fairminded and /497/ humorously wise Thomas More. Our present purpose is to suggest the critical basis for supposing that Hythloday and *persona* More represent the two polarities of More's own mind, by an analysis of *Utopia* in terms of its genre and its historical perspective.

As a literary technique, the dialogue is often used for purposes of refutation, for demonstrating the patent superiority of one idea over another. In this method the creator of the dialogue possesses the enviable advantage of being able to speak on behalf of his opponent, and to order his arguments in a fashion best suited to his own case. To such a type More's diatribes against Tyndale unquestionably belong.[4] Abstractly considered, however, literary dialogue would seem to lend itself equally well to a rendering of two balanced sides of a question. Such dialogue partakes of the nature of the drama: its author can create characters who speak as representatives of the many divisions of humanity. In analyzing a dramatic work we guard ourselves against identifying its author with any one of the characters, however much we may want to believe that some character summarizes our view of the author's mind. In this connection it is worth noting the kinds of early sixteenth-century drama with which More was most likely to be familiar: e.g., *Fulgens and Lucrece* (printed by John Rastell, More's brother-in-law), and a little later the interludes of John Heywood (More's nephew by marriage).[5] Nearly all of these interludes are characterized primarily by the element of rhetorical debate rather than dramatic action, and often present several sides of a question without preference for one side over the others. For example, Heywood's *Play of the Weather* reconciles all of Jove's petitioners with complete impartiality.

A balanced, two-sided dialogue is also analogous to the proceedings of a court trial, suggesting a parallel with the renowned impartiality of More's own judicial career. He served both as /498/ lawyer and judge on many

---

[3] Only recently have critics become interested in following Sir James Mackintosh's suggestion, that More regarded various aspects of his *Utopia* "with almost every possible degree of approbation and shade of assent." Quoted in J. H. Lupton, ed. *The Utopia of Sir Thomas More* (Oxford, 1895), p. xli. Lupton too is of the opinion that criticism has often attempted "to crystallize what More purposely left in a state of solution" (p. xli). The moderate Catholic point of view has recently been presented with admirable clarity by Edward L. Surtz, S. J., *The Praise of Pleasure: Philosophy, Education, and Communism in More's Utopia* (Cambridge, Mass., 1957), who declares that "More's personal attitude is manifested absolutely and unconditionally in neither [speaker More or Hythloday], but in both" (p. 182). See also Surtz, "Thomas More and Communism," *PMLA*, LXIV (1949), 549-64; R. J. Schoeck, "More, Plutarch, and King Agis: Spartan History and the Meaning of *Utopia*," *PQ*, XXXV (1956), 366-75; and Fritz Caspari, *Humanism and the Social Order in Tudor England* (Chicago, 1954), pp. 50-75.   /497/

[4] It is important to note that More's polemical dialogues tend to fall late in his career. The Reformation was to call forth in More the zealous defender of the Faith; in 1515-16 the atmosphere was one of less urgency, in politics as well as religion. When More wrote *Utopia* the time was not yet too late for dispassionate inquiry.   /498/

[5] A consideration of much non-dramatic debate in the fifteenth and early sixteenth centuries (e.g., Lydgate) leads to the impression that no firmly fixed line can be drawn between dramatic and non-dramatic debate. Some of Heywood's interludes, such as the *Play of Love*, are little more than forensic exercises presented between courses of a banquet.   /498/

occasions, and is known to have refused as a lawyer cases that he considered not worth a day in court. His overpowering sense of fairness inevitably found its way into his writings. Except for the occasions when he was refuting what he viewed as a palpable and gross public danger to society — such as a Tyndale or a Luther — More as a person was temperamentally inclined to grant any worthy cause a hearing and to arrive at the truth of the matter by the legal process of approaching every issue from two opposing viewpoints. As lawyer, More learned to argue for a case; as magistrate, he learned to receive conflicting arguments and to weigh them with justice.

More was capable, then, both of polemical dialogue and of a dialogue of genuine debate wherein real issues are to be decided. Which sort did he choose to employ in *Utopia*? An analysis of the literary method of this dialogue suggests that he viewed with detachment and fairness the presentation of both sides. The dialogue in Book I of *Utopia* contains a good deal more agreement than is generally supposed or recognized. Furthermore, the discussion moves in the direction of agreement. Amicable debate always is, or should be, a process of coming together, of discarding irrelevancies, of untangling those misunderstandings which are the artificial product of imperfect communication, of determining a basis of agreement in order to narrow the dispute to its elemental refinement of difference. The proponents concede points when convinced, until they have arrived at the distillation of their respective stands. Hythloday and *persona* More follow this generalized pattern, with the result that by the time they have discovered their ultimate positions they have left behind them a vast area of consent. They agree particularly with respect to their analysis of the historical facts: the condition of European society and government in the years of the early sixteenth century.

It is actually Peter Giles who begins the central discussion of Book I by posing the first major question, and accordingly it is important to account for More's literary purpose in introducing this third person to the conversation:

> Then Peter, much marvelling at the man: Surely, Master Raphael, quoth he, I wonder greatly why you get you not into some king's court.[6] /499/

Giles is indeed something of an innocent, for he supplements his query with two reasons for joining a king's court which are immediately demolished: (1) an official position in the government will enable a man to assist all his friends and kinsmen, and (2) public power will give a man an opportunity to bring himself "in a very good case," that is, to line his own pocket. These considerations are raised only to be answered, and Hythloday wastes little time or effort in doing so. Concerning favoritism and personal aggrandizement there could be no dispute, nor would it have

---

[6] Page 19. All quotations and page references are from the Everyman Edition of *Utopia*, rev. ed. (London and New York, 1951), as the most readily available edition of the Ralph Robinson translation. The Latin text has been consulted in Lupton's edition of *Utopia*. /499/

been appropriate for either of the two main contenders to have proposed such possibilities. We may see here the usefulness of having a third person present at a dialogue essentially between two persons. Giles's function is to pose the question and to state the superficial arguments that would be unsuited to either of his companions. Thereafter his part in the discussion dwindles to nothing. Throughout the rest of Book I Hythloday continually addresses "Master More" with only one mention of Giles (p. 21), and Peter's only speech in all this time is another touch of simpleheaded complacency: "Surely, quoth Master Peter, it shall be hard for you to make me believe that there is better order in that new land than is here in these countries that we know" (p. 52).[7]

It is doubtful that More wished deliberately to portray his good friend Giles as an intellectual lightweight. Clearly, More is consciously distinguishing between the *persona* and the actual man. Giles speaks in such conventional terms for dramatic reasons only. His function is an important one, for it is in the discrediting of Giles's suggestions of personal advantage and favoritism that Hythloday and *persona* More come to their first agreement. In fact, the very earliest utterance of *persona* More in the discussion is in support of Hythloday's deft answers to Giles:

> Well, I perceive plainly, friend Raphael, quoth I, that you be desirous neither of riches nor of power; and truly I have in no less reverence and estimation a man of your mind than any of them all that be so high in power and authority. (pp. 19-20)

Whenever we find an agreement between the two principals, we are surely safe in assuming the author's concurrence. In the /500/ analogy of the courtroom, it is as though plaintiff and defendant have stipulated concerning some fact that is plainly incontrovertible. Thus, at the beginning of his trial on the merits and limitations of counselling a king, More rejects out of hand the consideration of private gain. In fact, the case is put far more strongly: Hythloday and *persona* More agree that court service, if it is to be undertaken, must prove a real personal sacrifice on the part of the philosopher. The greatest loss will be liberty, insists Hythloday: "Now I live at liberty after mine own mind and pleasure, which I think very few of these great states and peers of realms can say" (p. 19). And *persona* More readily concedes that public office will be "somewhat to your own pain and hindrance" (p. 20). The only point of contention between them is whether or not the result would be worth the self-sacrifice; that is, whether court service would prove to be a public benefit. Both speakers agree that personal comfort must never stand in the way of "the profit of the weal-public," but they differ as to whether the philosopher can be of use at all, no matter what the individual cost.

The chief question is: if the philosopher offers counsel, will the king take heed and will he translate good advice into wise policy? Which way does monarchy tend, to tyranny or to benevolence? Hythloday and *persona*

---

[7] In answer to Kautsky, who contends that *persona* More is only posing the conventional arguments (see note 2, above), it might be argued that Peter Giles is the real dupe or stooge, not either of the chief contenders. /500/

More take sides from the start. For Hythloday, the record is almost entirely on the side of tyranny. To *persona* More, monarchy is at least a potential source of good, although he freely recognizes even at the beginning of the discussion the equal power for evil: "For from the prince, as from a perpetual well-spring, cometh among the people the flood of all that is good *or evil* (p. 20; italics mine). *Persona* More's position is not naive, like that of Giles. His statement is cautious but hopeful. Hythloday also speaks with qualifications about "the most part of all princes" (p. 20). In neither case is monarchy absolutely good or absolutely bad. Once again we find the spokesmen not so far apart as it first seemed. They agree that monarchy exists in various degrees of quality. The question hereupon becomes, for the philosopher who is to make the personal decision whether or not to offer counsel, what are the specific historical conditions at the time and place of his choice?[8] In Thomas More's case, this meant England under the reign of Henry VIII. /501/

Unquestionably an ambiguity existed in More's mind concerning the nature of the reigning monarch. Henry VIII was a young king of many virtues and liabilities. To More's sorrow Henry vain-gloriously insisted on emulating his great ancestor Henry V in "delight in warlike matters and feats of chivalry" to the neglect of home administration and to the depletion of the treasury. Yet at his succession in 1509 Henry was immensely popular. He was amiable and generous, skillful in archery and tennis. He was competent in Latin, French, and Italian, was a musician and encourager of the arts, and a friend to new sciences and Humanism. Hence there was a contemporary validity in each of the respective stands of Hythloday and *persona* More.[9] More, the lawyer and judge, argues each case as one who understands the issues involved. His presentation takes the form of a comprehensive and orderly historical survey of recent issues and events, embracing three chief areas of governmental activity: (1) domestic policy: unemployment, the farm problem, the penal code and question of capital punishment, and vagabondage (pp. 21-38), (2) foreign policy, principally concerning foreign conquest and colonization (pp. 39-42), and (3) fiscal policy: the valuation of money, benevolences and forced loans, monopoly grants, extortion, and bribery (pp. 42-46).

In the technique of literary dialogue, the factor which distinguishes the discussion of domestic policy from the other two major headings is that it does not take place between Hythloday and *persona* More. Hythloday relates it to his companions as an argument that took place many years before, in 1497, among himself, Cardinal Morton, and "also a certain layman cunning in the laws of your realm." The possible reasons for this removal in time are several. One obvious suggestion is that it is a form of self-protection for the author, an attack on Henry VIII under the guise of criticizing a former reign. Another possibility is that the author is paying careful heed to his fictitious chronology, and accordingly dates Hythloday's visit to England at a time consonant with his voyages under

---

[8] See Caspari, *Humanism*, p. 52.   /501/

[9] In an epigram entitled "The Good and the Bad Prince," More had defined the polarities thus: "What is a good prince? A sheepdog, who keeps away the wolves? And a bad prince? The wolf himself." Quoted in Kautsky, *Thomas More*, p. 125.   /502/

the flag of Amerigo Vespucci. In the context of our discussion, however, a third reason may be offered: /502/ that the writer More's chief motivation is a removal of these specific issues from the immediacy of the Hythloday-*persona* More debate. Hythloday and *persona* More are enumerating the counts for and against English monarchy in 1515-16; we shall see, however, that domestic policy was not an issue wherein either of them found Henry VIII seriously at fault. Hence it was no longer a live issue in terms of the debate between More's two *personae*. We never actually learn *persona* More's opinion on the question of enclosure. At the conclusion of Hythloday's account he acknowledges that the narrator has spoken "wittily and so pleasantly," but implies that the entire matter of the speech has been slightly irrelevant to their debating point:

> But yet, all this notwithstanding, I can by no means change my mind, but that I must needs believe that you, if you be disposed and can find in your heart to follow some prince's court, shall with your good counsels greatly help and further the commonwealth. (p. 39)

In other words, *persona* More gently reproves his friend for beating a dead horse, and proposes that they proceed to matters that will really test the nature of Henry VIII's intentions. Why does he consider the discussion of enclosure to be irrelevant?

When we read Hythloday's stirring pleas on behalf of the husbandman, and his defiance of the rich, we instinctively conjecture a denunciation of complacent governmental policy, and suppose that Hythloday has scored a telling point against Henry VIII. In point of fact, however, by 1515-16 the government was attempting to handle the crisis on a large scale, under the direction of Wolsey.[10] Royal commissioners were appointed to study the problem, and they reported a need for positive action. Hythloday urges the government to "make a law" (p. 28); important legislation was passed in 1514, 1515, and 1516. These acts were directed particularly against the evils which Hythloday mentions: engrossing and forestalling (i.e., buying up in advance to force up the market price), and the plucking down of farms and villages by rich men who were exploiting the demand for wool at the expense of other types of agriculture. The government actually ordered rebuilding, as Hythloday demands, and restrained numberless attempts at further enclosure. The problem continued, because it was too large /503/ an agricultural revolution to be stayed by any governmental policy: but there was at least no ambiguity in the government's position on the farm problem. Hythloday's strictures would have been relevant in 1497, but not in 1516. Hence More removes this topic from the present conversation not only in time but in persons involved in the discussion.

The debate on domestic policy is a discussion within a discussion, and in many ways it mirrors in microcosm the larger plan. The most striking resemblance is that we again find three persons present at a dialogue (the scoffer and the friar appear from nowhere much later in the

---

[10] J. H. Hexter, *More's Utopia: The Biography of an Idea* (Princeton, N.J., 1952), pp. 152-53. /503/

conversation). Once again the function of the third party—the irascible lawyer—is to serve as spokesman for the wrong point of view, and thus provide a basis of agreement between the principal characters. *Persona* Morton, like *persona* More, tends somewhat to the cautious side, but he receives Hythloday's declamation on enclosure reform without an objection. He is also willing to give the Polylerites' penal code a practical trial by deferring death sentences in England for a period of time, and adds his own suggestion that "vagabonds may very well be ordered after the same fashion" (p. 35). This amicable talk ends in a quarrel between the scoffer and the friar which has all the appearances of a digression (pp. 36-38). Hythloday afterwards apologizes to his hearers for a "long and tedious . . . tale." A digression it may be, but it is not without purpose. The sharp tongues and short tempers of lawyer, scoffer, and friar provide a meaningful contrast to the sane and considerate conduct of Hythloday, Morton, and *persona* More. The primary object of the satire in this digression is not the court or the clergy, but the folly of unreasonable argument.

The proposals concerning social legislation and penal reform are included in the Morton-Hythloday conversation for a very different reason from that suggested for the inclusion of the enclosure problem in this same section. In this latter instance the reason was that governmental policy seemed to be entirely in accord with More's wishes. The same could hardly be said to hold true for relaxation of the death penalty or improvement of regulations concerning vagabondage. Paradoxically, the precise opposite was true. In exploring these possibilities More was centuries ahead of his time, and his suggestions clearly extended beyond what he was ready to ask realistically of Henry VIII. No sixteenth-century /504/ government considered such social benevolence as its proper sphere of activity, much less as its duty. Hence it was an unfair test in distinguishing between a tyrant and a true prince at that point in history. More evidently had no doubt as to the essential rightness of this stand—both Hythloday and Morton agree to this—but More was not ready to propound such an advanced degree of enlightenment as a necessary condition of the philosopher's endorsement of any particular administration. In order to distinguish between the attainable and the unattainable, he relegated the latter to an abstracted conversation in a past reign. In summary, then, the material for the debate on domestic policy consists of a settled issue— enclosure—and an essentially impractical issue—social humanitarianism, both lying outside the realm of the central controversy concerning the nature of Tudor monarchy. It is for these disparate reasons that *persona* More can conclude the entire section with the easy dismissal, "But yet, all this notwithstanding, I can by no means change my mind" (p. 39). The crucial issues in the debate of the mind with itself lay yet ahead.

Plainly, it was to be in foreign and fiscal policy that monarchy would reveal its true inclination towards benevolence or despotism. The weight of evidence here would be decisive in persuading the philosopher to aid a government or to avoid its hopeless contamination. Policies of war and reckless expenditure were unavoidably interrelated, and were anathema to the Humanist scholar and supporter of London commercial interests.[11]

If, however, one could reason that a young king's sabre-rattling had stemmed from the effusion of adolescent vanity, one might pray for a change of temperament and for an era of peace at home. *Persona* More and Hythloday characteristically take sides. In the former's view any possibility for improvement, no matter how slight, would oblige the philosopher to assist and encourage the humane instinct. Hythloday is more inclined to expect the worst, and hints darkly at the incorrigible example of King Dionysius — with its obvious moral for the philosopher whose fate it is to be involved in duplicity beyond his control (p. 39). Here is an issue that would influence one's choice, unlike the uncontroversial issue of domestic policy. /505/

Consequently, in his consideration of foreign and fiscal policy the author shifts his scene from 1497 to the present (1516) and from the abstraction of a discussion within a discussion to the immediacy of the Hythloday-*persona* More debate. The foreign policy debate centers upon the example of the King of France, while fiscal policy is discussed abstractly with relation to "some king and his council." In neither case, obviously, is Henry VIII actually mentioned, and the extent to which his own actions partook of these evil examples is left unstated. The historical factors lie outside the scope of this study; we are interested in the literary method of debate and the extent of agreement between the two speakers.

In these terms, the fact of prime significance is that *persona* More and Hythloday agree entirely on the dangers involved. Although they implicitly differ as to whether Henry VIII in 1516 fell irretrievably into these categories of aggressive foreign policy and reckless spending, the two speakers do not question the essential perniciousness of these categories. In foreign policy the French king is plainly charged with meddling in affairs that are none of his business: laying claim to foreign dominions under pretext of an ancient hereditary line of succession, buying soldiers and alliances, encouraging pretenders to the enemy's throne, and the like. *Persona* More makes no pretence of finding a glimmer of hope in such a situation. When asked how well he thinks the French king would receive the philosopher's advice to "tarry still at home" and govern his own kingdom wisely, *persona* More readily concedes the point: "So God help me, not very thankfully, quoth I" (pp. 41-42). In a case like this, any philosopher would show his greatest wisdom in sparing his breath and saving his own skin.

Similarly in fiscal policy *persona* More has no answer for Hythloday's example of "some king and his council" who indulge in extortion, bribery, "benevolences" and forced loans, creating exorbitant taxes (largely at the expense of the middle class) for the purpose of levying unneeded troops. After stating his proposals and objections, Hythloday concludes:

> These, and such other information, if I should use among men wholly inclined and given to the contrary part, how deaf hearers think you should I have?

---

[11] A well-known example of More's opposition to Tudor fiscal policy was his successful defense against Henry VII's budgetary request for three fifteenths, forcing More's retirement from politics until the death of that king.   /505/

Deaf hearers doubtless, quoth I, and in good faith no marvel. (p. 46)
/506/

When confronted with completely "deaf hearers," *persona* More is ready
to abandon the cause of counselling a monarch, and to live in philosophic
retirement with Hythloday, pondering an impractical but ideal world
across the oceans. But who is to say that an administration at any particular
moment in history is entirely hopeless? Hythloday's examples of evil are
as theoretical in their way as his picture of the ideal life of Utopia in Book
II.

Somewhere between the ideally good and the perfectly evil stood Henry
VIII, and his intentions were as yet uncertain. Thomas More had to make
a decisive choice in answer to Henry's request for his wise counsel. The
actual decision is beyond our present scope, but it is central to an understanding of the dialogue to realize that in 1515-16 More perceived a
dilemma.[12] He gave expression to it in a pattern of two alternatives:
Hythloday's wariness of all Machiavellianism as an earnest of future ill
intent, and *persona* More's cautiously idealistic tendency to seize upon
any ray of hope as a basis for gradual improvement.

Now that the historical evidence is in, More's spokesmen proceed to
their summations, to the concluding arguments of counsel for both sides
(pp. 46-50). If one spokesman is merely serving as devil's advocate for
the other, it is difficult to understand why both addresses to the jury are
so coherent, rational, convincing, and essentially moderate in tone. *Persona*
More labels the distinction between their points of view with the terms
"school philosophy" (Hythloday's) and "another philosophy, more civil"
(his own). He does not use the term "school philosophy" pejoratively;
it is "not unpleasant among friends in familiar communication" (p. 47).[13]
Its only fault is that it is too forthright, too uncompromising; it lacks the
quality of tact and diplomacy, of knowing when to speak and when to remain silent. "Civil" philosophy is the /507/ ability to "make the best of it,"
to "handle the matter wittily and handsomely for the purpose; and that
which you cannot turn to good, so to order it that it be not very bad"
(pp. 47-48). This is no idle and naive humor, to be overturned and made
ridiculous by Hythloday. More as a responsible public servant had long
known the meaning of "compromise" in its best sense. He was eminently
a practical man of politics.

Yet a man of principle knows where compromise leaves off and appease-
ment begins. At least, he knows in theory. More's beloved classical master
Seneca found the dividing line to be exasperatingly thin and hard to
locate. A policy of compromise involves a frightening element of chance.

---

[12] J. H. Hexter presents a convincing thesis that it was a continuation of peace—as a part of
Wolsey's policy of retrenchment and non-intervention until the balance of power should
realign itself with the deaths of the old men Frederick of Spain and Maximilian of the Holy
Roman Empire—which provided a conclusive impetus for More's final decision to join the
government in 1518. *More's Utopia*, pp. 132-57. Compare Caspari, *Humanism*, who believes
with Russell Ames that More "probably entered royal service in 1516 after much hesitation"
(p. 226, n. 10).   /507/

[13] Caspari, *Humanism*, identifies Hythloday's point of view with that of Erasmus, supposing
conversations between Erasmus and More much like those in Book I of *Utopia* (p. 52).
/507/

In a very real sense, compromise is a braver course for the true man of principle than stoical indifference. The counsellor of state is forever in need of reappraising the situation, while the man of principle stands fast on his logic. The worst that can befall the latter is martyrdom. The counsellor is in danger of personal dishonor and ridicule. Nero's reign might well have been the worse without Seneca's attempts at compromise, but the stigma of "appeaser" will live forever with Seneca's name. More evidently had Seneca's example in mind as he wrote *Utopia,* for he refers to the passage "out of *Octavia* the place wherein Seneca disputeth with Nero" (p. 47).

It is possible to be at the same time a counsellor of state and a man of principle — possible but dangerous. At every moment in history such a man must decide whether to acquiesce or to stand fast. He holds as incontrovertible the axiom that "You must not forsake the ship in a tempest because you cannot rule and keep down the winds" (p. 48). On the other hand, no sane man would undertake to contravene Plato's similitude of the philosophers who, being unable to persuade others to come in out of the rain, "do keep themselves within their houses, being content that they be safe themselves, seeing they cannot remedy the folly of the people" (p. 50). More, in his own life, applied both courses of action to differing problems. The problem relevant to the dialogue in *Utopia* was a complex one, and depended on a great many variables. The choice was not easy, and by all indications it came months or even years after the composition of the work. What we hear in *Utopia* is the dispassionate voice of the author, laying before the world his view of the facts and of the philosophical basis for a decision.

The description of the island of Utopia in Book II deals similarly /508/ with the problem of the philosopher in deciding whether or not to participate in a government. The respective stands of *persona* More and of Hythloday are merely the obverse of their previous positions concerning tyranny. The former, who always tries to "make the best of it," is skeptical of a system that would overthrow entirely the established order of things. He is skeptical but not hostile; he is anxious to hear his friend's account of Utopia in all its details: "you shall think us desirous to know whatsoever we know not yet" (p. 53). Hythloday, who considers most princes to be beyond hope, is ready to try a more severe remedy. Yet even he does not reject the moderate solution out of hand. He readily grants that wise statutes may help somewhat to ease inequality of wealth, so that "these evils also might be lightened and mitigated. But that they may be perfectly cured, and brought to a good and upright state, it is not to be hoped for, whiles every man is master of his own to himself" (pp. 51-52). The description of Utopia is a body of theoretical material towards which More's inquiring mind develops a polarity of rational attitudes. The philosophical mind must contain within itself always a Platonic ideal as a frame of reference. Notwithstanding, the Platonist in his worldly life is a practical man, recognizing the need for temporizing with human imperfection. *Persona* More is this practical man. It is he who accentuates mortal frailty: "For it is not possible for all things to be well unless all men were good, which I think will not be yet this good many years" (p. 48). Still, Utopia belongs to the future; and *persona* More's practicality remained a living force for its author in his life's application of Utopian ideals to English society. The two sides of the question continued for More to be valid and essentially unanswerable. /509/

Aids
to
Further
Study

Principal Dates in More's Life

1478   Birth — February 6

1485   Accession of Henry VII

c.1490 – 1492   In the household of Lord Chancellor Cardinal Morton

c.1492 – 1494   Oxford

1494 – 1496   Law student at New Inn, then at Lincoln's Inn

1497   Made a barrister at Lincoln's Inn

1500   Intimate friendship with Erasmus

1500 – 1504   Lived at the Carthusian monastery in London (the Charterhouse) but without vows; pursued Greek studies with Lily, Grocyn, Linacre; practiced law

1504   Elected to Parliament

1505   Marriage to Jane Colt

1509   Accession of Henry VIII at the age of seventeen. Erasmus wrote *The Praise of Folly* in More's London home

1510   Under-Sheriff of London

1511   Death of Jane Colt; marriage to Alice Middleton

1515   Embassy to Flanders as King's ambassador; wrote Book II of *Utopia*

1516   Wrote Book I of *Utopia;* published in November at Louvain

1518   Accepted office on the King's Council

1521   Under-Treasurer

1529   Succeeded Wolsey as Lord Chancellor

1531   Cromwell appointed to the King's Council

1532   Resigned the Lord Chancellorship

1533 Cranmer consented to the divorce of Henry VIII and Catherine of Aragon; Anne Boleyn crowned Queen; More conspicuously absent at the coronation

1534 Refused to take an oath accepting the king as head of the church; imprisoned in the Tower

1535 July 6, beheaded after conviction on perjured evidence

Questions on Utopia

1.   Why does More urge Hythloday to become a counselor to the king? What moral reasons does he give?

2.   Which groups does Hythloday consider parasites of the commonwealth?

3.   What is Hythloday's proposed reform of England's penal law? Is modern penal law closer to his idea?

4.   What view of human nature does Hythloday's reform presuppose?

5.   What five results of the enclosures does Hythloday specify?

6.   With what reasons does More, in speaking to Hythloday, defend the notion of politics as "the art of the possible"?

7.   What three arguments against communism are given by More in Book I?

8.   Does the "fictional format" of *Utopia* have a clear beginning, middle, and end?

9.   Is there any development of character?

10.   In what do the Utopians suppose the felicity of life to consist? Are they consistent in organizing life to attain this felicity?

11.   How do the Utopians deal with the problem of population increase? Evaluate their solutions.

12.   Do the Utopians believe there is ever any justification for war? Explain.

13.   What fifth-column activities do the Utopians engage in?

14.   What is the Utopian view of euthanasia?

15.   Is the existence of a class of slaves or bondsmen a major defect in any ideal state? How do the Utopians justify their class of slaves?

16.   Comment on the desirability and practicality of the marriage customs in Utopia, particularly a) the physical inspection of spouses by each other before marriage and b) the divorce laws.

17.   How do the Utopians rate the art of diplomacy?

18.   What is the position of women in Utopia?

19.   What does More mean by saying that community of goods was instituted by Christ and that the custom was still in practice among the most sincere of the Christians?

20.   How is freedom of religion interpreted in Utopia?

21.   Can Utopia be called in any way democratic? Explain.

22.   What is the distinction afforded the prince? The priest? What are the robes of the priests?

23.   What is the role of the priests during war?

24.   What are the religious principles of the Utopians?

25.   How do the Utopians define virtue?

26.   Of what does the Utopian library consist?

27.   What is the position of the scholar?

Questions on Critical Selections

1.   What purpose does Erasmus ascribe to the writing of *Utopia?*

2.   What is the outstanding quality of the man Erasmus describes in his letter to Hutten? Evaluate the letter as a biographical essay.

3.   Does More's letter resolve any problems of whether or not he identified himself with Hythloday? Cf. Bevington.

4.   To what three "divine institutions" does Budé attribute the Utopians' maintenance of Christian wisdom? Is he accurate in saying that Utopia has assimilated Christian usages and wisdom? Cf. Chambers.

5.   What significance is there in Budé's changing the name of the state of Utopia to Hagnopolis?

6.   According to Budé, what are More's chief credentials? What is the significance of Budé's standards?

7.   What purpose does Busleyden ascribe to More in writing the *Utopia?*

8.   Comment on the fact that all the sixteenth-century commentators in this text praise More's conscious moral and practical purpose in writing *Utopia.*

9.   What view of society does Bolt propose? How does he place More in this view?

10.   Would More as Bolt interprets him—a man with an "adamantine sense of his own self"—have difficulties living in Utopia? Are individualism and the common good reconciled in Utopia?

11.   What ideal purpose for scholarship does Kautsky propose? Why is the fact that More was a scholar important to Kautsky's argument?

12.   How does Kautsky amplify Hythloday's picture of economic distress in England?

13.   Is Volgin's assertion that More thought the Utopian order "the best, . . . most rational and the most conducive to man's well-being on earth" defensible? Cf. Surtz.

14.   How does Chambers dispose of the charge of imperialism in *Utopia?*

15.   Chambers quotes Robynson's translation of *Utopia* in reference to those turned out of their homes, "Poor silly, wretched souls. . . ." Look up in the *New English Dictionary* the meaning of the word "silly."

16.   Compare Bolt's and O'Sullivan's opinions of More's relationship to law.

17.   What is O'Sullivan's statement of the right to private property? How does he support it?

18.   What aspect of *Utopia* does Ames consider central?

19.   What distinction does Surtz make between More as theoretical and practical philosopher?

20.   How is this distinction related to Surtz's examination of Christianity's defense of private property although the Christian ideal is community of goods?

21.   What reasons does Bevington propose for Hythloday's reminiscence about Cardinal Morton?

22.   On what points does Bevington find More and Hythloday in agreement?

23.   One of the more interesting features of the twentieth-century essays is the way in which they refer back to one another. Comment specifically upon the way this is done, and evaluate the scholarly "conversation" that results.

24.   How does Ames expand Chambers' argument that *Utopia* is not anti-Christian?

Topics for Papers

Some of the study questions might profitably be developed into papers or panel discussions as well as the topics listed below.

Short Papers

1. Describe a day in the life of a typical Utopian. [Description]
2. How does Ames support his argument that "the core of the book is republican, bourgeois, and democratic"? [Division]
3. Compare and contrast the political organization of Utopia (families, syphogrants, tranibors, etc.) with the political organization of the United States. [Comparison and Contrast]
4. Compare the opinions of Volgin and Chambers on More's purpose in writing *Utopia*. [Comparison and Contrast]
5. Compare Kautsky's and Ames' interpretations of the economic attitude of *Utopia*. [Comparison and Contrast]
6. By what reasoning do the Utopians determine their attitude toward and their customs concerning death? [Logical Analysis]
7. What is the ideal of the true prince according to *Utopia*? [Definition]
8. What examples does Ames use to support his argument that all of *Utopia*, not just Book I, refers to specific events with which More was often personally acquainted? [Example]
9. Why were the enclosures a major factor in England's economic and social problems? In your paper show how Kautsky amplifies Hythloday's picture of England's economic distress. [Causal Analysis]
10. O'Sullivan and Bevington differ on the meaning of what *persona* More says in *Utopia*. Explain and evaluate their arguments. [Exposition]
11. Comment on the skill and validity of Ames' comparison of Kautsky and Chambers. [Exposition]
12. Compare and contrast the problem of enclosures with the modern economic problem of automation. [Comparison and Contrast]
13. Why and how is the philosophy of pleasure dominant in Utopia? [Exposition]

Long Papers

1. The controversy over More's position on communism
2. *Utopia* and the political concept of democracy
3. Hythloday's history, character, and thought
4. Utopia—a humanist ideal?
5. Irony and satire in *Utopia*
6. The extent to which Book II is seminally in Book I
7. The dramatic ambiguity of *Utopia* as the chief cause of the book's continuing vitality
8. Comparison and contrast of the Renaissance and Modern commentators on *Utopia*

Research Papers

1. Erasmus as a model for Hythloday
2. More's *Utopia* as a "Praise of Wisdom," opposed to Erasmus' *Praise of Folly*
3. More's *Utopia* and Machiavelli's *The Prince*
4. The history of Marxist Communist interest in *Utopia*
5. The history of More's canonization; More and the Hagiographers
6. Comparison of More's *Utopia* with any one or several of the following Utopias:

Plato, *The Republic*
St. Augustine, *Civitas Dei*
Erasmus, *The Praise of Folly*
Rabelais, "The Abbey of Theleme" (from *Gargantua and Pantagruel*)
Montaigne, "Of the Cannibals" (from *Essays*)
J. Hall, *Mundus Alter et Idem*
J. V. Andreae, *Christianopolis*
T. Campanella, *Civitas Solis*
F. Bacon, *The New Atlantis*
S. Golt, *Nova Solyma*
J. Harington, *Oceana*
S. Berington, *The Adventures of Gaudentio di Lucca*
J. Swift, *Gulliver's Travels*
S. Johnson, *Rasselas*
S. Butler, *Erewhon*
W. Morris, *News from Nowhere*
E. Bellamy, *Looking Backward*
E. Bulwer-Lytton, *The Coming Race*
N. Hawthorne, *The Blithedale Romance*
W. D. Howells, *A Traveler from Altruria*
H. G. Wells, *A Modern Utopia*
A. Huxley, *Brave New World*
――――――, *Ape and Essence*
――――――, *Brave New World Revisited*
――――――, *Island*
G. Orwell, *1984*
W. Golding, *Lord of the Flies*

7. The problems in advising a king—as discussed in Book I of *Utopia,* as demonstrated in More's own last years, and as dramatized by Bolt in *A Man for All Seasons*
8. Christopher Hollis calls *Utopia* a "disappointingly futile book." (*Thomas More,* Milwaukee, 1934, p. 60.) Agree or disagree.

Bibliography

Bibliographical Works

Gibson, R. W. *St. Thomas More: A Preliminary Bibliography of His Works and of Moreana to the Year 1750.* New Haven: Yale University Press, 1961. (This volume is an earnest of the St. Thomas More Project of Yale University, which is now engaged in preparing an edition of the complete works of More, in fourteen volumes.)

Sullivan, Frank and M. P. *Moreana, 1478–1945.* Kansas City: Rockhurst College, 1946.

Works

Erasmus, Desiderius. *The Education of a Christian Prince,* trans. and ed. by L. K. Born. New York: Columbia University Press, 1936.

——————. *The Epistles of Erasmus, From His Earliest Letters to His Fifty-First Year,* trans. F. M. Nichols. 3 vols. New York: Russell & Russell, Inc., 1962.

——————. *The Praise of Folly,* trans. H. H. Hudson. Princeton: Princeton University Press, 1947.

More, Thomas. *Selected Letters of St. Thomas More,* ed. E. F. Rogers. New Haven: Yale University Press, 1961.

——————. *Utopia,* in Latin and English, with notes by J. H. Lupton. Oxford: Oxford University Press, 1895.

Biography

Bolt, Robert. *A Man for All Seasons.* New York: Random House, 1962.

Bridgett, T. E. *The Life of Blessed Thomas More.* London: Burns, Oates & Washbourne, Ltd., 1924.

Chambers, R. W. *Thomas More.* New York: Harcourt, Brace and Co., 1935.

Froude, J. A. *Life and Letters of Erasmus.* London: Longmans, Green and Co., 1895.

Smith, Preserved. *Erasmus.* New York: Harper & Brothers, 1923.

Roper, William. *The Life of Sir Thomas More,* ed. E. V. Hitchcock. London: Oxford University Press, 1935.

Historical Background

Adams, Robert Pardee. *The Better Part of Valor: More, Erasmus, Colet, and Vives on Humanism, War, and Peace, 1496–1535.* Seattle: University of Washington Press, 1962.

Allen, J. W. *A History of Political Thought in the Sixteenth Century.* New York: Barnes and Noble, Inc., 1960. (University Paperbacks)

Allen, P. S. *The Age of Erasmus.* Oxford: Oxford University Press, 1914.

Bouyer, Louis. *Erasmus and His Times.* Maryland: The Newman Press, 1959.

Caspari, Fritz. *Humanism and the Social Order in Tudor England.* Chicago: University of Chicago Press, 1954.

Huizinga, J. *Erasmus and the Age of Reformation.* New York: Harper & Brothers, 1957. (Harper Torchbook)

Kautsky, Karl. *Communism in Central Europe in the Time of the Reformation.* New York: Russell & Russell, Inc., 1959.

Seebohm, Frederick. *The Oxford Reformers: John Colet, Erasmus, Thomas More.* London, 1887. (New York: Longmans, Green and Co., 1913)

Criticism of Utopia

Allen, Peter R. "Utopia and European Humanism: the function of the Prefatory Letters and Verses," *Studies in the Renaissance,* X (October 1963), 91-107.

Ames, Russell. *Citizen Thomas More and His Utopia.* Princeton: Princeton University Press, 1949.

Bevington, David M. "The Dialogue in *Utopia:* Two Sides to the Question," *Studies in Philology,* LVIII (July 1961), 496-509.

Campbell, W. E. *More's Utopia and His Social Teaching.* London: Eyre and Spottiswoode, Ltd., 1930.

Donner, H. W. *Introduction to Utopia.* London: Sidgwick and Jackson, Ltd., 1945.

Hexter, J. H. *More's Utopia: The Biography of an Idea.* Princeton: Princeton University Press, 1952.

Kautsky, Karl. *Thomas More and His Utopia,* trans. H. J. Stenning. London: A. & C. Black, Ltd., 1927.

O'Sullivan, Richard. "Social Life and Theories of St. Thomas More," *The Dublin Review,* CXCIX (July 1936), 46-62.

Schoeck, R. J. "More, Plutarch, and King Agis: Spartan History and the Meaning of *Utopia,*" *Philological Quarterly,* XXXV (1956), 366-375.

Surtz, Edward, S. J. *The Praise of Pleasure; Philosophy, Education, and Communism in More's Utopia.* Cambridge, Mass.: Harvard University Press, 1957.

_____. *The Praise of Wisdom; A Commentary on the Religious and Moral Problems and Background of St. Thomas More's Utopia.* Chicago: Loyola University Press, 1957.

_____. "Richard Pace's Sketch of Thomas More," *Journal of English and Germanic Philology,* LVII (January 1958), 36-50.

Volgin, Vyacheslav. "Sir Thomas More," *News, A Review of World Events,* XXXIX (February 15, 1953), 14-15.

3549   32

50